CFO Insights

Library of Congress Cataloging-in-Publication Data:

Wulf, C. Cristian.
    CFO insights : enabling high performance through leading practices for finance ERP / C. Cristian Wulf.
        p. cm.
    Includes index.
    ISBN-13: 978-0-471-77083-1 (cloth)
    ISBN-10: 0-471-77083-3 (cloth)
    1. Business enterprises—Finance. 2. Business enterprises—Finance—Data processing. 3. Management information systems. 4. Business planning. I. Title.
    HG4026.W85 2006
    658.15'1—dc22
                                            2005037203

Printed in the United States of America

10   9   8   7   6   5   4   3   2   1

CFO Insights

Enabling High Performance through Leading Practices for Finance ERP

C. CRISTIAN WULF

John Wiley & Sons, Inc.

Preface

Organizations across the globe continue to look for ways to achieve high performance.

Recently, I met with an organization that was looking to integrate an acquisition and implement a standard set of Finance capabilities using their Enterprise Resource Planning (ERP) solution to reduce costs and improve capabilities. When asked about the biggest risk the organization faced with this effort, the CFO replied "*Manumation.* Automation of our existing manual processes. . . . How can I be sure we are enabling the right outcomes and not just automating what we do today?"

At Accenture, our research shows that Finance capabilities enabled through ERP solutions are both a primary driver and a key enabler to attain high performance. *CFO Insights: Enabling High Performance through Leading Practices for Finance ERP* focuses on leading practices in Finance and how those practices can be realized through Finance ERP solutions. The chapter authors offer their expertise and practical guidance supported by case studies to bring the experiences to life.

Through our Accenture High Performance Business research, we define high-performance businesses and governments as organizations that consistently outperform their peers over a sustained timeframe (five to seven years) and across business cycles, industry disruptions, and management cycles. These organizations deliver consistent upper-quartile total returns to shareholders. They create returns on invested capital significantly in excess of the cost of capital and drive profitable revenue growth faster than their industry peers. In short, high-performance organizations are lean, responsive to changing competitive fundamentals, and consistently rank as market leaders.

By examining organizations that met our criteria for high performance, we found that Finance capabilities matter. We found a correlation of more than 70 percent between organizations that were assessed as Finance masters and those that were also high-performance businesses. Finance masters were those organizations with progressive and pioneering practices across five key Finance capabilities: Value-Centered Culture, Enterprise Performance Management, Finance Operations, Capital Stewardship, and Enterprise Risk Management.

In this book, our chapter authors scrutinize each of the end-to-end business processes that enable leading practices in Finance. By reviewing business processes in their entirety, we are able to determine how business outcomes are enabled and what specific actions and integration points need to be managed to achieve those outcomes. This book examines the business processes of Record to Report (key closing and reporting cycles), Procure to Pay, Acquire to Retire (Asset Lifecycle), Order to Cash, and Tax Management. In each chapter, we discuss process, technology, and organizational considerations – all components of high performance. We also explore key implementation and operational imperatives such as: ERP in a Shared Services environment; Enterprise Performance Management; and Total Cost of Ownership.

In addition to our own research and experiences, this book includes metrics and insights from The Hackett Group in an effort to provide the latest information from their database of Finance operating cost and leading practice trends. The Hackett Group benchmarking methodology and database together are recognized as the "gold standard" to define and measure how Finance cost structures and leading practices have changed over time. The Hackett Group perspectives provide details on where Finance organizations are positioned today and how that has changed over time.

CFO Insights: Enabling High Performance through Leading Practices for Finance ERP is the third of the Accenture CFO Insights book series published by John Wiley & Sons. The other titles in our series include *CFO Insights: Achieving High Performance through Finance BPO* and *CFO Insights: Delivering High Performance.*

CFO Insights: Achieving High Performance through Finance BPO provides a strategic guide to the fast-growing Finance & Accounting business process outsourcing field for CFOs and senior management. *CFO Insights: Delivering High Performance* is based on exclusive, in-depth research with CFOs of some of the world's most distinguished organizations; it presents a new operating model that sets the Finance function of high-performance businesses apart from their peers, describes their five common characteristics, and explains what these organizations do differently and how to emulate them.

We wish to thank the many members of our global Accenture team for their support and contributions: Dan Hahn, Geoffrey O'Connell, and Scott Uelner, Chapter 1; Tiffany Brown, Elton Doi, Gary Duncan, Janet Hobbins, Denise Mitchell, and Geoffrey O'Connell, Chapter 2; Darby Brennan, Karisa Nava, Sean Norton, and Geoffrey O'Connell, Chapter 3; Greg Dyer, Christian Kaemmerer, Adrian Leaf, and Jessica Wang, Chapter 4; Tony Masella and Kimberly Morgan, Chapter 5; Adebayo Bankole, Troy Barton, David Santoro Jr., Richard Boustead, Melissa Brandebourg, Wilda Siu, and Joy Wei, Chapter 6; Scott Elsky, Sunil Tanna, and Mike Wallace, Chapter 7; and Jacqueline Bourne, Gary Duncan, and Gregg Taylor, Chapter 9.

We also give special acknowledgement to our external contributors and to the team that helped us put this publication together. We would like to thank Richard T. Roth, Chief Research Officer of The Hackett Group. In addition, special thanks go to Scott Uelner, senior manager in the Accenture Finance & Performance Management (F&PM) service line, Deborah Hinson, Director of Marketing for the Accenture F&PM service line, and their team (Haralds Robeznieks, Sarah Muskett, Deanna Finley, and others) for their efforts and contribution on our behalf.

Dan London
Managing partner,
Accenture Finance & Performance Management service line

Contents

Contents

Contents

Acronyms/ Abbreviations

ABC	Activity-Based Costing
ACH	Automated Clearing House
ASBN	Automatic Shipping & Billing Notification
ASN	Advanced Shipment Notification
BI	Business Intelligence
BPO	Business Process Outsourcing
CoA	Chart of Accounts
COSO	Committee of Sponsoring Organizations
CRM	Customer Relationship Management
CRP	Conference Room Pilot
DPO	Days Payable Outstanding
DSO	Days Sales Outstanding
EDI	Electronic Data Interchange
EFT	Electronic Funds Transfer
EPM	Enterprise Performance Management
ERP	Enterprise Resource Planning
ERS	Evaluated Receipt Settlement
ES	Enterprise Solutions
EU	European Union
FASB	Financial Accounting Standards Board
GAAP	Generally Accepted Accounting Principles
GAAS	Generally Accepted Auditing Standards
HFM	Hyperion Financial Management

IAS	International Accounting Standards
IASB	International Accounting Standards Board
ICR	Intelligent Character Recognition
IRR	Internal Rate of Return
IT	Information Technology
KPI	Key Performance Indicator
M&A	Mergers & Acquisitions
MRP	Material Requirements Planning
NPV	Net Present Value
OCR	Optical Character Recognition
OLAP	On-Line Analytical Processing
OTC	Order to Cash
P-Card	Procurement Card
P&L	Profit & Loss
PCAOB	Public Company Accounting Oversight Board
RFID	Radio Frequency Identification
RFQ	Request for Quotation
ROI	Return on Investment
ROIC	Return on Invested Capital
SCM	Supply Chain Management
SEC	Securities and Exchange Commission
TCO	Total Cost of Ownership
VAT	Value-Added Tax
XBRL	Extensible Business Reporting Language

CHAPTER 1

Overview of Finance Solutions Leveraging Leading Practices

INTRODUCTION: A NEW LOOK AT FINANCE ERP

Enterprise Resource Planning (ERP) solutions have consumed vast amounts of time, resources, and money as organizations strive to implement, upgrade, and operate these complex integrated solutions from vendors such as Oracle and SAP. Through our vast Accenture client experience, we have seen that successful organizations have learned that an ERP solution encompasses and affects all aspects of the enterprise. In fact, many organizations have found that these solutions end up redefining Finance organizations' processes, policies, technologies, and even organizational structures. Their ERP programs do not "end," rather, the ERP solutions become part of the fabric that makes up their Finance organizations – and continue to present challenges and opportunities long after the technology is in place.

The ERP journey has made Finance realize how directly and frequently it is affected by all areas of operation. In contrast, real-time participation in the operation of the organization that the ERP programs have enabled has also raised expectations around Finance's own services. Increased expectations have often led Finance to take the lead as ERP solutions are being implemented or upgraded, or as process and capability programs associated with ERP solutions are being undertaken.

Through *CFO Insights: Enabling High Performance through Leading Practices for Finance ERP*, Accenture executives offer readers an alternate view of ERP projects and programs by looking at end-to-end business processes, rather than individual functions. We review key end-to-end Finance business processes, such as Procure to Pay, Asset Lifecycle, Order to Cash, and Tax Management, along with key Finance functions such as the closing process, financial and management reporting, and compliance. Each chapter discusses process, technology, and organizational considerations — all components of high-performance Finance functions and, indeed, high-performance businesses and governments. By focusing on end-to-end processes, we want organizations to identify and understand the key integration points and areas of focus that impact Finance.

This book also provides key points of view on broader implementation and operational imperatives for an ERP solution, such as:

- Enabling Shared Services and Business Process Outsourcing (BPO)
- Enterprise Performance Management (EPM)
- Total Cost of Ownership (TCO)

CFO Insights: Enabling High Performance through Leading Practices for Finance ERP includes a number of case studies and lessons learned from Accenture clients that have implemented, upgraded, and operated Oracle, PeopleSoft, and SAP Finance solutions. Each case study highlights key thoughts, benefits, and considerations and provides relevant guidance for other organizations as they proceed with their ERP on their journey toward high performance.

The intended audience for this book is varied, as it includes organizations that are planning a software selection, embarking on a new ERP implementation (either the full Finance suite or perhaps adding a new module), or preparing to upgrade their existing ERP solution. We also believe organizations that are working to achieve real value from their implemented Finance ERP solution can follow the leading practices we highlight and discuss in the book. From the individual reader's perspective, the audience for this book is also broad, as it includes the CFO and direct reports, as well as CIOs and project managers.

We will discuss key success factors for Finance ERP programs, perhaps the most important of which is that Finance ERP programs should be business driven and IT supported and enabled. Organizations must realize that business and Finance requirements should drive the implementation of an ERP solution. The objective of the book is to highlight the "do's and don'ts" that organizations will face during the entire lifecycle of their Finance ERP programs.

DEFINING CORE FINANCIALS

The scope of Finance, also known as the "CFO Agenda," is represented as end-to-end processes (depicted in Figure 1.1). Typically these end-to-end processes can be grouped into two categories: Core Financials and Value-Added Finance.

Figure 1.1 *The CFO agenda*

This book focuses on the key Finance end-to-end processes described as Core Financials. Core Financials end-to-end processes include:

- Record to Report
- Procure to Pay
- Asset Lifecycle
- Order to Cash
- Tax Management

The functionality supported by the top-tier ERP packages (Oracle, PeopleSoft, and SAP) for these Core Financials processes is typically sound and stable. However, very few organizations can claim to have the full Finance set of modules implemented in one instance to support these core end-to-end processes. Even fewer organizations can claim they use a single ERP package solution on a global basis for the core Finance end-to-end processes. Finally, only a small number of organizations have achieved full Finance integration with other key functions, such as Human Resources or Supply Chain, on the same ERP software package. This lack of full implementation is often driven by the complexity of the organization – both the existing legacy technology and the Finance function – along with the overall business complexity (multiple business units, business models, and countries of operation). We find the challenge most organizations face is to optimize the capabilities of the ERP solution in these complex environments (see Figure 1.2).[1]

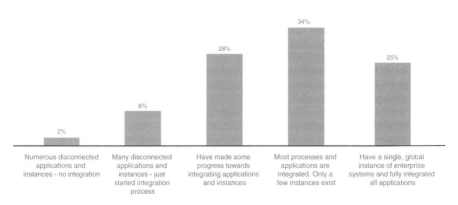

Figure 1.2 *Enterprise-wide integration of enterprise systems*

The Value-Added Finance scope of the CFO Agenda includes:

- Enterprise Performance Management
  - Planning and Forecasting
  - Management Reporting
- Treasury Management

Top-tier ERP software package vendors are focused on expanding functionality around Enterprise Performance Management (including planning, budgeting, forecasting, and management reporting) and Treasury Management. Although these processes lie beyond the scope of this book, the demand for these value-added processes is increasingly high. Key challenges faced by ERP programs focused on the Value-Added Finance scope center around vendor selection and quality of the data in the underlying source systems, including the Core Financials solution. Best-of-breed software vendor packages, such as Business Objects, Cognos, and Hyperion for EPM and Sungard, Trema, and XRT for Treasury Management, are still quite prevalent in the Value-Added Finance arena and probably a version or two ahead of the larger top-tier ERP packages (Oracle, PeopleSoft, and SAP) based on organizations' buying patterns. Organizations also typically face a difficult decision – to continue to invest in Core Financials to spread the footprint of the core ERP package or to focus limited resources on the primary expected benefits of improved decision making and management reporting as supported by the Value-Added Finance scope.

HIGH-PERFORMANCE FINANCE

Accenture defines high-performance businesses as organizations that consistently outperform their peers over a sustained timeframe and across business cycles, industry disruptions, and CEO leadership cycles. These companies deliver consistently upper-quartile total returns to shareholders. They create returns on invested capital significantly in excess of the cost of capital and drive profitable revenue growth faster than their industry peers. In short, they are lean, responsive to changing competitive fundamentals, and consistently rank as market leaders.

Accenture's research has identified key differentiators of high-performance businesses and government agencies, and one important finding has emerged: high-performance organizations have developed sophisticated capabilities in one or more of several strategically important business functions. Finance is certainly one of the most important business functions in any organization today. Our research[2] shows that there is a 70 percent or more correlation between a high-performance organization and Finance mastery, as measured by:

- The pervasiveness of a value-centered organization
- The depth of Enterprise Performance Management
- The efficiency of Finance operations
- The sophistication of capital stewardship
- The extent of enterprise risk management.

Organizations that achieve Finance mastery exhibit key characteristics that differentiate them and set them apart from their competitors. Our research shows that high-performance businesses and government agencies use Finance technology as a tool to help executives make better decisions for resource allocation, while at the same time increasing productivity. Finance ERP solutions enable integrated systems, a common source of data, timely information, and standardized processes that support Finance's contribution to these companies' high performance. High-performance organizations continually make technology investments at above-average industry rates and secure higher returns and value realization than their counterparts.

High-performance businesses and government agencies are typically also early adopters of leading technologies. In terms of the core financial end-to-end processes, examples of these leading technologies include scanning, electronic invoicing, and workflow processing. High-performance organizations are currently focused on leveraging their strong Core Financials-based ERP solution and expanding into business analytics tools related to Enterprise Performance Management.

In summary, high-performance Finance functions leverage technology as one ingredient to achieving Finance mastery:

- A world-class, leading practices-based Finance ERP solution is a necessary, but not sufficient, condition for high-performance Finance functions.
- A Finance ERP solution based on leading practices enables extremely efficient and effective Finance operations and is the backbone to successful EPM.

DEFINING ERP

ERP has been around for a long time. ERP solutions began as back-office solutions to the problem of automating complex, repetitive, time-consuming transaction processing. Although the names and acronyms have changed and the scope continues to evolve and expand, the basic objectives remain the same.

The earliest manifestation of an ERP model came in the 1960s, with the first Material Requirements Planning (MRP) systems, which focused on planning and scheduling for manufacturing companies. By the 1980s, Manufacturing Resource Planning (MRP II) systems were introduced. These mainframe-based solutions were the first to focus on the integration of manufacturing and financial applications; they can be categorized as "interfaced solutions" that share data across modules but maintain separate (and in many cases duplicate) master files (for example, Items, Vendors, Locations, and Company Codes). In the late 1980s, the next phase of ERP focused on integrating more and more functions of an organization. In the 1990s, these "integrated solutions" truly started focusing on the entire organization: across Finance, Human Resources, Supply Chain, and Manufacturing. The ERP solutions began sharing (and integrating) common data elements and master files, allowing additional information and tighter integration within the walls of the organization by leveraging the latest client/server technology.

The latest iteration of ERP, also described as Enterprise Solutions, leverages the Internet. Packaged software vendors are more and more focused on integration between organizations to connect with suppliers and vendors. Enterprise Solutions are software applications that connect and manage information flows across complex organizations, allowing managers to make decisions based on information that truly reflects the current state of their business.[3]

PROGRAMS — NOT PROJECTS

The history of ERP demonstrates that an ERP initiative is not a one-time effort — ERP as a technology solution is continually evolving. New functionality is added by way of new modules or new enhancements to existing modules, and more and more leading practices are incorporated into the basic off-the-shelf software packages.

Organizations that tackle ERP successfully address ERP as a program composed of multiple initiatives and projects. Leading organizations do not address ERP as a one-time project that is independent of other ongoing initiatives. The scope of the ERP program can be as large as entire suites of modules, such as Finance, Human Resources, Supply Chain, Customer Relationship Management, and Performance Management, and it can cover all geographies of the world. Other programs may be as narrowly focused as a new module within a family of applications, for example, Fixed Assets within Finance. Individual initiatives or projects within the ERP program will have to address strategy, technology, configuration, processes, policies, and organization in an integrated fashion. Those same programs are also established within the constraints of each organization and must address the interdependencies of other programs or organization charters. ERP is integral to the organization, and strong program managers will question how each of the current or planned programs, projects, or initiatives within the organization will affect the overall ERP program.

Organizations also need to view ERP as a series of ongoing projects that continually challenge the value realization of the existing solution. One of the typical downfalls of ERP programs is that they do not focus on achieving the business case or realizing the full value of the implemented solution. Typically program teams establish a business case early on in the lifecycle of the program; at best, the team continues to evolve and fine-tune the original business case until the final "go-live date." Only a very small number of organizations establish a mechanism or function to continue to track the actual value realization of the implemented solution up to and past the go-live date. Even fewer use this value realization process to continue to evolve and fine-tune the ERP solution while leveraging the value realization process to justify ongoing investments. Organizations should not view their ERP program as complete until the data stored in the ERP solution are transformed into information that changes the way the people in the organization conduct their work activities and make tactical and strategic decisions. We recommend that the key focus of successful Finance ERP programs be the achievement of ongoing business value, as opposed to delivering the project or initiative "on time, under budget."

An ERP program is a major undertaking, even if the scope of the program is focused only on Finance. Finance ERP programs need a delicate balance of strategy, process, organization, and technology.

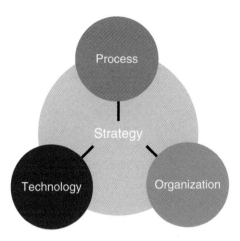

Figure 1.3   *Finance ERP program drivers*

A leading practices-driven Finance ERP program will drive key decisions around the new end-to-end process definition and system implementation considerations. Today's off-the-shelf ERP software packages support most of the generally accepted leading practices and continuously work to include enhancements and/or new modules, as more leading practices or more detailed leading practices are developed and refined. As Figure 1.3 shows, successful organizations plan and execute Finance ERP programs based on the premise of supporting the organization's overall strategy. The leading practices-based, end-to-end process definition drives the proper ERP package configuration for each organization. Successful ERP programs will then focus on process-driven configurations, as well as on process-driven organizational impacts.

The ERP software package by itself is not the solution to any organization's unique problems, issues, and constraints. Instead, ERP software packages should be viewed as the key technology enabler to the overall ERP solution at the same time that they establish the groundwork for transformational change. Successful ERP programs are focused on business results – not just software implementations or configuration exercises.

Our experience demonstrates that successful ERP programs are based on eight key elements, centered on the ERP solution, as shown in Figure 1.4:

1. **People:** deep proven software package technical and configuration skilled resources, coupled with the "know-how" to implement full business (for example, Finance) solutions. Successful ERP programs are staffed with their organization's best resources.
2. **Program Management:** established program management organization and methodology focused on business results — for example, leveraging a business case and delivery excellence.
3. **Risk Mitigation:** proactive risk mitigation, covering technology, business, delivery, and return on investment (ROI) risk mitigation.
4. **Enterprise Technology:** focus on Total Cost of Ownership and integration with the overall organization technology strategy.
5. **Business Value:** delivering differentiated business capabilities with an industry focus when appropriate.
6. **Business Readiness:** creating ownership and accountability in the business while developing key metrics to measure performance.
7. **Global Sourcing:** a program team that includes the appropriate mix of internal personnel and external consulting skills — from business consulting to low-cost implementation skills, including sourcing across the globe through off-shore delivery centers.

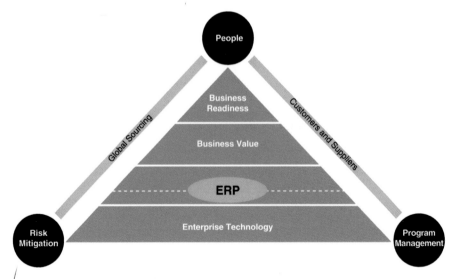

Figure 1.4 *The eight key elements of successful ERP programs*

8. **Customers and Suppliers:** internal and external stakeholders, including customers and suppliers that are actively engaged and measure the success and value of the program.

Typical ERP Program Objectives

We find there are many different objectives and goals for embarking on a Finance ERP program, just as there are different organizations and Finance functions. Most organizations group the program objectives and segment them within functional (Finance and business) benefits and technology (IT) benefits. This approach is the first sign that the overall vision for the ERP program may not be fully understood. Segmenting program objectives typically demonstrates a "siloed" approach or an unnatural response to assigning budget requests or business case responsibility across functions and departments. ERP programs need to be business led, for example, led by Finance while incorporating Finance stakeholders. Although IT is an integral part of the program, the key sponsorship for the ERP program must come from the business. If this is the case, there is no need to segment the benefits — the benefits are business driven and technology enabled.

With this ERP definition and these overall ERP solution objectives in mind, we can summarize the typical Finance ERP program objectives as follows:

Strategy

- **Better management decision making.** Although the Finance ERP program addresses Finance stakeholders' key needs and requirements specifically, the end goal needs to be improving the business' overall decision making based on the appropriate financial data.
- **Mergers and acquisitions (M&A) support to create an extendable platform.** A successful Finance ERP program will deploy not only a standardized common solution but also an extendable one. Finance must be involved in early discussions of future M&A strategies.

Process

- **Streamlined financial, management, and performance management reporting.** The Finance ERP solution needs to provide *all* reporting that is financial data driven. As Chapter 3 will discuss, there needs to be "one single source of the truth."
- **Increased Finance focus on value-added activities versus transaction processing.** Finance organizations typically spend most of their time

on transaction processing (including the data manipulation needed to create requested reports and information) versus planning or management reporting. Finance ERP programs typically address Core Financials modules first to address data quality concerns and to free up time for value-added activities.

- **Improved process and/or function management.** Finance ERP solutions result in organizational impacts to the Finance function, as well as to its key stakeholders.
- **Sarbanes-Oxley compliance and enablement.** ERP software packages have added compliance modules in response to the latest regulations. Although these modules provide greater visibility into the controls embodied within the new technology, the software itself does not address all compliance requirements.

Organization

- **Shared Services operating model support.** Finance and Human Resources are the most common functions to "lead the way" in implementing Shared Services. Leading organizations address the Finance ERP initiative and the Shared Services initiative simultaneously under the same program umbrella.
- **Business Process Outsourcing transition and transformation.** BPO is a logical extension to Shared Services. Every organization considering Shared Services should also consider Finance BPO for its future operating model.
- **Headcount reduction.** This key quantitative benefit needs to be considered in every ERP program business case, but it also needs to be carefully balanced with headcount redeployment, particularly for those Finance functions trying to rebalance their activities with a more value-added focus.

Technology

- **Process and systems standardization and simplification.** The top-tier ERP software packages enable policy, process, and procedure standardization across business units as well as geographies.
- **Systems/technology consolidation.** Legacy technology "sun-setting" is another quantitative benefit of Finance ERP programs. However, a detailed design is required to ensure that legacy systems can truly be retired, as heavily customized technologies rarely provide a one-to-one match with an ERP module.

Accenture research[4] (based on data collected from 340 distinct corporate headquarters, business units, and government entities across industries and geographies) demonstrates that ERP programs realize certain benefits more often or more quickly than others (see Figure 1.5). Interestingly, the typical ERP program benefits highlighted in original business cases tend to focus on the easier to quantify aspects of the program, such as headcount reduction or cost savings to be realized from increased operational efficiencies.

ERP Program Key Success Factors

Most of the typical program and project key success factors discussed in the following list certainly apply to all ERP programs. However, for Finance ERP programs, we believe some additional and more specific key success factors need to be considered:

- **Visible executive commitment throughout the program.** For a Finance ERP program, executive commitment typically includes the CFO (and business unit CFOs if applicable), the CIO, and, in some cases, the CEO. Executive commitment manifests through a strong governance model throughout the program and continues after implementation.
- **Business unit executive sponsorship across the business, including functions, lines of business, and geographies.** The newly implemented Finance ERP solution is not just an internal tool for the Finance function but is also a vital resource for Finance's key stakeholders. Executive sponsorship typically manifests in the ERP program's Steering Committee.

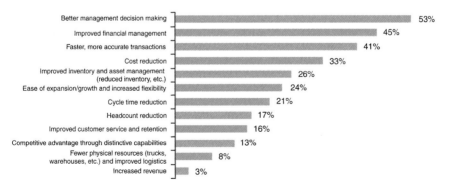

Figure 1.5 *Key benefits targeted by enterprise systems*

- **Program alignment with overall business strategy to support the business as well as the Finance vision.** The Finance ERP program is not an isolated event. Finance derives its vision from the overall organizational strategy, and the Finance ERP solution is a key tool to deliver Finance's vision. The Finance ERP solution should be value driven and should explicitly support the organization's strategy.

- **Strong change management, with a focus on people, not technology, as the main challenge.** An ERP program is not a software exercise. ERP success hinges on how the new solution is accepted and leveraged by the entire organization.

- **Design globally, roll out regionally.** Every country has its own regulations and requirements. The power in the ERP solution relies on the level of commonality and standardization successful Finance organizations can drive with the ERP program. Global ERP software solutions are designed to support local regulations and requirements. A global design with representation from countries and regions provides the correct balance to drive that standardization.

- **Funding by operational units, not by corporate.** Requesting funding support from the operational units will ensure their buy-in and participation at all levels throughout the lifecycle of the program (even though the overall budget for the Finance ERP program will not change in response to what part of the organization provides the program funding).

- **Strong management and program management office.** Success relies on identifying the right Finance resources (from Finance, business units, and geographies), with the right skills and appropriate level of decision-making power, supported by a proven ERP implementation methodology designed for the particular ERP software package.

The key reasons ERP programs "go wrong" are centered on people and process. Technology factors usually represent a small fraction of the reasons for failure. In fact, people and process factors typically outnumber technology reasons by a 4:1 ratio. The top "people" factors that lead to program failure include: change management, executive and stakeholder support, internal organization resource capabilities and/or allocation, project team training, and external resources. The top "process" factors leading to ERP program issues include process re-engineering, scope management, and value realization. Technical "program breakers" are software package functionality and enhancements/upgrades.

LEADING PRACTICES ENABLED WITH ERP

Throughout this book we will review and discuss leading practices for Core Financials end-to-end processes, as well as other leading practices that organizations should consider as they navigate through their Finance ERP program. There are many varying definitions for leading practices. According to The Hackett Group, a leading practice is a proven technique that delivers measurable improvements in either efficiency or effectiveness. The Hackett Group further defines "Hackett-Certified™ Practices" as those for which The Hackett Group has empirically established a correlation between practice adoption and world-class performance metrics obtained through benchmark studies.

For purposes of this book, we propose that the key for any practice to be considered a leading practice is that it needs to be able to be transferred from one organization to others, even across lines of business, industries, or geographies, and it needs to drive efficiencies and effectiveness in the organization. Specific to the ERP arena, a leading practice should leverage the power of existing technology and "systematize" the end-to-end processes it supports. It is important to remember that to implement most of these leading practices, there are impacts beyond the technology. For example, for the Purchasing approval process to be made common and electronic there will most likely be impacts to:

- Policy (defining and implementing a common approval policy across the organization)
- Process (adjusting the approval process to support the electronic process)
- Technology (implementing an integrated workflow solution to provide the technology support)
- Organization (revising key roles and responsibilities, as a reduced number of people will approve purchases).

We refer to these practices as leading, not best, practices for several reasons. Leading practices are continually improved, updated, and evolved, or even replaced by new leading practices. Some practices are more applicable in a specific industry or geography than others. Practices can typically be grouped into three categories: leading, common, and lagging. However, the bottom line is: there is no end game or right solution at a point in time. Practices evolve over time and we therefore do not refer to them as "best practices."

In Chapters 2 through 8 of this book we describe in detail and provide key leading practices for each Core Financial end-to-end process. In the remainder of this section we discuss some of the "building block"-type leading practices that organizations need to consider, during their Finance ERP program journey or after the "go-live date."

Business-Driven Solution

An organization's overall vision and strategies drive the mission of the Finance function. At the same time, the Finance function's mission and objectives should drive how Finance operates its end-to-end processes, how Finance defines key policies and procedures, and how Finance is organized. As shown in Figure 1.6, all three of these aspects within Finance – processes, policies and procedures, organizations – are the primary drivers of the Finance technology solution.

Successful Finance ERP programs are organized and executed from left to right in the diagram shown in Figure 1.6. This left-to-right approach has been proved to be effective and should be a fundamental premise irrespective of the Finance program's objective. Leading organizations follow this approach for full or partial implementations, for functional or technical upgrades, and for simple enhancements, such as new reports or queries.

Organizations that implement their Finance ERP solution from right to left execute a technology project – implementing the latest software for

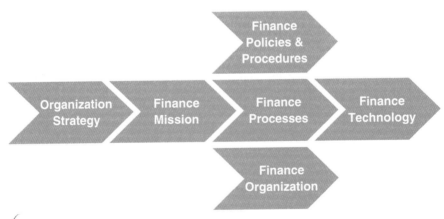

Figure 1.6   *The drivers of the Finance technology solution*

technology's sake. The Finance ERP solution may work in the short term, but in the long term these organizations typically face user dissatisfaction and internal customer complaints about Finance not being responsive or not understanding the business. The natural reaction to this dissatisfaction and complaints is to embark on another project to upgrade to the next version, to implement another Finance module, or to implement a third-party management reporting or planning tool (or even spreadsheets). However, until these organizations take a step back and approach the current crisis with the organization's strategy and Finance function's objectives in mind, they will continue in this endless loop trying to find the technology to fix all problems.

Finance Process Improvement

Successful ERP programs and implementations address a business problem or requirement and, in some cases, tackle technology issues in parallel. The key to these successful Finance ERP implementations is that leading practices are at the core of the solution, which includes processes, policies, organization, and technology. The top-tier ERP software package solutions are based, designed, and developed on leading practices. ERP vendors receive constant requests and feedback from customers, potential customers, and implementation partners, and work closely with leading researchers to incorporate the latest thinking into their development cycles and products. ERP vendors translate the feedback they receive through software selection processes and ERP implementations into enhancements to existing modules, new modules, or an entirely new family of products. Hence, business needs and requirements should be at the core of your ERP program. Organizations should view the ERP software and the technology components as the foundation and a key enabler to the overall ERP solution – not the other way around.

Figure 1.7 illustrates an approach that pulls leading practices into successful Finance ERP implementations.

Figure 1.7 *Leveraging leading practices in Finance ERPs*

We recommend that the initial focus of an organization's Finance ERP program should be around the definition of where the organization wants to be at the end of the ERP journey sometimes referred to as the end state, the "to-be vision," or "beginning with the end in mind." Our experience has shown that the best way to define this end state is to start with a review of leading practices and a "why would we not follow leading practices" approach. This approach certainly accelerates the definition of the end state by bypassing the "dreaded" documentation of the current state or "as-is." Certainly not all leading practices will be accepted or applicable to every organization – and others will be implemented over time – but at the end of this exercise, an organization will have a strong understanding of what leading practices will be implemented and when. Organizations will also by default define which leading practices will not be implemented and have a strong understanding of the reason why certain leading practices will not be followed.

The next logical step in the typical Finance process improvement approach is to define the end state for the end-to-end processes, in a scope specific to the organization. The most important element in this exercise is to use the leading practices as guiding principles and answer the key business and Finance operating model questions before diving into the details of software configuration.

After defining the end-to-end processes and documenting the end-state process flows, the Finance ERP program can then focus on the typical design, configuration, and development phases of the program lifecycle.

"Vanilla" versus Customizations

ERP software packages go through hundreds of reviews, software selections, and implementations of each major version or release as ERP vendors incorporate the latest thinking, research, and leading practices into their products, modules, and technology architectures. ERP packages are designed to be applicable across industries, geographies, and business models (although in some cases ERP vendors develop specific solutions, templates, or "starting points" for a particular industry or geography). For most organizations, the appropriate approach is to avoid customizations, modifications, extensions, and enhancements. In the Core Financials set of modules and products in particular, the going-in position for most organizations should be a "vanilla" design and implementation.

The definition of "vanilla" can differ. In most cases, it should refer to a Finance ERP solution with off-the-shelf functionality and technology.

In some cases key strategic enhancements are acceptable; customizations, modifications, or extensions to the delivered package and code, however, are not. When organizations deviate from the vanilla guiding principle they are typically also losing their focus on leading practices or trying to replicate the current state. Organizations need to support and live the vanilla guiding principle and approach while asking themselves why the delivered off-the-shelf functionality works for most other organizations across industries, geographies, and business models. The vanilla guiding principle supports other typical Finance ERP program goals such as simplification and commonality.

There are a few exceptions to the vanilla guiding principle that organizations may need to consider:

- **Reporting.** In the Finance arena, a proven approach is to utilize the ERP package-delivered reports for the subledgers or transactional modules (for example, Accounts Payable, Fixed Assets, and Accounts Receivable). The ERP package-delivered reports for these transactional modules certainly will not mirror the existing reports, but a Vendor Listing report or Outstanding Balances report is not strategic enough to warrant additional investments. In contrast, organizations should look at the delivered reports and queries in the General Ledger and Project Accounting modules. Here, organizations should be prepared to spend additional time, resources, and investment to develop reporting options that map more closely to their specific business models, organization responsibility matrix, and requirements, but only when absolutely necessary.

- **Strategic Impact.** Enhancements or customizations should be considered as exceptions to the vanilla guiding principle when these enhancements or customizations are a strategic imperative for the organization. For Core Financials functionality, these strategic requirements typically arise in the Order to Cash end-to-end process (as discussed in Chapter 6), as this is the touchpoint with the customer and is tightly integrated to the organization's revenue stream.

- **Payback or Tangible Benefit.** Each enhancement or customization should be researched and validated through a payback or some type of return on investment process. Typical exceptions occur in the Procure to Pay end-to-end process, particularly for organizations with significant spending volumes in indirect and/or direct procurement. An enhancement or set of enhancements can sometimes be easily justified by a small reduction in overall procurement spend.

- **Regulatory Requirements.** Leading ERP software vendors typically cover regulatory requirements in countries around the world. In certain cases, because of recent changes to regulations or limited software vendor market share in a specific country, organizations will be required to enhance the delivered functionality or develop additional reporting options.

The key message embedded in the vanilla guiding principle and approach is to enhance or customize the Finance ERP software package to gain a competitive strategic advantage and only when the Finance ERP program governance model justifies the enhancement or customization. ERP programs need to balance the value of the enhancement or customization with its Total Cost of Ownership. For tactical end-to-end processes that are routine and nonstrategic, the off-the-shelf ERP software solution should satisfy the business and Finance requirements.

End-to-End Processes

In the introduction to this chapter, we stated that this book is focused on the Core Financials end-to-end processes (for example, Procure to Pay), rather than on individual functions or modules, such as Purchasing or Accounts Payable. Nevertheless, the ease of integration with legacy systems as well as modularity requirements and fit with the typical Finance organization structure has forced the ERP software packages to be grouped, developed, and marketed on a function-by-function basis. Successful organizations tackle their Finance ERP program on an end-to-end process basis to minimize process and organization integration issues, to increase data and hierarchy definition commonalities, and to force Finance organizations away from their typical siloed structure.

As we said earlier in this chapter, an ERP program requirements definition should "begin with the end in mind" to address the organization's key business needs. In the case of a Finance ERP program, "beginning with the end in mind" requires a clear four-step process:

1. Focus on the definition of the organization's Finance-related reporting requirements for all in-scope end-to-end processes.
2. Leverage the Finance-related reporting requirements, in conjunction with the agreed-on leading practices, as the primary drivers to define the end-to-end processes.

3. Define the common standardized codeblock and Chart of Accounts for the entire organization, based on the updated reporting and end-to-end processes.

4. Define the ERP package configuration requirements.

The overall Finance ERP program will also have to understand, design, and implement the people and organizational impacts resulting from this four-step process. These organizational impacts will be reflected within Finance, as well as in other functions and groups outside of Finance. Finance-related reporting requirements are extensive and cover all parts of the organization as well as external stakeholders. These requirements can typically be grouped and categorized as shown in the table in Figure 1.8.

Reporting Category	Description/Examples	Audience
Transactional	Accounts Payable Accounts Receivable Fixed Assets	Corporate Finance Internal Management
Financial	Balance Sheet Income Statement Cash Flow Trial Balance	Corporate Finance Internal Management
Regulatory	GAAP IAS IFRS Tax	Government Tax Authorities
Consolidations External Reporting	Balance Sheet Income Statement Cash Flow Trial Balance	SEC Financial Institutions
Management	Balance Sheet Income Statement Cash Flow Trial Balance	Internal Management
Performance	Metrics Balanced Scorecards Dimensional Profitability	Internal Management

Figure 1.8   *Categories of reporting requirements*

A key objective of the end-to-end process approach is to force the Finance ERP program team members to cross the typical functional and departmental boundaries encountered in the Finance organization structure. Individual program team members will focus on reporting requirements, leading practices, and configuration requirements for a specific Finance module. Certainly, a multitude of key decisions must be made at the module level, but the biggest areas of risk are typically found in the integration points between modules, such as between Purchasing and Accounts Payable or between Project Accounting and Fixed Assets.

For example, key decisions made in Accounts Payable may force workarounds or increased processing or burden on users of Requisitions, or configuration decisions in Purchasing may limit the information available to Accounts Payable required during invoice processing or matching error resolution processing. The logical and physical architecture of the ERP package requires a combined effort between Accounts Payable and Purchasing — at a minimum to define a common vendor master file as well as a common item master file. Successful Finance ERP programs force integration decision making across modules and functions.

At an even higher level, the integration risks increase between application families such as Finance and Human Resources (for example, between basic Human Resources and Project Accounting to share personnel data).

An implicit benefit of the end-to-end process approach is the organizational impact requirements, definition, and design that result. The end-to-end process approach forces the Finance process owners assigned to the program team (and, by default, the Finance organization) to move away from functional silos and toward efficient and effective cross-functional processing. High-performance Finance organizations will leverage the ERP program to address the organizational impacts that are uncovered by the leading practices-based process and configuration design. They will use this information to transform themselves. By extension, if the Finance ERP program can successfully implement a value-driven Finance solution based on an end-to-end process approach, why would Finance as a whole not retool itself away from functional silos into a process-based organization?

Business Case and Value Realization

In the early stages of the lifecycle of an ERP program (just as in most other significant initiatives in the organization), the program team needs to focus on the business case. It is a key priority once the program is defined and envisioned. The first iterations of the business case will be at a very high level and have a significant level of variability. The key is to use the business case as one of the key decision points at each phase in the lifecycle. As the program team embarks on each new phase, it should refine the business case. The level of variability should decrease, while the level of detail may or may not change depending on each organization's procedures.

A consideration that organizations face when preparing their ERP program business case is determining whether or not to benchmark. Benchmarks provide an independent assessment of an organization's current performance; organizations cannot argue with the average and first-quartile metrics in these benchmarks, as they are empirically based on thousands of other organizations. An organization should determine its end target, in terms of quartile metrics, after the implementation of its ERP program. Some organizations choose to set the first quartile as their goal, whereas others may strive for median performance.

Companies such as The Hackett Group specialize in benchmarking back-office functions based on standard cross-industry performance metrics, while maintaining comparative metrics and information for organizations. The Hackett Group addresses the measurement of both efficiency and effectiveness to compare an organization with a peer group for both average and top-quartile performance. Throughout this book, we include key metrics, benchmarks, and insights from The Hackett Group.

Business cases have many different shapes, formats, and levels of detail, depending on the governance model followed by the organization. The costing aspects of the business case typically are the easier factors to define and estimate, including software license costs, maintenance fees, hardware costs, and internal and external labor. It is much harder to define and gain agreement on the benefits side of the business case, particularly in the case of Finance ERP programs. Such programs typically do not carry significant quantitative benefits (such as reduced headcount or legacy system maintenance costs). The quantitative benefits for Finance ERP programs truly come into play only if the organization's benchmarked performance does not currently fall in the first quartile or the second quartile. Therefore, in many cases, Finance ERP program benefits often include "cost avoidance" benefits. For example, the business case might describe the cost avoidance of additional headcount to support the organization's organic growth or growth through acquisition. For Finance ERP programs, particularly those that outline extensive reporting in their defined scope, business case benefits predominantly focus on qualitative benefits – for example, improved management reporting and better decision making.

As individual releases of the Finance ERP program go live (either by geography, or by function, or by business unit), the program team needs to continue to focus on the detailed business case for the remaining releases. At the same time, the program team (or a newly instituted "continuous improvement team") needs to shift some of the focus to value realization of the newly implemented releases. In the early days of ERP, these software packages and solutions delivered most of their value when they were finally implemented. They were basic solutions that replaced mostly manual processes and procedures. Today, ERP solutions are extremely complex and typically, organizations should expect an initial decline in productivity. Therefore, they should also expect a longer time before the newly implemented ERP solution starts to deliver value.

The key is for organizations to be outcome focused, as opposed to milestone focused, when defining their benefits and expected value. The fact that the new ERP solution has gone "live" will not provide value in and of itself; the new processes, policies, procedures, and technology need to become ingrained in the newly impacted organization. The entire organization, not just Finance, needs to accept and institutionalize the new solution.

Accenture research,[5] as illustrated in Figure 1.9, demonstrates that measuring the benefits obtained from enterprise solutions and holding people accountable for realizing the targeted benefits significantly speeds time to value.

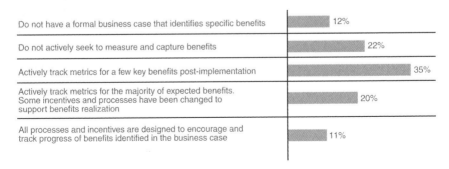

Figure 1.9 *Measurement of enterprise system benefits*

ERP JOURNEY CONSIDERATIONS

When Finance functions take the ERP journey, typically many decisions must be made that can be grouped under the heading of implementation lifecycle considerations. These usually include the following:

- **Software Selection.** The typical packaged software implementation methodology includes a Software Selection phase. Organizations should take a step back and define the true need for this software selection. Our experience and industry research demonstrates that vendor choice, particularly in the Core Financials scope, is not relevant. According to research from The Hackett Group, in fact, 96 percent[6] of all companies that implement leading ERP packages do not achieve world-class performance in Finance. Instead, The Hackett Group's research pointed to the importance of making process, organization, and policy changes and proactively configuring ERP to support best practices in Finance as part of any implementation effort. Top-tier Finance software vendors face an extremely commoditized market; as soon as one vendor incorporates a new feature or new module, the competitors quickly catch up. However, software selections are certainly still relevant in emerging areas of Finance, such as Enterprise Performance Management and Treasury. These functional process areas are still dominated by best-of-breed software vendors that continue to push the envelope and manage to stay ahead of the top-tier ERP software vendors through their focused investments.

- **Industry Templates.** Also called industry preconfigured solutions, these vendor-delivered package extensions are the focus of much debate during the software selection and planning phases. The objectives of the templates are to jump-start the design and implementation lifecycle by delivering a preconfigured, standard industry-specific solution. Our experience demonstrates that these templates are of great use as a starting point for conceptual design sessions. However, our experience has also shown that this preconfiguration is not as relevant for pure configuration activities. Global and large national organizations typically operate in a multitude of industries or under several operating models, making it difficult to define which industry template to use initially. For these types of organizations, we recommend using the industry templates as design enablers, rather than as a true starting point. For smaller organizations, or for entities that are extremely focused on one industry (for example, higher education or government), these preconfigured templates provide a strong starting point for the ERP journey.

- **Conference Room Pilot.** Packaged software methodology also typically includes a Conference Room Pilot (CRP) phase. CRP is also sometimes referred to as a "proof of concept" or "working demonstration." The objective of this phase is to incorporate the early design decisions into a working model of the final solution that can be used as a demonstration for Finance end users and key Finance stakeholders. The key is to configure the critical Finance end-to-end processes without spending time on developing proposed enhancements or customizations. The CRP should include sample organizational data and demonstrate typical scenarios for each end-to-end process. Certainly not all aspects of each end-to-end process should be set up and configured. The focus should be on those processes or subprocesses that will require the most change in the organization or are most strategic in nature. CRP should be approached as an important change management activity and training opportunity, remembering that people, and not technology, are the key challenge to a successful ERP implementation. To achieve this objective, the CRP needs to demonstrate key functionality within a module, across modules within an end-to-end process, and across end-to-end processes within Finance.

By carefully incorporating these additional ERP journey considerations, in conjunction with leading practices, we believe an organization will be able to realize the full value of their ERP solution.

THE HACKETT GROUP ON WORLD-CLASS FINANCE ORGANIZATIONS

According to The Hackett Group's research, world-class Finance organizations now spend 42 percent less than typical companies overall (0.73 percent of revenue versus 1.26 percent). Typical companies have seen an 18 percent increase in total Finance costs since 2003, while world-class Finance organizations have seen a 5 percent drop during the same period. World-class Finance organizations now operate with 44 percent fewer staff than typical companies (63 employees/billion of revenue versus 112).

More than half of the overall spending gap between world-class and typical companies is attributable to lower labor costs, even though

continued

world-class Finance organizations pay their staff more, with fully loaded wage rates being 11 percent higher than typical companies ($79,345 versus $71,411). According to Hackett, this higher wage rate is an indication that world-class Finance organizations are changing their staffing profile, focusing on more skilled employees capable of delivering higher value Finance activities.

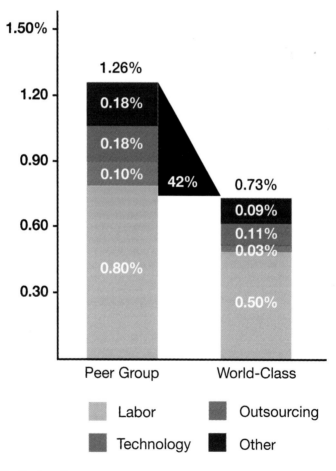

Total finance cost as a percent of revenue, 2005

Source: The Hackett Group

continued

---

continued

For organizations that have achieved world-class results, exceptional performance is no accident. The executive team is focused on both operational excellence and alignment with the overall business. Our data show that leveraging technology investments by simplifying and optimizing the infrastructure is a key ingredient in the mix they use to attain exceptional performance.

CFO INSIGHTS

- High-performance businesses and governments consistently outperform their peers over a sustained timeframe. There is a strong correlation between a high-performance organization and Finance mastery. Research shows that high-performance businesses and governments use Finance technology as one of the capabilities to help executives make better decisions for resource allocation, while at the same time increasing productivity. High-performance organizations continually make technology investments at above-average industry rates and secure higher returns and value realization than their counterparts.

- The functionality supported by the top-tier ERP vendors (Oracle and SAP) for Core Financials is typically very sound and stable. Differentiation between the software products is minimal. The functionality supported in the Value-Added Finance arena continues to advance. Top-tier ERP vendors provide strong support for the basic Value-Added Finance functionality, although best-of-breed vendors are still prevalent and probably a version ahead.

- The Finance ERP solution is not just a Finance tool; the key stakeholders include Finance, business units, operations, and external stakeholders. High-performance Finance organizations are aligned with the organization's overall vision. Successful Finance ERP programs are business driven and therefore involve business representation from the start (on both the Steering Committee and the core project team).

- Finance ERP programs are not a one-time activity, but a series of ongoing projects that help the existing solution to evolve. Thus organizations need to develop and monitor the business case throughout the lifecycle of the program, while continually refining assumptions and estimates. High-performance Finance organizations establish a continuous improvement process and organization to fine-tune the ERP solution and evolve the value realization beyond the initial "go live" date.

FROM INSIGHT TO ACTION

TREAT THE FINANCE ERP SOLUTION AS A PROGRAM, NOT A PROJECT

The Finance ERP journey is composed of multiple projects and initiatives and requires its own governance model and structure. The Finance ERP program also needs to work within the context of the overall business and other ongoing programs.

ENSURE THAT THE PROGRAM IS LEADING PRACTICE DRIVEN AND TECHNOLOGY ENABLED

Leading practices should drive key decisions around the new end-to-end process definition and system implementation considerations. High-performance Finance organizations first define leading practices-based end-to-end processes and then focus on process-driven configurations and process-driven Finance organizational impacts.

THINK IN TERMS OF END-TO-END PROCESSES

Finance ERP programs organized around end-to-end processes as opposed to functions will enable Finance to identify and understand key integration points. These integration points are between functions (such as Purchasing and Accounts Payable), between Finance end-to-end processes (such as Procure to Pay and Asset Lifecycle), and between Finance and other organizations (such as Human Resources).

BEGIN WITH THE END IN MIND

A core premise for successful Finance ERP programs is to "begin with the end in mind" — the reporting requirements for all Finance stakeholders. These reporting requirements will then drive the end-to-end process definition, as well as the codeblock/chart of accounts design as a basis for the software configuration.

FOCUS ON PEOPLE AND PROCESS, NOT TECHNOLOGY

People (within Finance and the business) and leading practices-based processes are the main challenges. The Finance ERP program is not a

continued

continued

software exercise; the Finance ERP solution success hinges on how the new solution is accepted and leveraged by the entire organization. Change management is key.

REFERENCES

1. Jeanne G. Harris and Thomas H. Davenport, *New Growth from Enterprise Systems*, Accenture Institute for High Performance Business, October 2005, http://www.accenture.com.

2. Accenture, *Finance & Performance Management Mastery and the High Performance Business*, 2004, http://www.accenture.com.

3. Thomas H. Davenport, Jeanne G. Harris, and Susan Cantrell, *The Return of Enterprise Solutions: The Directors Cut*, Accenture Institute for High Performance Business, 2002, http://www.accenture.com.

4. Jeanne G. Harris and Thomas H. Davenport, *New Growth from Enterprise Systems*, Accenture Institute for High Performance Business, October 2005, http://www.accenture.com.

5. Thomas H. Davenport, Jeanne G. Harris, and Susan Cantrell, *The Return of Enterprise Solutions: The Directors Cut*, Accenture Institute for High Performance Business, 2002, http://www.accenture.com.

6. The Hackett Group, *ERP Vendor Choice Is Largely Irrelevant in Achieving World-Class Finance Performance*, May 18, 2004, http://www.thehackettgroup.com.

CHAPTER 2

Leveraging the Financial Close to Gain a Competitive Advantage

FINANCIAL CLOSE: AN OVERVIEW

In the late 1990s, Cisco Systems and Motorola touched off the craze of the "virtual close," sending a message to companies around the world that a faster close is a better close. In 2001, Larry Carter, CFO of Cisco Systems, defined the virtual close to *Harvard Business Review*: "We can literally close our books within hours, producing consolidated financials statements on the first workday following the end of any monthly, quarterly or annual reporting period."[1]

The virtual close, which is enabled by end-to-end integration of application systems, is generally a costly and time-consuming process. However, for many organizations still struggling to close their books in 8 to 12 days, Larry Carter's words were inspiration enough to make a start. As a result, average time to close the books decreased from 5.9 days in 1997 to 5.2 days in 2003.[2]

As many organizations were working toward a virtual close, two major events took place that changed the focus of financial reporting and compliance. In Cisco's third fiscal quarter ending April 2001, the company posted a net loss of approximately $2.7 billion, as sales declined by

30 percent from the previous quarter and the company wrote off $2.2 billion in inventory. This financial setback made many question the value of a costly virtual close if it could not help Cisco forecast such a significant decline in customer demand. Then the high-profile corporate financial scandals of companies such as Enron and WorldCom induced Congress to pass the 2002 Sarbanes-Oxley Act, which, among other requirements, mandates publicly traded companies to accelerate their Securities and Exchange Commission (SEC) filings and executive management to certify the accuracy of these financial results.

Suddenly, corporate goals for the month-end close changed. The overriding driver was not the virtual close, but a world-class close that would not only be faster than the 8 to 12 days of old but also be more accurate and reliable.

The traditional close process is executed within the bounds of the "Record to Report" monthly cycle – recording transactions within sub-ledgers, reconciling those sub-ledgers to the General Ledger, adjusting the sub-ledgers or General Ledger as necessary, consolidating the General Ledger, and reporting the results. Figure 2.1 illustrates the Record to Report process.

Defining the Financial Close Process

Our experience shows that leading companies with a world-class close have been able to achieve an accurate month-end close cycle of three to five days by improving their entire Record to Report process. They have made these improvements by implementing leading practice process designs, coupled with an integrated Enterprise Resource Planning (ERP) and reporting solution. Their focus is less on reducing the number of days that it takes to close and more on improving the quality of the data, making incremental process improvements, and using their existing technical architecture for a more effective and efficient closing process.

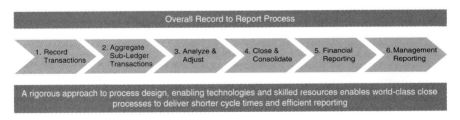

Figure 2.1 *Record to Report process*

The Challenge to Shorten the Close

When organizations are closing their books, they may find themselves challenged for a number of reasons, including:

- Decentralized/autonomously run operations
- Frequent organizational restructuring
- Merger and acquisition activity
- Limited use of enabling technology, such as ERP
- Lack of continuous improvement or process design initiatives.

For example, KeySpan, a gas and electrical utility in the northeastern United States, was formed in 1998 through a number of mergers and acquisitions. The disparate legacy systems and financial processes inherited from those merged businesses hindered KeySpan's ability to close its books in fewer than eight to nine days each month. BP, a global energy company, had also undergone a number of mergers and acquisitions, leaving it with disparate legacy systems and financial processes, which resulted in a lengthy close. In fact, the goals for their world-class close initiative revolved around:

- Providing management with faster, more reliable data
- Driving efficiency and effectiveness improvements through dramatic acceleration of the financial close process
- Enabling its Finance and control community to focus on value-adding work beyond making the merged systems perform.

Once an organization chooses to improve its close process, the process will not necessarily be easy. Typical financial system and processes characteristics we have seen that can challenge close improvements include:

- Multiple ERP platforms with custom-built or manual interfaces
- Continued use of legacy technology with inconsistent master and transaction data
- No common financial language (i.e., Chart of Accounts, codeblock, transaction consistency)
- Manual data entry required to create, adjust, reclassify, and correct journal entries

- Lengthy batch execution time to post transactions and generate reports
- Lack of a seamless and automated solution to report and analyze actual results versus plan
- Close schedule not tightly defined, managed, or controlled
- Complicated allocation method within the business unit or between corporate and business units
- Complex and disparate interorganizational processes
- Inconsistent financial policies and procedures across the organization.

When Should an Organization Address the Close?

An individual organization's circumstance drives when that organization should make major process improvements. Most circumstances would suggest that major process improvements be undertaken prior to or in parallel with a major ERP implementation or upgrade; therefore, the new process can be considered when designing the ERP configuration.

Our experience shows that there is no typical length of time for designing and implementing a streamlined close process. Not surprisingly, the presence of multiple geographies and business units, as well as the need to introduce complex financial technology, can often dictate the length of time needed to complete such an undertaking. For example, Niagara Mohawk needed to decrease its month-end close from eight workdays to two workdays so it could meet the closing schedule requirements of its merger partner, National Grid. Because Niagara Mohawk had limited geographic and divisional structure, it could implement process changes quickly.

BENEFITS FROM A WORLD-CLASS CLOSE INITIATIVE

Organizations that transform their close process have typically seen their month-end closing workdays substantially reduced – by two to ten days, depending on the starting point. For example, BP reduced the number of workdays it took its business units to report from ten working days to six working days. BP was also able to take a week out of its Group Centre Results Consolidation phase during quarters 1 through 3 each year as a consequence of error elimination, improved timeliness, reduced low-value adjustments, and so on.

In another example, KeySpan decreased the number of workdays it took to close (originally 10 to 12) to four workdays. Meanwhile, Niagara

Mohawk, now part of National Grid, shaved six workdays off its close. These reductions in workday efforts translated into significant man-hour reductions as well.

Although the quantitative benefits may seem reason enough to embark on a world-class close initiative, these organizations also experienced significant qualitative benefits from their initiatives. We find that these benefits can generally be classified into five categories:

1. **Strategy and Management.** More timely access to key metric data can help management make faster decisions that can lead to shareholder value creation.
2. **Organization and People.** By taking significant man-hours out of the close, accounting staffs are able to focus on other value-added activities.
3. **Process and Principles.** Common business processes and practices implemented across an organization enable consistent results.
4. **Technology and Solutions.** Common, standardized technology solutions enable consistent results across an organization and are often less expensive to maintain.
5. **External Stakeholder Satisfaction.** A streamlined and efficient close, executed over a shorter period, enables an organization to report results to external parties in a timelier manner.

WORLD-CLASS CLOSE LEADING PRACTICE INITIATIVES

As discussed previously, the close process is executed within the boundaries of the Record to Report monthly cycle. We will now examine the four subprocesses required to close the books: Record Transactions, Aggregate Sub-Ledger Transactions, Analyze and Adjust, and Close and Consolidate (depicted earlier in Figure 2.1). When you are improving the close process, it is important to keep these in mind. Implementing leading practices within your ERP solution for each of these subprocesses facilitates a reduction in the time to close the books.

The subprocesses for Financial Reporting and Management Reporting are discussed in more detail in Chapter 3.

1. Record Transactions and 2. Aggregate Sub-Ledger Transactions Leading Practices

Within the Record Transactions and Aggregate Sub-Ledger Transactions subprocesses, all the leading ERP vendors offer functionality to streamline the recording of transactions to the General Ledger. However, it is often difficult to take advantage of some of these capabilities because of the complexity of the existing technology platform, as well as the underlying business structure. Our experience shows that organizations able to streamline their business complexities are best able to take advantage of these capabilities.

Often, it is the CFO and the executive team who are required to drive the reduction of business complexity, as discussed in Chapter 1. For example, some organizations will force relentless standardization across the business. Executive team support is often a key success factor in successful ERP programs and close improvement efforts. A number of leading practices should be considered within the Record Transactions and Aggregate Sub-Ledger Transactions subprocesses, as follows:

Create a Single, Standardized Codeblock

The foundation for financial transactions is the ERP codeblock, which includes the Chart of Accounts (CoA), as well as other master data components, such as cost centers, profit centers, and others. A key success factor and leading practice to accelerate the operation and ability to close the books is a single and standardized codeblock and CoA. Companies that have been able to standardize all their divisions onto a single CoA and codeblock have been able to eliminate reconciliations between source systems and the General Ledger, leading to fewer analyses and adjustments. Oracle, PeopleSoft, and SAP all support this leading practice. (Additional information about defining the codeblock is given in Chapter 3.)

The development of a common CoA is driven less by the technology and more by an organization's desire for standards and commonality. To implement this structure, there is a strong requirement for executive support to develop the common definitions for the CoA.

For example, a comparison of SAP's approach to handling the codeblock structures with that of PeopleSoft demonstrates that there are a myriad ways to achieve a world-class close. The cornerstone of SAP financials revolves around its Master Data concept, whereby the codeblock is maintained centrally and integrated with the sub-ledgers and financial modules when necessary. PeopleSoft emphasizes the hierarchical nature of the codeblock and its natural tendency to drive the ultimate look and feel of the reporting output. Either way, the two platforms highlight the importance of the codeblock in integrating finance processes throughout the organization.

Once Niagara Mohawk was fully integrated into National Grid, National Grid implemented the PeopleSoft suite throughout the company. During the design phase, National Grid designed a new simplified codeblock that was adopted throughout the company. The new codeblock minimized the complexity of intercompany transactions and the number of reconciliations and adjustments from the General Ledger to the source system or from General Ledger to General Ledger. The company also standardized policies and processes.

Capture Management and Statutory Data Once, at the Source

As a common CoA and codeblock is defined, it is important to facilitate the capture of statutory and management data once, at the source. As the transactions are recorded within the ERP solution, it is important to record the transaction once and to support the statutory, management, and (if applicable) tax-reporting requirements. Organizations that use the same source transactions to derive both statutory and management reporting data (with a single codeblock to distinguish reporting hierarchies) can eliminate reconciliation activity during the close process.

From an ERP technology standpoint, SAP facilitates the integration between transaction and reporting data by designing its Enterprise Controlling (ECC) core financial system to stream directly into the Strategic Enterprise Management module (SEM). The two systems (ECC and SEM) share common codeblock structures, but the SEM reporting structures are configured to present the appropriate view of the business, depending on whether the delivered reports are for management or statutory purposes. An end-to-end solution such as this can quicken the time to report delivery and can increase the accuracy of the close.

Standardize Policies and Processes of Core Activities

Organizations that have been able to standardize core policies and processes in such areas as transfer pricing, intercompany transactions, payments, receipts, and stock valuations have found that they get the data entry "right the first time," limiting the amount of reconciliation and adjustments that could hold up the close.

Automate Intercompany Transactions and Other Recurring Entries

Organizations that have been able to automate intercompany transaction controls, recurring accruals, and reversals (and that have been able to conduct these activities prior to close) eliminate time as well as critical path items from the close.

For example, while analyzing the closing cycle, KeySpan found it had a significant number of manual journal entries booked each month. Upon analyzing the situation, KeySpan found it used a manual entry process to book entries recurring each month. It was also using an entirely manual process to book unbilled revenue accruals. An important medium-term close initiative for KeySpan was to set up automated recurring entries and automated bookings of unbilled revenue. By redesigning the process accordingly, KeySpan was able to reduce manual entries and processes within the entire closing process by 25 percent.

BP utilizes the SAP suite across many of its multiple business units and geographies. SAP requires dual-entry accounting, even with regard to intercompany processing. For many of BP's business units and geographies on one single instance of SAP, this functionality ensures that BP intercompanies remain in balance. This is not always the case outside of the United States, as BP is still implementing SAP in some of its international locations. Until a single instance of SAP can be rolled out globally, BP implemented an Intercompany Hub solution to manage global intercompanies.

Intercompany invoice information is fed from the originating sales system to the centralized Hub tool, providing the seller with earlier access to transactional information and an additional reconciliation tool. In addition, the Hub provides for automated settlement of intercompany activity on the due date, via direct linkages to the individual company financing accounts. Through this sophisticated global issue resolution process, intercompany issues no longer hold up the closing process.

BP uses SAP dual-entry accounting (even with regard to intercompany processing system requirements), coupled with strict process controls, to ensure that intercompany accounts are never out of balance everywhere they have been able to implement a single instance of SAP. BP does this by assigning the responsibility to book the simultaneous entries to the business unit purchasing from an internal entity. Understanding that the business unit selling to the internal entity may not always be in agreement with the business unit bookkeeping that is purchasing, BP developed an issue resolution system for intercompanies.

Intercompany issues may be logged into an issue-resolution tool: a document workflow system. Business units may use the issue-resolution tool to document discussions that take place to obtain resolution on the issue. If the intercompany cannot be resolved in a timely manner and is material in nature, BP has developed an escalation process, whereby controllers of the business units act as arbiters. If the business unit controllers cannot resolve the discrepancy, then the corporate controller will resolve the issue.

The daily U.S. close meetings provide a forum from which the controllers can mediate intercompany issues. This structured intercompany process allows a large company such as BP to maintain tight financial control over its many businesses and geographies that sell and trade products internally before products reach the end consumer. Through this sophisticated issue-resolution process, intercompany issues do not hold up the closing process within the U.S. geography.

Post All Transactions to the Sub-Ledger

By requiring all transaction activities to be posted to sub-ledgers and not to the General Ledger, organizations have been able to keep their General Ledgers clean and minimize the amount of reconciliation and analysis between the General Ledger and the sub-ledgers.

Aggregate Sub-Ledgers to the General Ledger Frequently

Many companies reduce the time it takes to close source systems by loading source system data into the General Ledger on an instantaneous, daily, or weekly basis. This approach takes some of the key activities out of the close process critical path, which allows for faster close cycles after month-end. It can also provide organizations with the opportunity to create interim flash reporting during the month.

Oracle, PeopleSoft, and SAP all offer the benefit of aggregating and integrating sub-ledger transactions to the core General Ledger. The benefits of this approach are realized via the reduction of external interfaces and by eliminating the number of manual postings to the General Ledger that result from sub-ledger activity.

Shift Noncritical Close Activities to Pre-Close

Many organizations have begun aggregating and closing their noncritical sub-ledgers prior to month-end to spread the closing activities over a longer period without adversely impacting the month-end closing cycle.

A variation of this practice is to execute selected processes prior to the close and then perform catch-up activities during the actual close. For example, SAP allows early executions for activities such as asset depreciation, settlements, and cost allocations ahead of time. Companies that execute these activities a few days prior to the actual close can review preliminary results, correcting any errors and posting adjustments in advance of the close. These activities can be run again during the close against any newly posted data, resulting in shorter runtimes and less exceptions to analyze and correct.

Provide Drill-Down from the General Ledger to Sub-Ledgers

Any integrated ERP solution can provide drill-down capability from the General Ledger to the sub-ledgers, allowing an organization to simplify its reconciliation process between the General Ledger and the sub-ledgers.

3. Analyze and Adjust Leading Practices

Evaluate Materiality Thresholds

With the passage of the Sarbanes-Oxley Act, many organizations have decreased materiality thresholds to levels lower than their external auditor requires. Organizations will sometimes miss a close deadline because source systems remain open to book a last-minute adjustment. Organizations should consider impacts at the consolidated level when determining materiality thresholds to avoid last-minute adjustments.

Simplify the Allocations Process

Many organizations make use of a complex system of formulas and calculations to allocate nondirect and corporate overhead expense. Often, these algorithms contain circular and convoluted references to generate the allocated amounts. Organizations have begun to simplify the allocations process as they have realized that the analytical value of these allocations does not justify the elongation of the close cycle and its effects on the timeliness of receiving key decision-support data. Organizations should restrict allocations to areas in which there is a business reason to justify the allocation rationale.

One of the areas that National Grid considered a high-value opportunity for improving its close was its complicated intercompany and corporate allocations process. The company made significant headway on its allocation process by simply standardizing its financial codeblock across the company. However, National Grid did not stop there. National Grid leverages its PeopleSoft solution by consolidating the number of allocation steps, minimizing the number of allocation bases used, and allocating at a more summarized level, using summary accounts instead of detailed accounts. The initiative required process and procedural changes at corporate as well as changes to the PeopleSoft system to automate the new simplified allocations process. National Grid could not have simplified and automated the allocations process if it had not first simplified and standardized its financial codeblock within PeopleSoft across the company. The functionality of the codeblock and the flexibility of the PeopleSoft system allowed National Grid to simplify and automate the corporate allocations process.

Reduce Management Adjustments

Organizations with complex business structures generally have leaned toward development of decentralized business units with fully accountable Profit & Loss (P&L) statements. This practice has generally created an atmosphere in which individual business units will negotiate with corporate for last-minute management adjustments that will affect their own P&L more favorably. However, this process usually adversely affects a company's ability to finalize the close. Therefore, many companies are moving their business units onto P&Ls that only reflect the unit's controllable revenue and cost, eliminating the need for a negotiation process for noncontrollable expense adjustments during the close process and reducing the closing cycle in the process.

4. Close and Consolidate Leading Practices

Structure the Close Calendar and Have a Single Process Owner

The close process typically touches multiple groups within Finance and the business. Only through a highly structured and rigorous process can organizations predetermine month-end close dates. Organizations have found that they have been able to shorten the closing cycle by implementing a single coordinated close calendar managed by a single process owner.

Often, we have seen that taking a holistic look at the close process and redesigning the close calendar and overall process can subtract days from the time to close. Niagara Mohawk, as it was merging into National Grid, realized that it waited until project accounting closed on workday five before beginning to close revenue accounting, even though project accounting was not critical for closing revenue accounting. So Niagara Mohawk moved many of these nondependent processes into parallel closing paths and took noncritical activities out of the overall close. The company also found that it performed little to no closing activities before month-end. Niagara Mohawk was able to move as much closing activity as possible to prior to month-end. Many of these activities were related to source systems. By keeping only critical close activities on post-work-day one and implementing parallel close processes, Niagara Mohawk was able to move from an eight workday close to a two workday close.

Maintain Data Centrally

Consolidating legal entities and standardizing to one CoA is a good first step in solving this issue of disparate data. However, a consistent and standard legal entity structure, CoA, and codeblock cannot be maintained properly unless the organization has centralized ownership of the General Ledger and codeblock. The organization needs to implement significant process and system controls within its ERP solution. Only through a structured and centralized control method can an organization ensure that its codeblock structure remains harmonized across businesses.

Automate Consolidations

Once the codeblock has been harmonized across businesses, an organization may automate the consolidation process through the use of a standard consolidation tool. All the major ERP vendors have consolidation tools available within their packages. SAP has its Business Consolidation System (BCS) for financial consolidations. Likewise, Oracle offers Financial Consolidation Hub and PeopleSoft Global Consolidations. Organizations sometimes use best-of-breed packages, such as Hyperion Financial Management (HFM) and Cognos Controller. Many companies opt for these best-of-breed solutions based on functionality. Regardless of the approach, we realize it is key to have automation and integration between the transaction and reporting systems to minimize manual interfaces and intervention.

The ERP providers facilitate the consolidation process through their consolidation modules. As stated previously, SAP allows for a data stream from General Ledger into its business consolidation system (SEM-BCS). Oracle offers similar functionality with its Financial Consolidation Hub.

Further efficiencies in the consolidation process can be realized by automating the consolidation of the investments function (which is a manual effort in many organizations today). Most consolidation packages allow users to define the ownership structure of a company's legal entities and will automatically generate the appropriate accounting treatments as needed.

Measure Close Improvements

Organizations can monitor continuous improvement of the close (and other key process areas) by developing close metrics and evaluating these metrics from month to month. Typical metrics include: days to close, days to report, cost per journal entry process, journal entry processes per person, days to complete account reconciliations, days to earnings release, manual journal entries per billion dollars of revenue, number of manual entries booked each month, material exceptions booked each month, percentage of time spent on transaction processing versus analysis, and General Ledger reports per billion dollars of revenue.

Implement a Soft Close

Some companies have successfully implemented a soft close on nonquarter months. During these nonquarter (soft close) months, companies perform less analysis, do not perform all reconciliations, do not book all adjustments, and lessen materiality requirements. A company should only consider a soft close during nonquarter months when it has implemented a seamless closing process that incorporates most close-process leading practices and a robust systems architecture with integrated ERP, data warehouse, consolidation, and reporting capabilities. Only a company confident that its closing and reporting process has strong internal controls and a low risk of financial misstatement should attempt to introduce a soft close.

Even though KeySpan has multiple business units, it was able to design a close calendar effectively and then designate a single process owner to communicate and enforce deadlines across those business units. In contrast, BP, having a globally functioning close calendar, found that its business units and regions were still missing report deadlines, as source ledgers did not close according to close-calendar deadlines. BP underwent an internal change initiative, which entailed focusing management's priorities on the importance of timely closing and reporting of financials. Through this change initiative, managers were reminded of the importance of closing source systems on a timely basis and of only deviating from the calendar because of exceptions of material items. As a multibusiness unit company, BP could not rely on a single process owner to ensure adherence to a close calendar. Instead, it needed to develop methods of coordinating the close activities and issue-resolution process, which in some cases included daily close meetings of key business controllers.

Alternatively, KeySpan was able to reduce its close significantly through process improvements and made more significant strides by moving all group consolidation and reporting onto Hyperion, a robust consolidation and reporting tool that interfaced with Oracle financials and provided a robust and easy method for consolidating subsidiaries and producing company-level financial statements. The Hyperion reporting tool allows KeySpan to produce consolidated financial statements not only enterprise wide but also by legal entity and division.

SYSTEM/ERP-SPECIFIC LEADING PRACTICE IMPROVEMENTS

On their own, leading practice process improvements can significantly reduce the time to close. They can enable an organization to close within five to six workdays. However, we find that organizations wishing to close their books in less than four days will probably require significant technology investments and improvements.

Global Single ERP Solution Instance

Many organizations are moving all their divisions and geographies onto one ERP platform and logical instance. Although the rise in mergers and acquisitions for many of these companies has limited their ability to accomplish this task quickly, the benefits are worth the effort. One of the more tangible benefits is that organizations that have been able to move onto a single ERP instance have found a significant decline in reconciliation activities that need to take place, thereby decreasing the closing cycle. Of course, implementing a single ERP instance is no small task, but even taking the small step of moving an organization toward using common data definitions, configuration decisions, and transaction policies can help streamline the close process.

Management Reporting through a Data Warehouse

Many companies are interfacing their ERP solutions to a data warehouse. This warehouse may hold operational as well as financial data and may be used to create key performance indicator metrics for companies to track and measure performance. A robust reporting tool that works with the data warehouse can be used to produce both simple financial and operational reports. Many companies are moving to the use of a data warehouse as their "one version of the truth" for both external financial reporting and internal management reporting. This approach can significantly decrease the closing to reporting cycle at each month-end close, since companies without a robust data warehouse often have to undergo many hours of reconciliation between financial information reported to the SEC in the United States and financial information reported to management. Many of the ERP vendors provide consolidation tools, reporting tools, and data warehouses in their ERP suites. Companies may choose their ERP vendor's product or a best-of-breed product, depending on their business requirements. (Chapter 3 covers this topic in additional detail.)

Autoprocessing and Workflow

Although many organizations have a comprehensive ERP suite of modules, most organizations have not fully configured their solutions to utilize all capabilities available within the solution modules. Examples include daily autoposting from source systems to the General Ledger, formula-based accruals, validation of codeblock in sub-ledgers to minimize suspense, automated workflow for proper entry routing, and approval and drill-down capabilities from the General Ledger to the source systems for review.

All three organizations showcased in this chapter have implemented comprehensive ERP solutions. KeySpan uses Oracle, and National Grid uses PeopleSoft. BP is moving to multiple instances but the same template/configuration of SAP globally. All three of these companies have mandated a single instance of these systems across their divisions and geographies. Because of its size, recent merger and acquisition activity, and magnitude, BP is still moving all the businesses onto the same template/configuration of SAP. According to The Hackett Group, companies with world-class Finance operations still rely on an average of 1.7 ERP solutions for their information, significantly less than average companies, which utilize 2.7 ERP solutions. Lack of a single global ERP solution by most companies represents a serious roadblock to a world-class close.[3]

DECIDING WHICH WORLD-CLASS CLOSE LEADING PRACTICES TO ADOPT

When companies consider adopting a leading practice-driven approach to the close process, they must consider the value of adopting the practice versus the cost of implementation. Figure 2.2 is an illustrative opportunity matrix of leading practices, plotted according to their value and cost.

Organizations that are determined to implement their ERP based on leading practice should track both the leading practices implemented, as well as those not implemented, as discussed in Chapter 1. In the case of implemented leading practices, organizations can use information in their ERP solutions to measure the effectiveness of the leading practice.

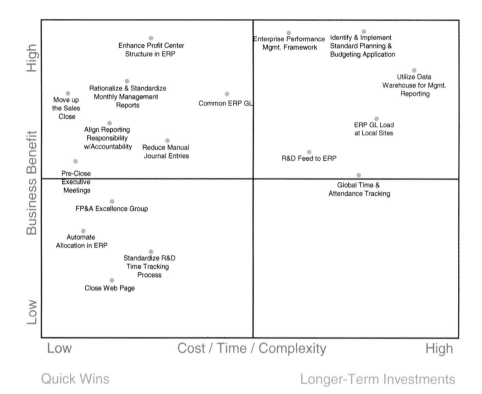

Figure 2.2 *An illustrative opportunity matrix of world-class close leading practices*

Leading practices that are not implemented should be tracked for future implementations or upgrades.

FUTURE WORLD-CLASS CLOSE TRENDS

Future trends suggest that a timely month-end close is becoming more of a challenge to companies. According to The Hackett Group benchmarking, the month-end close for average companies increased from 5.2 days in 2003 to 5.5 days in 2004. According to the same study, the month-end close for world-class companies increased from 4.3 days in 2003 to 5.1 days in 2004. The Hackett Group forecasts that the month-end close for average companies will inch up again and top six days in 2005.[4]

Many possible reasons explain the longer month-end close trend. Sarbanes-Oxley Section 404 requires more and better disclosure of forecasted and current financial results from companies and also requires CEOs and CFOs to certify these financial results. Amended filings for financial restatements of public companies owing to accounting errors totaled 414 in 2004, a dramatic 28 percent increase over the 323 restatement filings identified in 2003[5] (see Figure 2.3).

As a result, companies are becoming much more careful with their numbers and making time up in the back-end by lengthening the close and reporting cycles.[6] As companies spend more time ensuring that accurate financial results and forecasts are reported externally, they have gained greater confidence in their overall forecasting and results reporting. According to The Hackett Group's 2004 World-Class Performance study of corporate Finance departments, 67 percent of companies surveyed say they are confident with their forecasting and reporting output, an improvement of 58 percent over the results of the same survey in 2003.[7]

Finance organizations are also undergoing increased pressure from their own executive management teams to provide more accurate and timely financial information internally. As senior managers seek to improve their performance management capabilities, they are looking to their accounting departments to provide more accurate data for the key performance indicators they use to evaluate corporate performance and make decisions.

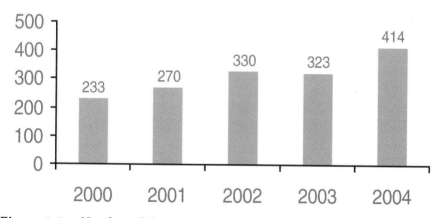

Figure 2.3 *Number of financial restatements by year filed*

CASE STUDY SUMMARY

Figure 2.4 provides a summary of the experiences of National Grid, Keyspan, and BP that have been discussed throughout this chapter. This table provides an overview of their respective situations, along with examples of leading practices implemented and key results by each company.

	National Grid	Keyspan	BP
Organization Background	▪ Electric and gas utility with nearly 4 million customers in New York and New England. ▪ 8,000 employees and $7 billion in revenue. ▪ Uses PeopleSoft.	▪ Fifth largest distributor of natural gas in the United States, with 2.6 million customers in New York and New England. ▪ Uses Oracle.	▪ One of the largest energy companies in the world, with over $200 billion in sales. ▪ Provides transportation fuel, heating and lighting energy and petro-chemicals. ▪ Uses SAP.
Business Challenges	▪ Niagara Mohawk needed to meet National Grid's consolidation and reporting timeline. ▪ Needed to reduce the month-end close from 8 workdays to 2 workdays. ▪ Sought to provide more timely information for decision-making and free up resources to provide more value-added activities.	▪ KeySpan had a 10-12 workday close. ▪ Finance executive management saw potential based on past experiences and case studies of other companies. ▪ Needed to meet stricter deadlines for submitting financial reports, driven by Sarbanes-Oxley requirements.	▪ Accelerate earnings and release dates. ▪ Internal management wanted financials sooner for appropriate review, analysis and business decisions. ▪ It was taking 10 workdays for division to report to corporate. ▪ Address the work/life balance issues confronting staff due to the long hours.
Leading Practices	▪ Moved as much closing activity as possible to prior to workday 1. ▪ Moved activities that were on consecutive processes to one parallel process. ▪ Used estimates for accruals for things such as labor, transportation, tax, electricity, purchasing and gas purchasing. ▪ Gained an understanding of the critical path and not waiting for non-critical path activities. ▪ Created and strictly enforced a close calendar. ▪ Identified a close process owner to manage the close calendar. ▪ Streamlined the allocations process by decreasing the allocation steps, minimizing the number of allocation bases and allocating at a more summarized level. ▪ Simplified the financial codeblock.	▪ Reduced manual entries where possible, such as setting up recurring entries and automating unbilled revenue (which reduced manual processes by approximately 25 percent). ▪ Monitored data throughout the close to understand and predict financials better. ▪ This approach allowed Keyspan to book accruals earlier, based on data known and reconciled as of the last day of the month. ▪ Developed a close calendar and designated a process owner to monitor close activities and ensure adherence to deadlines. ▪ Moved all consolidation and reporting into Hyperion, a robust consolidation tool.	▪ Moved up the dates for closing source systems. ▪ Strictly enforced the closing of source systems and General Ledger to meet the close calendar, only allowing exceptions for material items. ▪ Focused management priorities onto the importance of timely closing and reporting of financials. ▪ Improved communication and issue resolution between groups early in the close process through the introduction of US close meetings for the downstream business. ▪ Developed an understanding of the critical path for month-end close activities and interdependencies to streamline the business. ▪ Ran close processes in parallel where possible, to prevent wait time between interface runs. ▪ Limited the number of non-material accruals.
Key Results	▪ Niagara Mohawk decreased the close and reporting timeline from 8 workdays to 2 workdays. ▪ Paved the way for a subsequent PeopleSoft implementation. ▪ Subsequent improvements decreased the National Grid US close, consolidation and reporting process from 5 workdays to 4 workdays. ▪ Finance and accounting staff have been freed up to partner with the business. ▪ The faster close allows for more timely decision making.	▪ Decreased the close from 10-12 workdays to approximately 4 workdays (with final management reports available between day 4 and day 5). ▪ Increased visibility and management of the close process by developing a close calendar and holding individuals accountable. ▪ Improved data integrity by adding reviews during and after the close process. ▪ Enabled more timely and thoughtful decision-making as information is available sooner to upper management. ▪ Improved productivity by allowing people to focus on activities other than closing.	▪ Decreased the close timeline of its business units to corporate from 10 workdays to 6 workdays. ▪ Boosted employee morale by reducing the amount of overtime required by employees during the close. ▪ Enabled more timely and thoughtful decision making as information is available sooner to management. ▪ Improved quality of financials. ▪ Improved productivity by allowing people to focus on activities other than closing the books.

Figure 2.4 *World-class close case studies*

THE HACKETT GROUP ON LEVERAGING THE FINANCIAL CLOSE TO GAIN A COMPETITIVE ADVANTAGE

The ability of global Finance organizations to provide financial perform-ance results rapidly for their management teams is a lofty goal for most CFOs. However, for a few leaders it has been their badge of courage. The advantages of the quicker close have been clear: better access to finan-cial performance, less time spent on lower value-added activities such as reconciliations, and improved reporting cycle time with Wall Street. When we look at the monthly close process as a high-level indicator of the impact of corporate governance on the typical Finance organization, we see that the cycle time for the peer group has remained essentially the same from 2003 to 2005, whereas it has actually increased for world-class organizations.

Percent of companies that close their books in less than 3 days, 2005

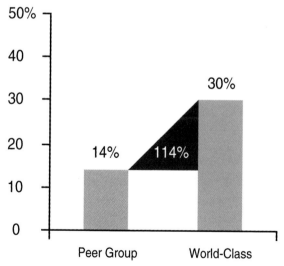

Source: The Hackett Group

continued

continued

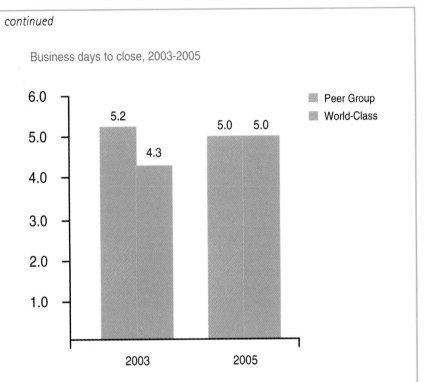

Business days to close, 2003-2005

Source: The Hackett Group

Given the recent changes in regulatory requirements because of Sarbanes-Oxley and Regulation FD (Fair Disclosure), the race to the quick close has slowed for many. The monthly close process has become increasingly complex, characterized by ambiguous compliance guidelines and a growing number of people who are involved in the close process. As a result, many CFOs have broadened their focus to include both risk management and financial transparency as part of the financial close process. Business Days to Close has been a performance metric for The Hackett Group that we have tracked for 13 years; until recently, there was a consistent trend toward shorter cycle times. We believe that the current trend toward longer cycle times will continue until the financial reporting processes have matured sufficiently to provide the appropriate control levels and financial transparency.

CFO INSIGHTS

- Leading organizations have been able to achieve an accurate month-end close cycle of three to five days. The focus is now less on reducing the number of days that it takes to close and more on improving the quality of data, making incremental process improvements, and utilizing existing ERP solutions for a more effective and efficient closing process.

- Many organizations have been able to achieve a higher quality close by improving their entire Record to Report process and implementing leading-practice end-to-end process designs coupled with an integrated ERP and reporting solution.

- CFOs are under increasing pressure from the financial markets, government regulators, boards of directors, and executive management teams to improve the financial transparency, accuracy, and speed of their financial close while also continuing to reduce the overall cost of Finance. Studies suggest that the financial markets reward organizations with outstanding transparency and timeliness of external reporting, while penalizing other organizations that are not transparent and timely.

- Although the immediate forecast is for longer close cycles, many believe organizations will eventually return to shorter closes, as organizations eventually catch up to the stricter compliance measures. As organizations continue to improve process design, controls, and process execution, they will automate compliance and shorten the close cycle yet again.

FROM INSIGHT TO ACTION

ANALYZE POTENTIAL MONTH-END PROCESS IMPROVEMENT ACTIVITIES TO DETERMINE WHETHER THE ORGANIZATION IS POSITIONED TO EXECUTE THE CHANGE

An individual organization's circumstance drives when that organization should make major process improvements in the end-to-end close process in conjunction with an ERP implementation. Most circumstances suggest that major process design improvements be undertaken prior to or in parallel with a major ERP implementation; therefore, the new process can be considered when designing the ERP configuration.

continued

---

continued

CONSIDER THE VALUE AND IMPACT OF EACH LEADING PRACTICE ON
THE OVERALL CLOSE PROCESS

All leading practices and process changes related to the close should be
compared and weighed against each other to determine which leading
practices provide the most value for the least amount of cost and business disruption.

REVIEW ALL CLOSE PROCESS REQUIREMENTS TO DETERMINE THE BEST
TECHNOLOGY SOLUTION

Certain processes such as consolidation may be better supported within the ERP solution, but outside of the ERP core transaction engine.
Proactively investigate how functions such as the consolidation process
are supported by the ERP solution and whether additional applications
outside the core financials modules are required.

REFERENCES

1. Larry Carter, "Cisco's Virtual Close," *Harvard Business Review* 79
   (2001): 22–23, http://www.hbr.com.

2. The Hackett Group, *The Hackett Group Book of Numbers (c) Research
   Series*, 1997–2003.

3. Stephen Taub, "Are These What You Call Worst Practices?" *CFO.com*,
   February 13, 2003, http://www.cfo.com.

4. Marie Leone, "Better Forecasts Mean Tougher Closes," *CFO.com*, May
   20, 2004, http://www.cfo.com.

5. Huron Consulting Group LLC, *2004 Annual Review of Financial
   Reporting Matters*, March 25, 2005, http://www.huronconsultinggroup
   .com.

6. Lori Calabro, "Compliance Creep," *CFO.com*, July 6, 2004, http://
   www.cfo.com.

7. Marie Leone, "Better Forecasts Mean Tougher Closes," *CFO.com*, May
   20, 2004, http://www.cfo.com.

CHAPTER 3

Financial and Management Reporting

FINANCIAL AND MANAGEMENT REPORTING: AN OVERVIEW

With ever-increasing pressure from financial markets and regulatory agencies to deliver financial data faster and more accurately, organizations must refine their financial, management, closing, and reporting processes or face significant market consequences. In addition to the newly reduced timeframe of 60 days for submitting annual financial statements, U.S. organizations are facing new Securities and Exchange Commission regulations (e.g., the Sarbanes-Oxley Act) that call for faster, more accurate reporting and greater CEO and CFO accountability. The International Accounting Standards (IAS) mandated in 2002 by the European Commission called for common accounting principles and methods to be implemented for consolidated accounts in 2005 for most European listed companies. Our experience shows that an organization's ability to meet these increased demands depends largely on streamlining the reporting process and automating the preparation of many aspects of the reporting and regulatory filing process.

Defining the Financial and Management Reporting Process

In the area of financial and management reporting, the key end-to-end process area calling for streamlining and automation is Record to Report (see Figure 3.1), which includes the subprocesses described in Chapter 2.

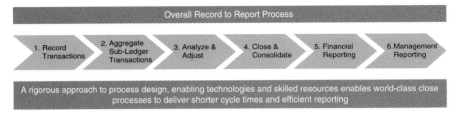

Figure 3.1 *Record to Report process*

In this chapter we focus on how successful companies are leveraging their ERP solutions to achieve leading practices related to the financial and management reporting components of the Record to Report process. Figure 3.2 illustrates these financial and management reporting sub-processes. The management reporting component of this process focuses on alternative views of the information such as Business Unit Profit and Loss (P&L) and Operating level information. Management reporting may also expand beyond traditional financial reports to complete Balanced Scorecards, which track financial and nonfinancial metrics across the organization. Regardless of the information captured and how it is reported, leading practices organizations capture this information only once to reduce the amount of time spent on the manipulation of data.

The Benefits of Leading Practices for Financial and Management Reporting

We believe that using leading practices in these six key capabilities of financial and management reporting will not only help organizations meet new regulations but also help avoid quarterly earnings surprises. When applied holistically, leading practices in these six areas can lead to reduced costs and increased performance. Also, by implementing these leading practices within the core ERP solution, investors and external readers of financial information can be provided significantly more information

Figure 3.2 *Financial and management reporting subprocesses*

Process/Function	Benefits
General Ledger, Real Time, Reporting, and Information Delivery	**Timelier Access to Information:** The automation of manual activities accelerates reporting, providing actual financial information in a timelier manner and shortening reporting cycles.
General Ledger and Convergence	**Reduce Effort and System Complexity:** Savings arise from the transition from decentralized to centralized data processing, as well as through the elimination of data and applications logistics.
Compliance	**Reduced Compliance Effort:** Improved transparency allows straightforward comparability and benchmarking with competitors.
Integrated Financial Planning and Analysis	**Time & Resource Savings:** Integrating disparate and duplicative processes enables time savings. **Reduce Variability:** Enhanced planning and reporting functionality minimizes unexpected earnings surprises.
Data Integration	**Enhanced Quality:** Integration enables efficiency gains by reducing processing times, synchronizing processes and eliminating data redundancies. Furthermore, inconsistencies are eliminated and data integrity is secured.
Information Delivery and Consistency	**Better Business Partners:** Management support becomes proactive across business units, and all legal entities and business units receive consistent reports.

Figure 3.3 *Financial and management reporting leading practices benefits*

regarding an organization's fair value, debt levels and liquidity, capacity to distribute dividends to shareholders, and, on the whole, its true performance in a more timely and transparent manner. Figure 3.3 shows a summary of these benefits.

DESIGNING FINANCIAL AND MANAGEMENT REPORTING WITH ERP SOLUTIONS

Critical Capability 1: General Ledger as Strategic Application

Regulatory reforms and an increased focus on the quality and timeliness of an organization's financial results heavily influence the configuration and implementation of the General Ledger, while supporting the shift to a centralized repository that provides a single version of the truth (versus a wide-scale use of spreadsheets and distributed applications). This shift allows the ledger to be leveraged for management and statutory reporting, as well as for viewing operational details that can offer a more transparent view of the organization. In addition, as discussed in Chapter 2, organizations are moving to the leading practice of a single codeblock and Chart of Accounts (CoA) – the core of the General Ledger – to ensure that information can be expressed and analyzed consistently. A common financial language reduces the manual work required to consolidate results, perform cross-business unit reporting, and minimize account reconciliations. We see that the General Ledger, when constructed properly, can be used not only to automate and shorten an organization's closing cycle, but also to serve as a strategic application that improves efficiency and generates value-added reporting capabilities (see Figure 3.4).

Although the capabilities exist, few organizations have transformed the General Ledger from a repository of financial transactions and account balances into a strategic application that improves employee efficiency and generates value-added information. Figure 3.5 reflects how ERP functionality can transform transaction-intensive processing into value-added decision support.

Current Practice	Leading Practice
Hard monthly close focused on reconciliation, adjustments and standardized reporting packages for all months	Financial close is structured to meet needs of the business (e.g., hard close on the quarter for regulatory requirements, soft close off-quarter to support management reporting)
Standard reporting hierarchies focused on geography and individual business units	Flexible reporting hierarchies and summary rollups provide a multi-dimensional view of the business
Standard reporting package that results in heavy reliance on MS Excel for further analysis	OLAP (On-line analytical processing) reporting with drill-down to sub-ledgers for easy analysis

Figure 3.4 *General Ledger leading practices*

The General Ledger functionality available in Oracle, PeopleSoft and SAP can transform transaction intensive processing into value added decision support.

Functions	Value
Chart of Accounts Setup Provide centralized maintenance of Chart of Accounts values Use a standard chart of accounts for all legal entities	Common financial language Chart of Accounts supports internal and external reporting requirements Centralized ownership of accounts limits proliferation of accounts
Reporting & Analysis Drill down capability and ad hoc analysis Exception based reporting Predictive and historical	On-line analytical reporting (OLAP) drill-down from the General Ledger to sub-ledgers facilitates analysis Actuals and budgets combined seamlessly for variance analysis

Figure 3.5 *General Ledger functionality and value*

Finance organizations can use the General Ledger as a strategic application to facilitate the financial and management reporting processes when the ERP:

- Is used as both a primary reporting vehicle and a link to data stored in ledger subsystems.
- Can be seamlessly integrated with best-of-breed consolidation, planning, budgeting, and business intelligence packages to provide a powerful enterprise-wide solution.

We find that the ERP vendors offer strong capabilities in this area:

- Oracle uses the account flex field to facilitate dynamic reporting hierarchies and scenarios that allow for a single data set with multiple views, depending on the business need.
- PeopleSoft offers more flexibility for CoA setup, which can allow an organization to use the ledger as the primary source of information.

- SAP's mySAP ERP 2004 "ECC 5.0 – General Ledger Accounting (New)" provides additional flexibility to the General Ledger codeblock. (We discuss this new functionality further in the "Convergence of Financial and Management Reporting" section of this chapter.)

The following case study highlights how an organization used the PeopleSoft General Ledger functionality as a strategic application to facilitate operational reporting, on-line reporting functionality, and more.

CASE STUDY
Large Global Banking Institution

Recognizing the inefficiencies and challenges presented by their legacy accounting environment, which consisted of more than 30 General Ledger applications, a large global banking institution embarked on a journey to replace and integrate General Ledger applications into one common platform. This resulted in a single set of numbers based on a single, logical source of data to feed their financial management and statutory reporting system.

The program included the implementation of a new General Ledger, housed within PeopleSoft 8.4, in multiple business lines (Personal and Commercial Banking, Capital Markets, Investments, Insurance) and all locations.

This new General Ledger became a critical initiative to:

- *Achieve efficiency and effectiveness through streamlined processes and greater integration across all divisions of the bank*
- *Expedite future merger & acquisition integration through a standardized, yet open and flexible system*
- *Increase risk management and control through improved auditing functions and tighter security*
- *Provide faster access to more and better financial information through a common financial language and one centralized General Ledger, with consistently detailed information across all business lines, legal entities, and operating units.*

The implementation yielded some considerable benefits. A common financial language offered daily access to worldwide information, a universal Chart of Accounts and definitions, and fewer reconciliation points and hand-offs, which facilitated a faster close process and reduced systems development and mainte-nance costs.

Control functionality provided visibility of accounts as a mechanism to enforce strict accounting principles and global policies and practices in audit and control functions across the globe.

After the PeopleSoft implementation, operational reporting was conducted out of the PeopleSoft General Ledger through queries and operational reports.

Critical Capability 2: Compliance — Parallel Accounting Standards

Global companies face many challenges in trying to comply with multiple government regulations. Although accounting methods may differ across countries and may require special handling, the information must be easily standardized and consolidated across the entire corporate entity to provide consistent, comparable reporting information. In Europe, the adoption of IAS and International Financial Reporting Standards (IFRS) will improve reporting quality, harmonize accounting and reporting standards, and provide greater transparency. Additionally, the changes in accounting rules should better protect investors through increased access to high-quality, reliable information, which will allow for more informed, confident decision making.

These regulations, however, significantly impact the construct of financial statements and the base valuations. As these accounting regulations emerge, it is critical that financial reporting applications, including ERP solutions, be equipped to handle the requirements and to provide a complete and compliant solution. Flexibility and adaptability of applications are vital in ensuring that the required changes can be integrated into the system. These challenges will prove to be difficult in many legacy system environments, in which hard-coding introduces limitations to adding new dimensions and processes.

For listed companies in the European Union, new financial reporting regulations such as IFRS apply to all consolidated financial statements filed as of 2005. In addition, local requirements remain in effect, and so parallel reporting is critical to an organization's ability to meet these new standards. Many organizations have had difficulties gathering, storing, and reporting the valuation bases required to settle the various accounts, making parallel reporting a challenge. The major ERP vendors have developed functionality to achieve the leading practice of providing multicountry Generally Accepted Accounting Principles (GAAP) capability in addition to meeting local reporting requirements. The ERP software vendors are addressing these requirements by offering prepackaged technical and process solutions that incorporate business leading practices and related documentation.

For example, the new General Ledger capabilities of mySAP ERP allow parallel financial reporting in several ledgers, which are populated through a unified posting transaction. Alternately, the ledgers may be analyzed through a unified reporting tool, for purposes such as the balance sheet or P&L statements. In addition, SAP has developed an IAS/IFRS-specific Leading Practices package that provides predetermined business process content, as well as the related technical configuration settings for SAP components, for an overall solution. This Leading Practices package details the procedures for converting organizational structure, CoA, valuations (e.g., fixed asset, currency, adjustments), and reporting in accordance with IAS/IFRS requirements.[1] Because IAS/IFRS regulations will affect the design of the CoA and posting rules, the Leading Practices documentation includes both procedures and configuration settings to allow parallel valuation in accordance with IAS/IFRS regulations as well as local legal requirements. In addition, SAP provides functionality for a country-specific CoA to help organizations generate financial statements to meet a country's legal requirements.

Oracle has also introduced a new solution in its Oracle Corporate Performance Management suite of analytic applications – "Oracle Financial Consolidation Hub" (FCH). Oracle FCH can bring together financial data from disparate sources to create a single source of financial information that can be used for compliance (as it facilitates accelerated reporting, expanded disclosures, and the certified internal controls now required by various governance mandates). FCH provides rules-based processing and standard functionality that support full, proportional, and equity consolidation methods. This capability facilitates compliance with IFRS and, eventually, IFRS/US GAAP harmonization. Oracle FCH also provides an open architecture and flexible solution that are capable of accommodating changes in corporate structure or compliance regulations. Finally, when used throughout the Record to Report process, FCH can accelerate access to information and improve management reporting, as well as feed strategic planning and budgeting.

PeopleSoft also provides a solution for IAS/IFRS compliance in the form of the PeopleSoft Financial Management Blueprint, which consists of a technical solution and leading practice business process models, accessed through a roles-based portal. A key component of the PeopleSoft design is the option to manage and streamline multi-GAAP entries; it also provides a consistent data source for reporting and analysis. An organization can choose to standardize a single instance of the PeopleSoft General Ledger, while managing IFRS and local GAAP entries in multiple instances. The solution allows several accounting standards to coexist simultaneously.

Critical Capability 3: Convergence of Financial and Management Reporting

Historically, most companies have had two separate sets of reporting: financial (external) reporting and management (internal) reporting. Financial reporting refers to the statements or financials an organization is required to publish in keeping either with legal requirements or with binding requirements established by a stock exchange as a condition for trade. Management reporting is not subject to legal regulations and serves the exclusive purpose of supporting management in its decision making. Management reporting generates information relevant to decision making for business units and business areas (independent of legal units) at any given level of detail and, in contrast to financial reporting, usually involves less gathering of detailed, relevant consolidation information, such as partner or affiliate information. This dual-reporting approach has led to an information disconnect between strategy and transaction processing. This disconnect has driven the need to integrate transaction processing with the financial and management reporting requirements.

To overcome the information disconnect, we recommend that an organization strive for corporate reporting excellence. Corporate reporting excellence provides information in a consistent, timely, and efficient manner to guide a global business. Corporate reporting excellence:

- Provides high-quality and consistent data that avoid redundancies by using integrated systems and processes
- Includes processes and structures to meet the requirements of global capital markets
- Achieves high process efficiency and avoids redundancy by integrating management reporting and legal consolidation

- Allows access to financial data from any location at any time by utilizing a company-wide data pool and individual on-line analyses
- Provides information in a timely manner through processes that are highly automated.

To achieve reporting excellence, organizations are seeking ways to leverage their ERP solutions by linking or embedding the following key elements into their ERP: consistency, decision support, flexible real-time access, flexibility, and performance management (see Figure 3.6). These organizations are also working to standardize their information by establishing common enterprise-wide definitions across geographic and legal entities, business segments, and reporting formats for statutory and management reporting. In addition, high-performance businesses and governments are rationalizing and standardizing their technology infrastructures in an effort to reduce costs and increase efficiency.

The Benefits of Embedding Leading Facets
of Corporate Reporting Excellence into ERP

Consistency

A single web-based information source for financial and nonfinancial data ensures consistently correct and transparent reporting data through the entire corporation and in different reporting dimensions, based on shared

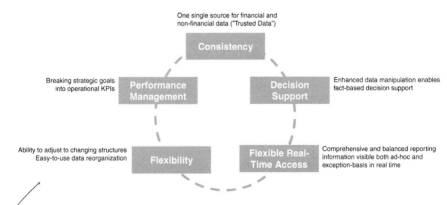

Figure 3.6 *Corporate reporting excellence vision*

and common standards and definitions ("Trusted Data"). Consistency of structures and content allows consolidated reporting and integration across all dimensions (e.g., organization, management entities, geography, functions, actual, forecast, budget).

Decision Support

Enhanced data slicing manipulation and simulation enables fact-based analysis for decision support. Reporting excellence provides for cause-effect hypotheses, which allow linkage of financial and nonfinancial measures.

Flexible Real-time Access

Comprehensive and balanced reporting information is visible immediately for both ad hoc and exceptional inquiries and is available for the organization's central functions and the business segments, independent of the location and in real time. Figure 3.7 illustrates the implications of flexible real-time access.

Flexibility

Reporting excellence provides the ability to adjust to changing structures (such as organization, products, or channels) through easy-to-use data reorganization and restatements of historic data. Financial and management reports are table driven, with no hard coding, which allows maximum flexibility.

Real-time data enabled

	Traditional Reporting	Corporate Reporting Excellence
Content	Pre-defined; limited	Broad data availability
Format	Pre-defined	Flexible
Skills	Expert Request	Self-extraction
Time	Slow and Periodic	Fast and at anytime
Location	In Headquarters	From everywhere

Figure 3.7 *The implications of flexible real-time access*

Performance Management

Breaking strategic goals into operational key performance indicators based on reliable forecasts and detailed variance analysis is essential to effective performance management. The Enterprise Performance Management (EPM) framework depicted in Figure 3.8 gives the ability to make decisions and take actions quickly. This structure is aligned with strategy and value creation at key points in the organization.

In contrast to the corporate reporting excellence vision, many organizational reporting infrastructures today rely heavily on complex, inefficient spreadsheets to produce their monthly reporting packages. Additionally, when key leading practices are not incorporated – even when there are standard systems – organizations face the challenge of nonstandard formats, which make it difficult to consolidate information rapidly and accurately.

Achieving Financial and Management Reporting Convergence within an ERP

As highlighted previously, efficiently meeting the new regulatory requirements and effectively managing the business require that financial and management reporting converge. The impact that the separation of financial reporting and management reporting has had on organizations is

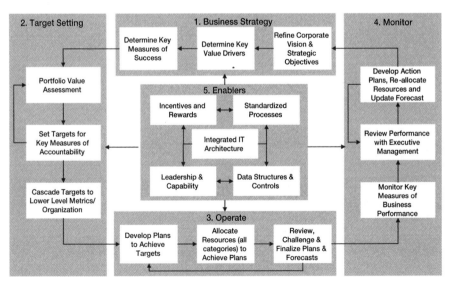

Figure 3.8 *An integrated framework for EPM*

very clear to us. The separation of departments, applications, and processes presents a considerable barrier for organizations trying to meet more demanding regulations. If companies truly desire a single version of the truth, they must evaluate and improve their reporting systems to integrate the two reporting silos.

Many companies are beginning to focus exclusively on aligning content between management reporting and external reporting. Harmonizing content, however, is only one element of an integrated reporting solution. To comply with the new reporting standards – in particular with respect to faster reporting time – processes, procedures, and the organization itself must also be integrated. Only a truly integrated, holistic framework will enable companies to meet the new global requirements.

For simplicity, Figure 3.9 shows only two extreme cases (no integration and full integration). Intermediate levels of integration are not included, although we have seen that they do exist for many organizations.

Full integration is the ideal scenario, but it is not feasible for all organizations to achieve in the short term. Nevertheless, a high level of integration can be achieved relatively quickly, even by companies that have complex group structures and highly dynamic landscapes. Organizations

Key Factors for Integration/Integration Levels	No Integration	Full Integration
Harmonization between management reporting and external reporting	Multiple data collections	One data collection
Database Integration: common database of booked source data	Separate databases	Common database for booked data
Data deliveries: Data impacting management reporting and external reporting booked once	Multiple	One
Sequences: Standardization of the management reporting and external reporting processes	Several	One for management and external reporting
Validations: Corresponding checks of management reporting and external reporting	No checking of correspondence	No validation necessary
Charts of Accounts: Corporate guidelines for management reporting and external reporting with a reconciliation to common accounts	Separate Chart of Accounts without clear reconciliation	One accounts plan
Recording level for consolidation information: The level where consolidation information is recorded	Legal unit	Strategic business area
Systems: the number of systems and necessary IT procedures	Multiple	One
Structural Organization distinguishes levels based on their degree of process orientation	Separate IT and reporting departments for external and management reporting	Process-oriented

Figure 3.9 *Key factors for integration*

can realize integration through a series of interim steps that can ensure a smooth transition:

- The first step focuses on the consolidation hierarchy. Reconciling the structures enables the alignment of management reporting and external reporting.
- The second step involves integration into a single system and database, as well as the integration of organizational departments responsible for reporting. This allows for validation to be carried out much more quickly and errors to be reduced, resulting in the convergence of both reporting schedules and content.
- Step three introduces the transition to harmonization and process integration.
- In step four the degree of integration is increased further with the introduction of automatic validation at some levels.
- In the fifth and final step, full integration is achieved with complete harmonization – single data delivery, process, and organization.

Integrating external reporting and management reporting represents a major challenge for the entire organization and often entails a break with traditional structures and procedures. Changes of this magnitude can only work if they are introduced in a way that aligns with the organization's strategy and only if the entity's organizational process and technological structure are taken into consideration. By following a carefully staged roadmap, however, full integration can be incrementally achieved.

From Thin Ledger to Thick Ledger

Financial and management reporting should serve to give a singular view of an organization's performance. With an integrated ERP solution, key stakeholders and decision makers have easy, quick, and accurate access to information, which leads to management action and value-minded business decisions. When an organization is designing an ERP-based reporting solution, it should strive to drive all financial information through the ERP, avoiding the use of disparate data sources whenever possible. This can reduce the total cost of operations for the ERP solution, as it reduces the burden on the Finance organization to reconcile reporting outputs to verify that data interfaces have been executed properly. (Chapter 9 discusses reducing the total cost of operation in more detail.) Likewise, it better positions the IT organization to support fewer application platforms and interfaces.

A single data set drives the information flow from the operational sub-ledgers (such as Accounts Receivable and Accounts Payable) through the General Ledger to the business intelligence and financial reporting modules. An integrated solution fosters greater confidence in reported information and further reduces the time commitment of maintaining disparate reports outside the ERP solution (spreadsheet reporting). The goal of an integrated solution is to drive a migration from the traditional General Ledger codeblock (thin ledger), which was meant to meet external reporting only, to a more comprehensive codeblock (thick ledger) to meet additional requirements (see Figure 3.10).

Although many companies have invested heavily in ERPs, we see that they continue to face the following business challenges:

- **Speed/Control.** Fragmented systems and processes elongate monthly close to the middle of the next month, slowing decision making and reducing control.
- **Customer.** P&L is managed by product and business line rather than by customer profitability.
- **Cost.** Cost of finance as a percentage of revenue is greater than benchmark values, with a high percentage of transaction-processing activities and little value-added analysis.
- **Complexity.** Mergers and acquisitions require significant spend to integrate increasingly complex legacy processes and systems.

Typical "Traditional" Codeblock Account	Representative Thick General Ledger Extensions
• Account • Currency • Legal entity • Cost center or Operating Unit • Product type • Internal counterparty (affiliate trading partner)	• Detailed cost center • Profit center • Client/Customer • Sales code • Transaction • Tax codes
Traditional Codeblock supports legal reporting.	Aggregate level elements such as Legal Entity/Operating Unit are replaced by detailed cost centers. Additional detailed elements support tax, local GAAP, IAS, regulatory and Line of Business management reporting.

Figure 3.10 *Extending the traditional codeblock to a new level of detail*

- **Responsiveness.** New regulations and changes in business direction almost always require corresponding increases in Finance headcount.
- **Globalization.** Complex legal entity structures multiply the effort required to close the books.

Figure 3.11 outlines the benefits achieved via a thick ledger, compared with a traditional thin ledger codeblock.

To help organizations achieve this convergence of external and internal reporting, the ERP vendors are reconsidering the General Ledger codeblock. This is most apparent in SAP's enhancement to its Financials module. SAP has introduced the New General Ledger, which includes additional dimensions in the General Ledger (such as profit center, functional area, segment, and so on). Whereas SAP's Classic General Ledger solutions required the reconciliation of multiple applications – such as

Traditional Thin Ledger Financial Architecture	Thick Ledger Architecture
Speed/Control ▪ Management information is time-consuming and expensive to produce from multiple sources ▪ Monthly close involves multiple sets of adjustments to different systems and multiple reconciliations	▪ All information can be sourced from one system ▪ Adjustments are made once in a single place ▪ Reconciliations are minimized
Customer ▪ A separate workflow is required to manage customer profitability	▪ Customer view and management view are integrated, ensuring accuracy and reducing cost
Cost ▪ Finance activities are predominantly transaction processing and reconciliation, e.g. inter-companies	▪ Information flow is streamlined and simplified enabling straight-through processing
Complexity ▪ Acquisitions involve the integration of multiple ledgers, and their associated business processes	▪ New subsidiaries are absorbed into a single financial platform and process
Responsiveness ▪ Changes to accounting rules or regulations need to be applied multiple times across line of business and finance solutions	▪ Changes are restricted to one ledger, one set of posting rules and one set of reports
Globalization ▪ Regions or line of business support volume and complexity of global organization ▪ Ledgers are consolidated into single corporate view for legal reports	▪ All global financial information stored in one place

Figure 3.11 *Benefits of a thick ledger architecture in comparison with a thin ledger*

the cost-of-sales ledger, profit center accounting, and the consolidation staging ledger – the mySAP ERP New General Ledger now provides a unified structure. As a result, it speeds reconciliation, ensures transparency and the ability to conduct audits, and enables an organization to meet both internal and external reporting requirements. The General Ledger capabilities within mySAP ERP are based on a broader unified database. For instance, company code, segment, and profit center are all contained in a single data record, which can easily be extended to include other fields. This functionality increases data quality, eliminates reconciliation measures, and allows faster execution of period-end closing. Likewise, both Oracle and PeopleSoft, via their flexible General Ledger codeblocks, provide similar functionality. Oracle's flexible account fields are a prime example of the benefits of a thick ledger, as they facilitate all applicable segments of the business in a single repository within the General Ledger.

As discussed in Chapter 2, each of the ERP vendors leverages this functionality to allow financial and management reporting within a single system. SAP has its Business Consolidation System, Oracle its Financial Consolidation Hub, and PeopleSoft its Global Consolidations. Their consolidation functionality ensures that management numbers reconcile with legal results. The resulting single set of consolidated financial information supports multiple perspectives and satisfies the needs of a wide range of users, from a general manager responsible for a stable of products, to a country-specific controller responsible for the finances of a geographic region, to a corporate controller responsible for fulfilling federal regulatory requirements.

The following UBS case study highlights how UBS used the Oracle-based thick ledger solution to provide the foundation for a consolidated financial and management reporting initiative.

CASE STUDY
UBS

UBS, one of the world's leading financial firms, is the largest wealth manager globally, a top-tier investment banking and securities firm, a key asset manager, and the market leader in Swiss retail and commercial banking.

UBS's Global Environment for Accounting and Reporting (GEAR) project used the General Ledger functionality of Oracle ERP to provide the foundation for an integrated financial and management reporting initiative. The overall goals of the

GEAR project were to provide a centralized General Ledger with common and consistent accounting logic (a single version of the truth), to enable faster downstream reporting, and to reduce the overall cost of ownership through application reduction and elimination of manual reconciliations. Oracle's thick ledger capabilities allowed UBS to create a single, multidimensional General Ledger capable of processing approximately 20 million journal entries per hour and able to scale for future growth. In the GEAR solution, all financial transactions, including relevant sub-ledgers, are now executed through this single source. With all key data elements captured in a common and consistent manner, UBS has created a solution that speeds information delivery to end users, allows resources to shift focus to value-added analytical tasks, simplifies compliance with complex regulatory requirements such as Sarbanes-Oxley, IAS, and U.S. GAAP, and enables faster integration of new businesses.

Critical Capability 4: Integrated Financial Planning and Analysis Reporting

Integrated financial planning and analysis reporting implies merging the business processes of target setting, planning, budgeting, forecasting, monitoring, and analysis, with the goal of converting business strategies into actionable plans. An organization's planning begins with an in-depth understanding of past performance and business trends, from which it can forecast potential future results.

Many organizations struggle to access, aggregate, and dissect the information necessary to draw conclusions. Historically, they have approached the problem with separate planning systems or spreadsheet-based analysis. However, these solutions are difficult and expensive to maintain. They create silos of stale, incomplete information and lack accurate comparisons of plans, actuals, and forecasts over time. Although the root causes vary, often the inability to provide adequate forecasting stems largely from systems being fragmented across operations, as well as from a lack of an integrated reporting and controlling mission. We find that the planning process returns more value when information can be reported, analyzed, and delivered on a frequent basis. Thus, reporting and multidimensional analysis are the core technologies for budgeting and planning and should be seamlessly integrated within the budgeting and planning application to enhance usability.

The ERP vendors have made significant strides in improving their planning and budgeting functionality through tight integration with financial and management reporting. For example, Oracle's Enterprise Planning and Budgeting (EPB) provides analysis tools that increase visibility into the organization. Furthermore, it provides a framework to manage the critical business processes of budgeting and forecasting via user-defined rules, tasks, and schedules. EPB enforces consistency, while supporting the flexibility needed in many decentralized environments. Up-to-date access to business information improves results.

Oracle's EPB is delivered with a reporting environment based on a common data model, and provides users the flexibility to select and change report parameters, run ad hoc calculations, and add visual representations to highlight key variances. Oracle's iterative "reporting-budgeting-reporting" process, linked as users prepare plans and budgets, provides a robust solution for managing the business. This integrated approach allows users to remain in the EPB environment to gather information efficiently as they move through the process and make budgeting decisions. EPB's reporting solution also allows reports to be published or shared, and comments can be added for authorized users to view. EPB provides an opportunity to automate the variance analysis processes performed in many organizations. It reduces the time spent gathering data and provides for auditing of the analysis and explanation process.[2]

SAP has revamped its module-specific planning functionality (e.g., cost center, profit center, sales planning) with its new Strategic Enterprise Management – Business Planning Simulation (SEM-BPS) component. This new functionality allows users to:

- Import/export sales forecast and production quantities and perform sales and operational planning for make/buy determinations
- Perform demand planning to determine capacity and ability to meet sales and operational plans
- Perform cost-center planning and/or product costing, using planned activity rates and/or product costs to derive P&L
- Perform planning at the profit-center level.

In addition, all reporting can be produced via the Business Explorer/Report Painter applications, giving designated business users the ability to produce reports.

The SEM-BPS functionality provides an organization with the ability to set and manage strategic direction across functions. It also provides the ability to import and conduct external competitive analysis, to provide context for setting targets, and to identify and prioritize key drivers of value. The improved reporting and forecasting capabilities in the new solution allow monitoring of performance against the critical key performance indicators. This improved functionality provides the ability to forecast dynamically, while highlighting the need to make course corrections based on changes in the competitive landscape or in actual performance.

Finally, PeopleSoft Planning and Budgeting also offers a solution for gathering, evaluating, and adjusting financial objectives across the organization in real time. Users can view actual results against department-level and company-wide business goals to evaluate performance and respond when required. PeopleSoft's reporting and analysis capabilities can enable an organization to access data and present it effectively to the people who need it. Specifically, it can[3]:

- Analyze business plans and line-item budgets with on-line reporting, including variance and trend analysis across multiple scenarios, versions, positions, and asset data
- Customize views of data with real-time, interactive drag-and-drop functionality
- Expand and collapse hierarchical data on rows and columns to drill into details or view data at a summary level
- Easily filter the on-line analysis to display only the rows and columns of the data of interest and then simply return to the original analysis view.

Critical Capability 5: Real-Time Reporting

An integrated ERP solution enables real-time reporting and greatly increases the speed of information delivery to key stakeholders. As discussed throughout this chapter, many organizations rely on spreadsheet-based reports to distribute information across the organization and even to satisfy statutory reporting requirements. In today's Sarbanes-Oxley environment, this practice can present significant compliance challenges. As previously highlighted, a real-time reporting module fully integrated with the organization's core ERP solution is a key way to foster confidence in reported results across the organization. Real-time reporting allows for the ability to satisfy statutory reporting requirements quickly, and it can give management greater confidence in the results requiring their certification (as required by Sarbanes-Oxley Section 409, for example).

Integrated, real-time reporting can be satisfied through the ERP solution's reporting module or through an add-on on-line analytical processing (OLAP) module integrated with the core financial modules, such as SAP's Business Information Warehouse (SAP BW) or Strategic Enterprise Management application (SEM). An example of real-time reporting visibility that leverages an ERP solution is SAP's Business Consolidation System (SEM-BCS).

By extensively automating all standardized consolidation operations and status indicators of data input and processing, the consolidation monitor of SEM-BCS integrates all relevant process steps. It also provides a graphical representation of the relevant steps in the consolidation process by legal entity. The consolidation-unit hierarchy is arranged vertically in the consolidation monitor, and the process steps (for example, data entry, reclassifications, and currency translation) are arranged horizontally, with a visual depiction available for status. This easily accessible visual depiction simplifies both users' effort and corporate headquarters' monitoring tasks.

By centrally monitoring a decentralized process, an organization can increase process transparency and decrease the time to complete financial close and statement publication.

Each of the major ERP vendors provides real-time reporting capabilities as part of its core financial reporting package. Their functionality ranges from real-time update of the General Ledger to drill-down capability through lower levels of the hierarchy back to the original source document. For instance, with Oracle General Ledger's integrated inquiry, reporting, and analysis solutions, managers can quickly investigate and reconcile balances on-line using the Inquiry Workbench. They can drill down to any level of detail, including detail balances, journals, and the underlying sub-ledger transactions – all from a single drill path.

Critical Capability 6: Information Delivery

Our experience shows that information delivery is a critical but often undervalued component of the financial reporting process. Recent competitive trends and legislation have sharpened the focus of many leading organizations on using improvements in technology to improve their delivery mechanisms. Successful organizations are implementing information-delivery solutions that deliver the lowest cost of ownership across the organization.

In the current environment, many organizations (on both non-ERP and nonoptimized ERP solutions) employ manual and labor-intensive processes. As discussed throughout this chapter, their spreadsheet-based reporting solutions require resources to spend a high percentage of time rekeying, calculating, formatting, and manually distributing information. By leveraging an integrated ERP environment, leading organizations are able to create a single, consistent chain of information, from original transaction through statutory and management reporting.

For example, an SAP R/3 environment, integrated with SAP-BW and SAP-SEM, eliminates the wasted effort of data rekeying and calculation, while increasing overall information transparency through the ability to drill down to source data. This is a key enabler for Sarbanes-Oxley compliance. Furthermore, the ability of an ERP solution to provide information on demand (e.g., via portals, web-based report generators) or to provide alerts via e-mail minimizes the manual report distribution activities common with most spreadsheet-driven report solutions today. The elimination of these labor-intensive activities frees time for increased analysis and better decision making, which positions an organization to take advantage of the information it has.

Another theme emerging within information delivery is one of organizations using ERP technology to create a cost-effective solution and reduce the total cost of ownership, as discussed in Chapter 9. In today's world, the data collection and data distribution activities within information delivery are often fragmented, duplicative, and manual. Different business units within an organization often have distinct reporting tools, separately created and maintained. Not only does this scenario result in data integrity issues, but it also drives duplicative implementation and maintenance costs.

We see that organizations are now looking to leverage their investment in ERP environments – to extend them beyond the traditional walls of transaction capture. This desire to broaden the footprint of traditional ERP implementations has been answered by the major ERP vendors with the development of more open and flexible solutions, best exemplified by the increased adoption of information portals. An information portal provides an easily accessible, web-based application from which a user can access a single source for enterprise-wide information. Robust portals are often personalized, with content specific to the end user (based on role), and they support the leading practice of moving to a "pull," rather than a "push," reporting environment. The key point of a pull environment is that information should be readily available when an end user wants it, rather than being pushed to them in static forms on a set schedule.

Furthermore, leading organizations are empowering end users with "slice-and-dice" reporting capabilities that allow users to customize their queries based on need. Often, this type of flexible analysis has historically been done via a download to a spreadsheet; a system solution with flexibility eliminates the inefficiencies associated with these spreadsheet solutions.

The Investor Relations (IR) function has realized considerable benefits from Internet-based financial reporting, as integrated ERP platforms have allowed IR web sites to be updated easily with SEC filings and statutory reports. The benefits of efficient information delivery are demonstrated by the results of one of the world's largest mySAP.com implementations. Siemens achieved a 25 percent cost reduction through streamlined information delivery and improved access to financial information. It also enhanced its reporting capabilities from 70 percent to nearly 100 percent through increased intranet availability.

CASE STUDY
Siemens

Siemens is one of the world's largest electronic and electrical engineering companies. Siemens operates world-wide, delivering advanced solutions for e-business, mobile communications, manufacturing, transportation, health care, energy, and lighting. During 2003, Siemens achieved:

- *Global Revenue*   *US$89.0 billion*
- *Market Capitalization*   *US$55.0 billion*
- *Worldwide Employees*   *417,000*

BUSINESS CHALLENGE
The globalization of financial markets, the significantly increased need for timely finance information, and a desire to gain process efficiencies have forced Siemens Corporate Finance to architect a leading-edge Management Reporting and legal Consolidation business capability. The organization's primary drivers included:

- *Access to financial markets that required transition to U.S. GAAP*
- *Reporting and closing cycle times that needed alignment to international standards*

- *An opportunity to reduce total cost of information delivery by more than 25 percent*
- *Existing complex IT architecture with numerous applications and interfaces that needed to be simplified.*

SOLUTION

Efficient eReporting is centered around the global integration of management reporting and legal consolidation based on a global SAP EC instance and enabled through a Siemens-wide web architecture involving:

- *The architectural integration of management reporting and legal consolidation into eReporting capability*
- *The blueprinting of eReporting centered around a one SAP EC instance fully utilizing the Siemens intranet/web architecture*
- *Facilitation of a transition to U.S. GAAP standards Siemens wide*
- *Deployment of the solution in a four-stage release to approximately 800 Siemens entities globally during a 28-month period, mobilizing approximately 32,000 days of joint project effort*
- *Continual provision of application management and help desk services to the Siemens Finance community.*

RESULTS ACHIEVED

- *Aligned closing cycle time to international standards and reduced time from 46 to 28 days (40 percent reduction)*
- *Reduced monthly and quarterly reporting events by 70 percent*
- *Further reduced complexity through harmonization of reporting positions into a single harmonized global Chart of Accounts*
- *Deployed globally an eReporting capability to approximately 3,000 finance users, covering 800 Siemens entities in 180 countries. This deployment represented the largest SAP ECCS application worldwide*
- *Delivered a harmonized eReporting architecture, which retired 60+ applications through one global web-centric SAP EC application*
- *Increased Siemens finance e-enablement from 70 to 98 percent.*

NON-PROCESS-RELATED CONSIDERATIONS

Implementation Considerations

It almost goes without saying that effective implementation is a critical factor in realizing the benefits of leading practices-based ERP design. However, we believe two critical elements warrant mention. First, begin with the end in mind for reporting, and second, critically assess individual report needs to determine the appropriate source of data and information.

ERP implementations are large and complex undertakings that require a significant amount of long-term planning. Often, when projects face budget and time pressures, reporting analysis and design become less of a priority. This decreased focus on reporting analysis and design is a highly significant decision, with long-term consequences. Because ERP solutions are extremely integrated, key design decisions made early in an implementation have ripple effects to the back-end processes, including reporting. Furthermore, once key configuration decisions and master data approaches are implemented, it can be extremely difficult to implement changes. Therefore, it is imperative to involve reporting resources in the beginning of an implementation and across process areas; an organization must begin with the end in mind.

The second major point to consider during implementation is the proper sources for relevant reporting. There are various reporting requirements and audiences across an organization, and for an optimal solution, these requirements must be mapped to the appropriate source. We find an excellent way to begin is by creating a reporting inventory: listing out all required (as opposed to current or "wish list") reports, as well as the key attributes of each report (e.g., data elements, criticality, frequency, complexity of calculations). Once the reporting inventory is complete, the organization can evaluate whether each report should be sourced from the transactional ERP (more real time) or through a data warehouse (less frequent, but best for large volumes of data and complex calculations). Careful evaluation of this decision will ensure that reporting requirements are met in the most effective and cost-effective manner.

Technical Considerations

To integrate management and financial reporting, the enabling technology must be able to support both types of reporting. All major ERP vendors, including Oracle, PeopleSoft, and SAP, offer modules that support both management and financial reporting. Today's standard ERP solutions have various modules that support a large percentage of the user's needs. Standard ERP software also can often be extended or configured for specific company conditions. In addition, standard ERP software offers:

- Minimal development time and costs
- Regular updates, including both technological and business innovations
- Long-term support from the manufacturer
- Standardized interfaces
- Broad adaptability to individual needs.

In addition to accommodating the requirements of management reporting and financial reporting in a single system, the software must possess high scalability and Internet backbone functionality. If an organization has complex group structures, the scalability of databases and applications is an important selection criterion, as a large number of organizations, accounts, movements, and segment information requires a system with a high degree of adaptability.

Leading-practice reporting requires a system architecture that is supported by an intranet/Internet backbone. Internet technology allows peripheral company subunits to be integrated via a virtual network, which is a precondition to:

- Location-independent access to company data, evaluations, and representations
- Immediate processing and forwarding of data and information
- A continuously consistent and uniform database
- A standardized data transfer.

When a central installation of an ERP solution is selected, there is no decentralized installation at individual business units and subgroups. These subunits work directly in the central application. As Figure 3.12 illustrates, the ERP solution (as a central corporate data pool) comprises the main components for input, processing, and output. All process participants, such as associated entities, business areas, and headquarters, can enter data, initiate process steps, and view data via standard ERP functions. Cost-intensive peripheral installations of applications and multiple data maintenance become unnecessary. Via their PCs, users at remote locations can record data directly into the common ERP modules and database. In the end, all participants have access to a common database and to consistent data that are generated through uniform calculation logics, provided in input and output reports tailored to the individual user. Because all process participants have direct access, they avoid redundant information and work duplication.

As the reach of business processing extends beyond the individual enterprise to a wide range of partners, we realize it is critical that an effective, supporting architecture be in place to provide ease of accessibility. Additionally, system landscapes consisting of multiple enterprise applications can benefit from a single overall architectural framework to facilitate total system integration. Some of the leading ERP vendors have begun to bring this concept to fruition through their development of an Internet-based technology foundation that not only supports their own application but also provides a mechanism for integrating with other existing applications. This Internet architecture solution also introduces process efficiencies and more effective communication and collaboration between the enterprise and its business partners (such as customers, suppliers, and employees) through increased access to the enterprise's applications.

Organizational Considerations

Implementing an enhanced reporting environment can enable significant organizational benefits. By harmonizing financial and management reporting, an organization reduces redundancy and rework, which in turn allows redeployment of skilled resources to additional activities. More

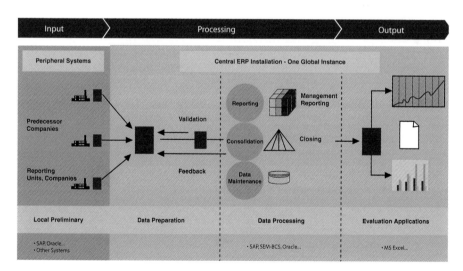

Figure 3.12 *ERP as a central corporate data pool comprising components for input, processing, and output*

specifically, financial personnel can focus their time on value-added analysis tasks, rather than mundane data entry and validation activities. Aside from the benefits to the organization, because these are the tasks Finance personnel would rather perform, the shift can create a more motivated and engaged workforce.

ROLE OF THIRD-PARTY SOFTWARE SOLUTIONS

The focus of this chapter has been primarily on the functionality provided by the leading ERP vendors. The ERP vendors have made significant strides in closing the gap with best-of-breed third-party vendors in financial and management reporting, specifically in the integrated financial planning and analysis area. Where the ERP vendors do fall short (for example, SAP's rigid financial statement formatting via Report Painter or SAP BW Excel-based solutions), they have opened their systems to allow relevant data to be transferred to third-party tools. Furthermore, most of the major ERP vendors have formed alliances with third-party providers, to leverage the capabilities of these solutions and provide greater levels of integration and support.

PeopleSoft Financials Warehouse supports all leading business intelligence tools, including those from Business Objects, Cognos, and Hyperion. With these flexible information access tools and PeopleSoft Financials Warehouse, knowledge workers, business analysts, and managers can perform sophisticated business analysis with ad hoc querying and reporting, personalized scorecards and dashboards, multidimensional analysis and exploration, and formatted production-style reports.

Oracle's Financial Consolidation Hub brings together financial data from disparate sources to create a single, global view of financial information across the entire enterprise. By providing one consistent view of an organization's financial position across boundaries, a basis for enterprise performance management is established. These tools also support third-party BI applications such as Business Objects, Cognos, and Hyperion. Oracle's table structure offers a great deal of flexibility for integrating the ERP solution with third-party solutions when a best-of-breed option meets business needs better.

FUTURE TRENDS

Recent advances in information technology (for example, web-centric architecture) allow for completely new business process designs and models. In a holistic financial and management reporting approach, end-to-end processes depend on technology for implementing requirements. At the same time, technology enables innovative end-to-end process models.

One financial and management reporting trend to watch will be the development of Extensible Business Reporting Language (XBRL), a framework focused on standardizing the creation, exchange, and analysis of financial data. All major ERP vendors have developed some degree of XBRL functionality. Current XBRL capabilities exist for creating key financial statements, such as a balance sheet, income statement, and statement of cash flows; using XBRL allows these financial statements to be published digitally to an external audience. Although the challenges to creating an easily adoptable solution are significant, XBRL functionality presents significant potential benefits in the areas of information transparency, data consistency, and timeliness of reporting. A key component of XBRL is the definition of common and consistent taxonomies that are reusable across organizations. These predefined specifications will increase data transparency through common definitions and facilitate simplified comparisons across organizations. Furthermore, the consistent structure associated with XBRL has significant potential to expedite and simplify regulatory filings. With this in mind, XBRL has the potential to grow in significance in the years to come.[4]

THE HACKETT GROUP ON FINANCIAL AND MANAGEMENT REPORTING

World-class CFOs are actively involved in establishing enterprise performance targets, typically during the annual budgeting process. The difference between the average CFO and the world-class performer is that the leader develops processes and people that will actually enable enhanced performance of the organization.

One critical tactic in achieving enterprise performance targets is to ensure alignment between the organization's established targets and its enterprise-wide priorities. The balanced scorecard is a widely recognized tool to help measure and achieve this alignment. It is not simple either to create or maintain balanced scorecards.

continued

continued

Nevertheless, when properly constructed, they offer management a useful way to look at financial results and operational drivers, leading and lagging indicators, and metrics that track a wide range of activities. According to The Hackett Group, world-class companies are almost twice as likely as the average company to use balanced scorecards. They are also faster at generating ad hoc business performance reports and reports from the General Ledger, providing faster access to critical information.

A recent rise in the number of CFO-to-CEO transitions at major corporations indicates a swing back to seeking leaders from inside the organization, particularly in Finance. For companies to retain their best and brightest Finance minds, they will need to do more to develop these people as future leaders of business, not just Finance. An increased emphasis on developing processes, professional skills, and business experience focused on enterprise performance management is crucial to help Finance executives adopt a broader, operational perspective.

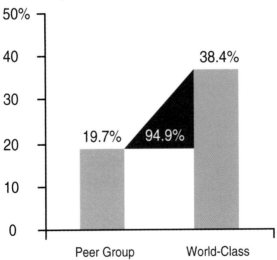

Percent of companies utilizing mature balanced scorecards with both operational and financial measures, 2005

Source: The Hackett Group

CFO INSIGHTS

- Successful organizations establish leading practices in the Record to Report end-to-end process to enable leading practices in financial and management reporting. Robust financial reporting infrastructures in successful organizations begin with a solid Finance ERP foundation.

- The General Ledger is a strategic application to meet reporting requirements and is the basis for shortening the time between the close and the reporting cycle. Forging harmonization between financial and management reporting drives redundancy out of the organization while simultaneously increasing confidence and accuracy of information.

- Leading organizations are leveraging increased regulatory requirements as an opportunity to enhance reporting processes and tools for a competitive advantage. To help organizations meet ever-changing regulatory and management reporting requirements, ERP vendors are rapidly developing or improving their existing solutions.

FROM INSIGHT TO ACTION

RATIONALIZE REPORTING REQUIREMENTS PRIOR TO DESIGNING THE SOLUTION

Begin with the end in mind. Design reports based on your "to be" vision, not on the "as is" state. Design the CoA with the reporting requirements in mind, as the General Ledger serves as the source for management and regulatory reporting.

LEVERAGE ERP PACKAGE FUNCTIONALITY TO MINIMIZE MANUAL REPORTING

Leverage the integrated ERP functionality or best-of-breed planning and reporting software to reduce the reliance on spreadsheets and other manual mechanisms for combining planning and forecasting data with actual results.

continued

> *continued*
>
> ENSURE THAT REPORTING IS DELIVERED TO THE USER COMMUNITY
> FROM THE PROPER SOURCE
> Real-time reporting requirements should be retrieved from the ERP; less
> time-sensitive but calculation-intensive information should come from
> the data warehouse.

REFERENCES

1. SAP Help Portal, *SAP Best Practices for IAS and IFRS*, V1.470, http://help.sap.com.

2. Henry D. Morris and Kathleen Wilhide, *IDC White Paper: Oracle EPB: Planning and Analysis as the Hub of Performance Management*, April 2004, http://www.oracle.com.

3. Oracle, August 2005, http://www.oracle.com.

4. Jim Richards and Barry Smith, *An Introduction to XBRL – Working Paper*, XBRL International, November 2004, http://www.xbrl.org.au.

CHAPTER 4

Procure to Pay for the Next Generation

PROCURE TO PAY: AN OVERVIEW

Across industries and geographies, high-performance businesses and governments routinely demonstrate consistent shareholder value creation and market leadership. These organizations develop a clear strategic mission and optimize business processes and technological capabilities to remain profitable consistently. Given the strategic nature of the Procure to Pay process, both in driving down costs and in assembling the materials required to introduce products to dominate the market, it is hardly surprising that mastery of this function is essential.

Beginning the Transformation: Required Capabilities

Taking the Procure to Pay process to the next level does not begin by just implementing, upgrading, or expanding an Enterprise Resource Planning (ERP) solution. Accenture experience shows that recognizing and understanding the challenges in transforming the process are the first steps toward achieving the benefits targeted. Such challenges include insufficient utilization of ERP investments, confronting existing processes and requirements, and gaining cross-functional support.

Build a Single End-to-End ERP Landscape

In a recent study by The Hackett Group, cross-industry executives identified their key challenge as misaligned business operations that were preventing effective collaboration with multiple partners. The study identified several factors that set world-class organizations apart from the competition. The goals of these organizations include minimizing system complexity, limiting the number of discrete systems used across the organization, and mandating ERP integration with legacy systems.[1]

Simply put, world-class organizations are striving to achieve a single instance of their ERP applications while eliminating or minimizing the legacy systems. With global supply chains, the need for a single global instance to streamline the Procure to Pay process becomes crucial in order to obtain real-time purchasing and spend information and to minimize total cost of ownership of the solution. For instance, an organization may have sites in Asia and Europe that source from the same supplier; to leverage the potential relationship with the supplier fully, global visibility into purchasing commitments and spend for that particular supplier is critical to operations. Much of these data could be consolidated through a data warehouse, assuming strict adherence to naming and coding standards. However, this additional effort and ongoing maintenance just adds cost to the overall process. Internally too, organizations often have global supply chains whereby, for example, sales organizations in South America may source goods internally from North America. In this case, a single global ERP instance will allow the South American entity to communicate electronically with the North American entity without burdensome interfaces or archaic exchange of paper documents.

Create Standard Global Processes

Achieving a single ERP instance may be the easy part, given that most organizations will see this as beneficial on face value, even if significant technical challenges exist. The biggest challenge is developing a standard global Procure to Pay process to leverage the ERP solution. Local customs and ingrained processes can create roadblocks to establishing a global process. However, although it is true that some countries have varying statutory requirements, we find that global processes are achievable when stakeholders are included in the design sessions and the ultimate goal of creating a global process is supported by all stakeholders.

Moreover, a global Procure to Pay process should not have a single, inward focus. The process should integrate supplier processes and alter the subprocesses as necessary, if possible. Creating seamless hand-offs between entities is the key to a successful end-to-end process. Several ERP options can integrate an organization's Procure to Pay process with that of its suppliers; these options are explored in detail later in the chapter.

Gain Cross-Functional Support

ERP solutions typically shift many tasks to the front end of the process. For instance, common ERP-based Procure to Pay processes require requisitioners to obtain the appropriate account coding prior to submitting the requisition. Gone are the days when the purchasing agent, the Accounts Payable clerk, or even an accountant had to track down the requisitioner to determine the purpose of the procure and identify the appropriate coding. This shifting of responsibilities requires cross-functional support. Purchasing, Receiving, Accounts Payable, General Accounting and Management all need to understand and support the new process. Just as it is important to bring in stakeholders from across the globe during the global process design sessions, including stakeholders from across the various functions is important too. Having a sponsor represent each function is essential to a successful transformation.

Benefits of Optimal Procure to Pay

Traditionally, organizations view Procure to Pay process improvements as a way to drive organizational efficiency and manage cost. Leading organizations, however, take that philosophy a step further as they seek to transform their Procure to Pay process into a vital driver of value with numerous tactical and strategic benefits:

Tactical Benefits

- Maximize buying power
- Control spending
- Maximize working capital
- Reduce support costs.

Strategic Benefits

- Improve capacity for differentiation in the marketplace
- Incorporate flexibility to react to market change
- Better assimilate mergers and acquisitions
- Enhance overall product quality.

Depending on an organization's long-term procurement strategy and capacity for leading practices adoption, optimization initiatives can offer powerful opportunities for economic value creation. We find that for an organization with an average cost of procured materials equal to 55 percent of the cost of goods sold, a reduction of as little as 1 percent in this cost could result in the same margin lift as a 12 to 18 percent sales increase.

By understanding the importance of developing a world-class Procure to Pay capability, successful organizations excel in creating value-centric Procure to Pay organizations and delivering superior results to their shareholders.[2]

For example, Chevron achieved significant cost and cycle time reductions in the Procure to Pay process by implementing world-class purchasing. The organization reduced the time required to approve procure requests from 5 days to 2 days or less; generated additional early pay discounts by demonstrating to suppliers the ability to pay promptly and according to terms; and moved more than 50 percent of its total spend to catalogs – thus ensuring compliance with contract terms. The Aberdeen Group estimates that "for a typical enterprise, it takes an increase of $5 in sales to equal the impact of a $1 reduction in procurement costs." With such an impact, analyzing procurement opportunities from both a strategic and a tactical perspective clearly makes sense. Accenture recently polled 100 procurement executives and found that optimizing nonstrategic sourcing would yield an average of 11 percent year-over-year savings, with one-fourth of the executives estimating the opportunity for savings in their organizations to be as high as 15 percent. In a $5 billion organization, assuming an average of 10 to 20 percent revenue spend on nonstrategic procurement, this improvement can translate into $55 million to $110 million in savings annually, as shown in Figure 4.1.[3]

Organizations have a wide range of options in their drive to maximize value through the Procure to Pay process. Leading organizations choose opportunities for value creation depending on their capacity for risk, applicability to their current and future strategy, organization leadership's support of supply chain management and the feasibility of an initiative's business case. The value creation is summarized in Figure 4.2.

Average baseline spend on non-strategic goods and services (typically 10%-20% of total revenue):	$500 million - $1 billion
Average annual reduction in spend achievable through leading practice sourcing/Procure to Pay performance:	11%
Average annual increase in operating income**:	$55 million - $110 million

*Illustrative
**For a public/government organization, the economic return is 1 to 1

Figure 4.1   *Organizational Procurement opportunities*

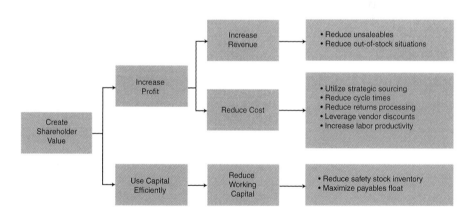

Figure 4.2   *Factors that influence the Procure to Pay process*

PROCESS DESIGN: LEADING PRACTICES & EMERGING TRENDS

The Procure to Pay process increasingly falls under the microscope of cost-reduction efforts. However, given that external forces extend ever greater influence on an organization and its internal capabilities, a strictly process-driven model no longer provides a complete perspective. The new model shown in Figure 4.3 illustrates an outward-facing process, driven to maximize efficiency by adapting to the current market environment. The external pressures of globalization, the increasing compliance requirements, and the drive toward shareholder value bring the flexibility, profitability, and adaptability of internal processes under scrutiny. In response to these factors, successful organizations place maximum emphasis on leveraging their ERP solutions and related technology investments to lower costs, improve product quality, and react to changing market and organizational conditions. Accordingly, over the past several years, Oracle and SAP have continued to enhance their products' functionality to allow organizations to adapt quickly to this changing external environment.

Leading organizations adhere to five principles in designing their procurement capability:

- Viewing Procurement and Accounts Payable as one end-to-end process and managing the efficiency of the entire chain
- Aligning the organization to support the new process instead of aligning the process to fit the organizational silos
- Capturing procurement activity in one ERP solution and leveraging Electronic Data Interchange (EDI) and other paperless capabilities
- Managing all data in one central repository and using decision-support tools to push reports to the appropriate personnel and allow on-line access to both standard and ad hoc reporting
- Ensuring that policies and procedures are well documented and enforced

Once this procurement foundation is in place, the organization is ready to design its world-class process, step by step, as illustrated in Figure 4.3.

In this section, we will discuss how organizations can create and stabilize each component of the Procure to Pay process (see Figure 4.3).

Figure 4.3 *The Procure to Pay process*

1. Vendor Management

Organizations often begin with a review of current purchasing activity, spend patterns, and vendor relationships. Armed with concrete facts, procurement professionals can then focus on managing vendor relationships:

- Which products do employees procure to enable daily production and office functions?
- Are the products strategic?
- Which vendors are used most often?
- What contracts and relationships already exist?
- What is the external market value of these goods and services?
- How is the value of that vendor tracked?

We see that one of the most frequent findings of a vendor review is that multiple records exist for the same vendor. Typically, this situation arises from significant merger and acquisition activity, or because systems have grown up in silos within individual entities. Multiple vendor records often lead to inaccuracies in the ability to track and manage individual vendor activity. Furthermore, each separate record may tie to a separate contract with different prices and payment terms for identical items.

In response, the Oracle, PeopleSoft, and SAP software solutions now offer significantly enhanced vendor master data management capabilities to allow better visibility across the organization and identify where duplication may exist. By consolidating vendors and establishing long-term agreements, an organization can lock in a cross-enterprise advantage in managing cost and vendor relationships. With the robust tools now standard in ERP solutions (e.g., EDI, automated inventory fulfillment, and on-line catalogs), establishing preferred vendor relationships has developed into a proven method for developing process efficiency and market response.

Traditionally, organizations equated vendor management with the establishment of a preferred vendor relationship, and assumed that they would automatically realize ongoing savings through economies of scale. Increasingly, organizations place greater value on more actively managed vendor relationships, and Oracle, PeopleSoft, and SAP ERP solutions have evolved to support this trend. As technology changes almost daily, vendor relationships have grown more flexible – with greater emphasis on "covenants" and a partnership focus rather than on "contracts." In industries requiring rapid technological innovation, procurement executives may regard traditional contracts as too limiting. For example, in an era in which top-of-the-line computers become obsolete within six months, a multiyear contract to supply a specific chip type no longer makes sense.

Furthermore, as organizations seek to manage cost drivers better, closer vendor relationships and accountability make sense. In fact, vendors and customers should collaborate to accelerate speed to market and to minimize production cost. For example, during the design stage of a new product, the development team can typically estimate 90 percent of the final product's cost. For that reason, preferred vendors should join in the product development lifecycle early on to help identify purchasing requirements at the outset.

Oracle, PeopleSoft, and SAP ERP solutions facilitate this new type of relationship, allowing more general flexible agreement setups and vendor functions within the customer system. Figure 4.4 shows the key dependencies and ERP solution features to meet vendor management leading practices.

Leading Practice	Key Dependencies	ERP Capability Fit
Centralize vendor master record maintenance **Centralize control of the vendor master file**	Single Procure to Pay solution	Oracle, PeopleSoft and SAP have end-to-end ERP solutions with functionality that support vendor management in a Shared Services environment
	Vendor management performed by a Shared Services organization	
View vendors as business partners whose goals are aligned with yours, sharing both the risks and rewards	Preferred Supplier programs	Oracle's iSupplier and SAP's eBuyer provide vendor & customer collaboration
	Self-service via web-based tools	
	On-line catalogs to get the right items from the right vendor at the right price	

Figure 4.4 *Vendor management leading practices*

From Day 1 in the product development lifecycle, vendors can access Oracle's iSupplier Portal to review design team specifications and suggest modifications to drive down cost or improve production efficiency and then route the documents back to the team with comments and suggestions.

Given the market trend toward up-front vendor collaboration, managing the vendor relationship ensures ongoing quality, participation, delivery, and predictability. Leading organizations regularly hold open discussions with their vendors to establish supplier performance metrics jointly. This practice actually improves vendor compliance. By giving visibility into and participation in the measurement process, an organization lays out concrete and reasonable expectations to which the vendor has agreed to adhere. Once both parties agree to the measurement process, an organization can design ERP and data warehouse reporting to deliver the performance metrics to both the vendor and the customer. For example, SAP's Business Warehouse (BW) can extract data from the Supply Relationship Management (SRM), Materials Management, and Accounts Payable modules and can generate metrics to analyze vendor and purchasing efficiencies.

2. Order Placement

Similarly, the trend in traditional goods procurement or order placement has evolved toward incorporating vendor capabilities from the very beginning of the process. To minimize time to market, more and more successful organizations choose to partner with vendors up front and closely involve them in their procurement function. By including vendors in the process – and when possible, aligning technology solutions – organizations can expect to realize significant improvements in speed to market and in overall quality of product.

For example, SAP's SRM solution allows document exchange, supplier portal capabilities, and process collaboration functionality for remote and on-site partnerships. Considering that today a preferred supplier for a key component could literally be located anywhere in the world, SAP's SRM module includes functionality to bridge the geographical gap through self-service functionality and paperless capabilities.

The evolution of ERP solutions to incorporate vendor management functionality through self-service portals has given rise to the opportunity to shorten the Procure to Pay cycle by permitting suppliers to submit procure orders electronically or through direct entry (see Figure 4.5). Increasingly, business-to-business exchanges are seen as part of the overall Procure to Pay capability for organizations, requiring integration to organizations' ERP solutions. Solutions such as Ariba (for procurement) and Xign are effective means for organizations with ERP solutions to extend their process capabilities.

3. Order Fulfillment

High-performance organizations employ a variety of strategies to streamline their processes for goods receipt (see Figure 4.6). The strengthening of the vendor/customer relationship means that organizations can leverage each other's ERP capabilities to ensure product availability. First, vendors can monitor their clients' database of materials, and ERP solutions can automatically trigger an alert when inventory falls below an acceptable threshold. This in turn will create an Advanced Shipment Notification (ASN), which prepares the customer's system for goods receipt. When the materials arrive, the ASN acts as the purchase order and materials are quickly replenished in stock. Through improved vendor

Leading Practice	Key Dependencies	ERP Capability Fit
Use EDI to streamline ordering, price change notification and processing receipt reports and invoices	Electronic data interchange (EDI) standardized around ANSI formats	Oracle and SAP feature integrated purchasing functionality to respond to Requests for Quotations (RFQs) and generate POs
	Available information about transaction volumes to prioritize vendors	
Utilize online purchase requisition systems with web-based supplier catalogs **Use Procurement cards (P-card) for small-dollar purchases**	On-line catalogs	Oracle and SAP have been adding functionality to support interaction with external sources of data
	Clearly defined policy and procedures regarding use of the P-card	
	Software that allows allocation of expense by card, Merchant Category Code (MCC), Vendor, Unit, Expense Type, and so on	

Figure 4.5 *Order placement leading practices*

Leading Practice	Key Dependencies	ERP Capability Fit
Release orders automatically based on system-generated demand Leverage vendor-based forecasting and replenishment systems by outsourcing inventory management to vendors	Implement automated reorder point (ROP)	Oracle, PeopleSoft and SAP have ERP functionality that support ROP and ASBN
	Implement automatic shipping and billing notification (ASBN)	
	Self-service via web-based tools	

Figure 4.6   *Order fulfillment leading practices*

self-service functionality, vendors can also ensure their clients have received their orders and view the status of their invoices.

4. Invoice Processing

Collecting and channeling information gathered during the requisitioning, purchasing, and receiving activities is critical to minimizing and automating the tasks of processing invoices and paying vendors.

Although scanning invoices and routing digital images are wonderful advancements, imagine eliminating the invoice all together. Organizations on the leading edge work actively with their vendors to transmit invoice information electronically, creating real benefits to both parties (see Figure 4.7). Whenever possible, organizations no longer print, place in an envelope, seal, mail, receive, open, sort, scan, and manually enter paper invoices into a system, as all of these steps require significant and unnecessary manual intervention. They also negatively impact an organization's ability to optimize working capital through payment terms optimization. Consider these comparisons of invoice processing standard times from the Institute of Management and Administration (IOMA)[4]:

Average	6.8 days
Best-in-class process	3.0 days
Best-in-class + automation	1.5 days

Leading Practice	Key Dependencies	ERP Capability Fit
Transmit electronic invoice data	Invoice data fit to established EDI conventions	Oracle Accounts Payable module features integrated AP EDI functionality for invoice data upload
	Vendor compatibility	All major ERP vendors provide approval workflows functionality
Implement Evaluated Receipt Settlement (ERS)	Manageability of price changes	SAP integration in Materials Management (MM) allows for Item catalog capabilities in the material master record
	"Tier One" vendor relationships	All major ERP vendors provide approval workflows functionality
	Item price stability	Oracle, PeopleSoft and SAP CRM modules allow for vendor portals to facilitate purchasing activities

Figure 4.7   *Invoice processing leading practices*

In an environment in which the ERP solution is aligned with leading practices, all invoice data are generated, passed, and received electronically via XML standards or mutually agreed protocol standards. Oracle and SAP offer functionality for receiving electronically transmitted invoice information. This eliminates most of the manual effort, which results in a reduction of the overall AP workforce and aligns an organization with the emerging trends toward a more global standard for EDI invoice delivery.

Electronic transmission of invoices requires significant initial coordination for both the customer and the vendor; as a result, some organizations have decided to eliminate the invoice altogether. Evaluated receipt settlement (ERS) functionality generates an invoice on receipt of the goods or services. In ERS, the pricing information is obtained from the purchase order and the quantity is derived from the goods receipt. This is enough information to generate the invoice; however, the process only works if Purchasing and Receiving enter accurate information up front.

With ERS, the three-way match among purchase order (PO), goods receipt, and invoice is no longer a control point, but this should not dissuade organizations from implementing ERS. Purchasing agents and receiving dock workers should be held accountable for accuracy. Additionally, preliminary payment run reports can be reviewed and large or unusual payments investigated. In some global organizations, certain countries still require the use of primary documentation in a paper format; however, to the extent that a paper-free environment is a viable option, IOMA reports that "moving from a low to a medium level of automation will cut the cost to process a vendor payment by 30–60 percent."[5] Cost savings such as these create a tangible increase in company shareholder value.

When electronic invoicing or ERS are not viable options, organizations are not limited to achieving greater efficiencies within the proven Accounts Payable practices (see Figure 4.8). Technology advances have significantly improved process efficiency in invoice recognition. Optical character recognition (OCR) technology digitally reads invoices and eliminates the need for manual data entry upon scanning. Assuming that invoices follow a standard format from a particular vendor, the OCR application can be "trained" to read invoices and pull the required information from the procure order number to the item prices. Once an invoice is scanned, the OCR process automatically feeds the invoice data into the ERP solution. Oracle, PeopleSoft, and SAP have standard open interfaces to upload the OCR invoice data into their Accounts Payable modules. Human intervention is only needed if the OCR application has difficulty reading a particular invoice.

5. Vendor Payment

Once an invoice has been generated and a liability established, the liability needs to be relieved through payment. Effective management of an organization's vendor payments accomplishes two objectives: 1) further cost reductions of the Accounts Payable function and 2) allowing effective management of access to cash and float. Implementing an ERP solution creates significant opportunities for managing the vendor payment process and achieving shareholder value.

Leading Practice	Key Dependencies	ERP Capability Fit
Implement Optical Character Recognition (OCR)	Standard invoice templates	Oracle, PeopleSoft and SAP have partnerships with Independent Software Vendors (ISV) that facilitate compatibility with imaging scanning solutions with OCR and ICR technology
	Widely relevant template recognition	
	Approval workflow	
Character Recognition (ICR) Implement Intelligent	Approval workflow	Oracle, PeopleSoft and SAP have functionality that support batch purchase order matching with scanned invoices and electronic approval workflows

Figure 4.8 *Electronic invoice scanning leading practices*

Oracle, PeopleSoft, and SAP enable organizations to minimize the Accounts Payable function when it is used in conjunction with leading practices that optimize the ERP environment. For those involved in ERP implementations, the challenge of creating a leading practice payments capability lies in optimizing the fundamental design of the payment model and having the initiatives in place to drive suppliers to use Electronic Funds Transfer (EFT). Following are some ERP design considerations:

- **Cash pooling** is a leading practice within Finance and treasury, with the idea that organizations should fund payables from one bank account; however, the complexity of cash pooling rises with the number of entities, countries, and currencies that need to be supported. Organizations may decide to use the momentum of an ERP implementation to introduce organizational change in this area, although doing so will cause additional challenges and design considerations for the project team and the Treasury function.

- Even though check processing is expensive, **electronic payments** still elude most organizations. The IOMA Accounts Payable Benchmarking Report for 2005 indicates that 15 percent of all payments across all industries are electronic, with a high of 40 percent in the communications and high-tech industry. Organizations may choose to adopt new policies to enforce the use of electronic funds as part of the overall ERP implementation effort.

- When an organization cannot implement electronic payment capabilities, **automating the check printing process** via an ERP payment program reduces the volume of checks and the labor required to produce the checks.

- **Payment consolidation by vendor** is another basic capability of ERP applications that allows for payment of multiple invoices as a part of a single payment transaction. This reduces the number of overall payments.

- **Netting Accounts Payable and Accounts Receivable** potentially reduces the volume of payments and also creates a safety net against paying a vendor who is also a customer with overdue payments. If the Accounts Receivable balance for the supplier/customer is greater than the Accounts Payable balance, a payment will not be issued.

- An organization may seize on the opportunities to reduce invoice and payment volumes by using **procurement cards** (P-Cards) to eliminate individual supplier payments in exchange for consolidated electronic invoice summaries and payments with financial institutions. By combining a P-Card process with EDI from the service provider, organizations can gain both greater spend visibility and payment processing efficiency.

Figure 4.9 provides a summary of these leading practices, in terms of the key dependencies that will determine whether each practice is a good fit for a particular organization, as well as the corresponding ERP solution features that support it.

A key component of maximizing value from Accounts Payable is maximizing Days Payables Outstanding (DPO); however, maximizing value from payment terms demands systems that will accurately capture that information for monitoring. Once in place, Oracle Accounts Payable can calculate the optimum payment date to delay payment as long as possible without sacrificing early-payment discounts. Optimum payment dates coupled with cash disbursement forecasting capabilities allow an organization to improve its working capital position and free capital for return-generating investments. Of course, an optimum payment date only works if the payments themselves are created and dispersed efficiently.

Leading Practice	Key Dependencies	ERP Capability Fit
Implement cash pooling	Single currency	SAP offers single paying company code functionality. Oracle Payable's functionality allows both single and multiple paying company codes
	Vendor EFT payment receipt capability	Oracle, PeopleSoft and SAP all offer forms of Vendor payment configuration
Encourage EFT payments	Use of automated clearing house (ACH) for electronic payments	All major ERP vendors can enable ACH payments
Automate check printing	Varying payment terms which can be grouped together	Oracle, PeopleSoft and SAP all offer Payment schedule functionality
Consolidate payments by Vendor	Payment cycle schedule compatibility	Batch payment cycle processing designed to consolidate payments by cycle, by vendor and by payment type is available with all major ERPs
Institute netting of Accounts Payable and Accounts Receivable	Accounts Receivable and Accounts Payable managed within the same ERP	All major ERP vendors have netting functionality
Use Procurement cards	Vendor capability	P-Card transaction requests and approval workflows
	High-volume, low-dollar purchases	Oracle, PeopleSoft and SAP all offer P-Card detail to be exported into their respective purchasing modules at vendor level
	Integration between merchant data and internal general ledger accounts	System-enforced P-Card policies
	Effective policies and limited access to P-Card purchasing capabilities	Procurement forecasting from historical transactions

Figure 4.9 *Procure to Pay leading practices as they relate to ERP capabilities*

6. Self-Service Enablement

When trying to manage procurement costs, organizations often benefit by pushing procurement activities to the end users in a self-service model. Self-service in the Procure to Pay process can take shape in many forms, as shown in the following examples:

Internal Self-Service

- **On-line requisitioning** allows a user in need of goods or services to create an on-line requisition either directly within the ERP solution or via a portal. The requisitioning process can be tied directly to product catalogs to link the product identification electronically with the request process.
- **Order status tracking** allows requisitioners to check on the status of their orders through the supply chain. An advanced system will link the requisition with the supplier inventory tracking information and the distributor or delivery services.
- **P-Cards** reduce the number of purchase orders and invoices when the volume of purchases is high and the value is low. Empowering employees to purchase these items with an organization-backed credit card reduces the overall transaction processing for low-value items.

External Self-Service

- **Vendor payment inquiry** capabilities can be enabled through portal and/or interactive voice functionality. The capability allows vendors to check on the status of their invoice and the payment.

Self-service models achieve process efficiency extremely effectively, as long as process owners ensure that they have appropriate controls to prevent abuse.

7. Policies, Procedures, Workflow, and Compliance Monitoring

Clearly, self-service functionality across an organization requires effective control mechanisms to prevent abuse and deviation from corporate policy. In addition to providing self-service capabilities, Oracle, PeopleSoft, and SAP ERP solutions all include various tools for managing policy compliance through robust on-line and reporting control capabilities in addition to drill-down capabilities from the invoice line in the Accounts Payable module to the original Purchase Order document.

On-line catalogs maximize vendor relationships and negotiated volume discounts. By tying a catalog to one to two negotiated vendor suppliers, organizations can monitor the transaction volume of specific supplies through reporting, and they can use this information to negotiate further discounts. Managing this capability requires that the organization set up clear governance structures and procedures and implement role-based workflows consistent with purchasing approval authorizations and robust exception reporting to ensure compliance.

THIRD-PARTY SOFTWARE: ENHANCING THE ERP SOLUTION

This chapter has focused primarily on working within the boundaries of a single ERP solution; however, third-party software providers exist that either enhance or fill gaps in existing ERP functionality. Such providers fall into two categories: licensed software and hosted services. They can enhance the overall ERP solution by providing:

- Robust catalog functionality
- Electronic marketplaces
- Invoice-scanning capabilities
- Check-clearing tracking.

When you are working with third-party software providers, it is important to understand the required level of integration to the ERP solution. This integration needs to be appropriately designed and implemented to ensure that the correct data are passed between applications.

FUTURE TRENDS

When Accenture researched[6] how organizations transform Procurement to deliver real benefits, generally we found that the organizations' largest problems stem from not executing the leading practices that will maximize value. Successful organizations seek to maximize ERP capabilities, align operations with suppliers, enforce process efficiencies, and drive value out of their investment. Every organization can benefit from analyzing and optimizing its Procure to Pay process in order to increase shareholder value. In this section, we discuss emerging trends that should affect organizational efforts to transform procurement.

The following case study shows how a European grocery retailer used ERP functionality to transform its Procure to Pay process for savings that totaled in the millions.

CASE STUDY
European Grocery Retailer

A European grocery retailer has to purchase a staggering amount of uniforms, sta-tionery, carrier bags, and other goods and services not for resale. Any products needed to run the business, from pens and pencils to the buildings themselves, had been ordered, paid for, and accounted for through complicated legacy processes and systems. At times, different stores were ordering from the same suppliers using completely different procurement approaches. The company needed a single procurement system to handle its purchases more effectively and to reduce both operating and procurement costs.

They decided to design an eProcurement system that would consolidate the tech-nologies and processes behind purchasing goods and services not for resale. They also needed the new capability to be web based and easily accessible to its geographical-ly dispersed workforce. Using Oracle's purchasing capabilities, the new eProcurement system is now live throughout more than 500 stores and all locations. In addition to millions saved annually on Goods Not For Resale spend, other benefits include:

- *Transparency of management information. Now the company can tell "who is spending what and when and how much it is costing." They put con-straints in place to achieve additional cost savings.*
- *Processes are easier and less fallible with eCommerce efficiencies. With elec-tronic ordering, "lost paper trails" are no longer a concern.*
- *Electronic invoicing is matched to purchase orders to allow skilled resources to focus on other, more value-added tasks.*

As an example of the increasing focus on procurement processes as legitimate sources of shareholder value, consider that in a recent Economist Intelligence Unit Report, 60 percent of executives from more than 350 global firms believe that by 2015, their organizations will have a CPO – a Chief Procurement Officer – and that the officer in this strate-gic position will report directly to the CEO.[7]

Shared Services and Outsourcing
As the market matures, many leading organizations have begun to reor-ganize the procurement functionality into a shared services function or

have outsourced the capability entirely. As Figure 4.10 illustrates, the scope of opportunities ranges from pushing functions back to the vendor (for example, the checking of quality), to outsourcing procurement functions ranging from travel and entertainment processing, to complete strategic procurement.

Clearly, as market forces continue to impact industry, the procurement function will receive greater and greater organizational focus. Successful organizations cannot miss the opportunity to capitalize on its potential. Today's organizations are working to coordinate Accounts Payable, Procurement, and Strategic Sourcing activities, while also modifying their processes to improve information sharing. Centralized management of these activities supports optimal vendor selection, negotiation, and management.

E-Auctions

According to a recent study commissioned by Visa International,[8] which surveyed 52 companies considered to have leading Procure to Pay practices, a new trend is emerging: electronic reverse auctions (e-Auctions). In the Visa study, 17 percent of participants had already implemented an e-Auction solution. An additional 22 percent of study participants planned to implement e-Auctions in the near future.

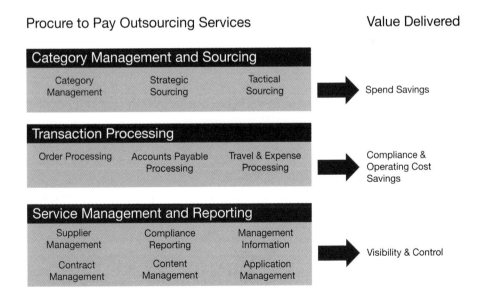

Figure 4.10   *Procure to Pay outsourcing services*

E-Auctions is an innovative procurement technique that uses Internet-based technology. Suppliers compete in real time by bidding lower as the auction progresses. E-Auctions offer efficient, open, and transparent negotiations as part of a full procurement process. This means that the time needed to carry out competitive negotiations is reduced as bidding starts at or near the market price. E-Auctions have proved to be particularly successful when they are used with requirements that have clearly defined specifications and when a vibrant market exists. The SAP SRM module allows for functionality that can facilitate an organization's e-Auctions and even inform vendors of upcoming auctions.

According to an Accenture pan-European study[9] that surveyed 30 companies, those that adopted e-Auctions experienced significantly higher economic returns upon using e-Auctions. The whole sourcing cycle was faster than before and typically generated savings of 10 to 35 percent.

THE HACKETT GROUP ON PROCURE TO PAY

World-class organizations excel at leveraging technology. Unlike their peer group, they streamline and automate both low-value and high-value processes to reduce labor requirements. The increasing stabilization of technology platforms has enabled world-class organizations to focus on delivering greater business value and overall strategic alignment throughout the entire procure-to-pay process.

This technology-for-labor swap frees up funds that are invested in higher value processes such as strategic sourcing initiatives, supplier analysis, supply base rationalization, and supplier collaboration and development.

Organizations support these processes not just by best practices and tools such as cross-functional teams and e-sourcing applications. They also support them by using the money freed up in transactional processing labor costs. Simply put, world-class procurement organizations work faster, incur less cost, and make fewer errors. For example, world-class procurement organizations, aided by technology, process 4.4 times the number of orders annually than their more typical peers, at a cost

continued

---

that is 61 percent less. They also make significantly fewer errors in quantity and pricing in items ordered.

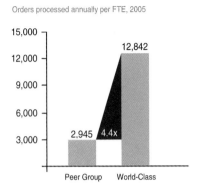

Source: The Hackett Group

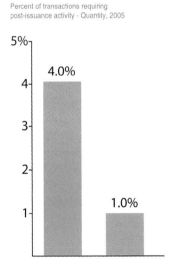

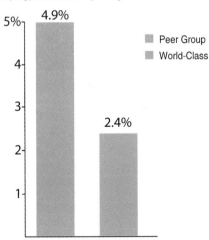

Source: The Hackett Group

Although the cost of transactional processes will never be completely eliminated, the more that increased productivity and accuracy can lower costs, the more firms have to invest in high-value processes, which ultimately increase the visibility and credibility of the procurement function at the company's most senior levels.

CFO INSIGHTS

- Successful organizations use the Procure to Pay end-to-end process to create and enhance shareholder value. Procure to Pay is no longer just a cost management tool; now it can positively impact shareholder value by optimizing key strategic value drivers.

- Active vendor management has become a critical success factor in designing a leading-edge Procure to Pay process. Technology is enabling organizations to involve their vendors at the earliest stages of product development to drive out real gains in product costing, quality, and market acceptance.

- Many of the traditional cost management initiatives prevalent in a leading Procure to Pay process continue to be valid. The role of Oracle, PeopleSoft, and SAP ERP solutions in implementing these initiatives is critical, particularly in invoice processing and vendor payments. Leading practices such as netting of payables and receivables and cash pooling payments are possible only with integrated ERP solutions.

FROM INSIGHT TO ACTION

ENSURE THAT THE PROCURE TO PAY PROCESS INCLUDES INTERNAL
AND EXTERNAL REQUIREMENTS

The Procure to Pay process should not have a single, inward focus; supplier processes should be integrated and subprocesses altered as necessary. Seamless hand-offs between entities are required to improve the process. Today's solutions can integrate an organization's Procure to Pay with that of its suppliers.

THINK IN TERMS OF VALUE CREATION RATHER THAN COST
CONTAINMENT

Leading organizations leverage the strategic value drivers of the Procure to Pay process. By employing leading edge technology and processes, these organizations have been able to forge lasting partnerships with vendors that not only impact traditional Procure to Pay functions but also affect product cost, quality, and time-to-market.

continued

> EMPOWER YOUR VENDORS AND EMPLOYEES THROUGH SELF-SERVICE
> Providing end users with self-service capabilities, such as on-line requisitioning and P-Cards, reduces costs and processing time. Self-service models drive process efficiency and effectiveness, as long as organizations ensure that they have appropriate controls to prevent abuse.

REFERENCES

1. The Hackett Group, *Best-Practices-Driven Management: Profile of World Class Finance*, 2003, http://www.answerthink.com.

2. Accenture, *Getting Real Results from Your Procure-to-Pay Opportunities*, January 2005, http://www.accenture.com.

3. Ibid.

4. Institute of Management and Administration (IOMA), *A/P Department Benchmarks and Analysis*, 2003, http://www.ioma.com.

5. Ibid.

6. Accenture, *Getting Real Results from Your Procure-to-Pay Opportunities*, January 2005, http://www.accenture.com.

7. Economist Intelligence Unit, *The New Face of Purchasing*, April 2005, http://www.sap.com.

8. David Cramer, "Best Practices to Optimize the Procure-to-Pay Process," *GTNews,* July 4, 2005, http://www.gtnews.com.

9. Accenture, *Unlocking the Full Potential of eProcurement*, 2001, http://www.accenture.com.

CHAPTER 5

Asset Lifecycle Management

ASSET LIFECYCLE MANAGEMENT: AN OVERVIEW

In every economy, there are times when nearly any capital investment can be justified with the promise of growth and capturing market share. Such eras of free-flowing capital investments, however, are both rare and short lived relative to more general market conditions. The prevailing corporate finance environment is characterized by heavily scrutinized performance, financial controls, and limited capital resources. Under these normal conditions, the Asset Lifecycle Management process plays a vital role in Finance organizations – particularly those operating in capital-intensive industries.

Defining the Asset Lifecycle Management Process

The traditional Asset Lifecycle Management process for tangible assets is defined within the bounds of the Acquire-to-Retire process, beginning with asset procurement and ending with the eventual disposition once the asset's useful life has expired. In today's leading organizations, our experience shows that the Asset Lifecycle Management process (see Figure 5.1) is far more comprehensive, with a footprint that extends well beyond these traditional endpoints and throughout the entire organization.

Progressive organizations begin this process well before capital items are ever procured by incorporating Asset Lifecycle Management into a well-designed capital planning and budgeting function. This process should align asset acquisition plans with the corporate strategy and should be enforced by formal capital allocation and approval functions to ensure that expenditures are properly authorized.

Figure 5.1 *Asset Lifecycle process*

Following planning and authorization, the transactional components of the Asset Lifecycle Management Process are administered through Enterprise Resource Planning (ERP) procurement modules. Organizations use transaction processing modules such as Purchasing, Inventory, and Accounts Payable to record the asset acquisition or issuance. Then, in the case of capital projects, costs are accumulated in a Project Accounting module while the asset is being constructed to enable precapitalization reporting and management. When the asset is placed in service, the transaction processing or Project Accounting module (depending on the type of asset being created) integrates with the Fixed Asset module to begin depreciation. After capitalization, the asset should be actively tracked and maintained until it is eventually retired or disposed.

The Asset Lifecycle Management process involves tracking, analyzing, and reporting performance metrics across the entire capital base, including both in-service assets and construction in progress. To be done properly, we advise that this reporting should include total cost of ownership, value realized from the investments, and analysis of capital investments across multiple dimensions. The insight gained from this analysis should feed back into the planning and capital allocation processes so the portfolio can be adjusted accordingly.

Is Asset Lifecycle Management Critical?

Although every organization needs to effectively manage its assets effectively, the necessity for advanced Asset Lifecycle Management capabilities is dictated by factors such as the amount of capital deployed, the investment options availability, the resources required to administer the process, and transaction volumes. Leading organizations recognize the impact these factors have on their ability to achieve capital efficiency and maintain cost-effective Finance operations. We have seen that organizations that take action by building a robust Asset Lifecycle Management process and associated tools gain a position of strength over competitors that fail to make this connection.

When Regularly Deploying Large Amounts of Capital

Successful organizations focus attention on areas that have the greatest potential shareholder value impact. For those operating in capital-intensive industries with substantial annual capital expenditures, Asset Lifecycle Management is clearly an area that should receive leadership's undivided attention.

When Many Investment Options Exist

The typical organization has a pipeline of desired strategic and tactical investments that far exceeds the funds available from operations. Organizations in this situation find themselves facing tough decisions about which investments to fund. Naturally, the organization wants to select the investment mix that produces the highest overall return, but, too often, these decisions are made using very basic methods such as top-down allocation, baseline from a previous capital budgeting cycle, or the investment's net present value estimated by the requestor. With effective capital allocation and portfolio management capabilities in place, this problem can be overcome, enabling the organization to deploy capital where it will generate the highest return.

When Administration of Capital and Asset Processes Requires Many Resources

Unlike some back-office functions that are administered over relatively short durations by a specific group of individuals, the Asset Lifecycle tends to span multiple years and touch many parts of the organization. Leading organizations understand the cross-functional interdependencies of this process and establish the streamlined processes and reporting necessary to minimize the resources consumed by managing capital projects and assets over time.

When Processing High-Transaction Volumes

The primary challenge facing an organization with hundreds of thousands or millions of assets is maintaining real-time visibility across the enterprise.

Each day, the complexion of the asset base will change, with new additions, transfers, and retirements. Simply capturing and depreciating this volume of data require a sophisticated, integrated capability that supports automated asset additions from the ERP Procurement or Project Accounting modules. After capitalization, the organization must track subsequent asset movements to ensure property tax compliance as well as maintenance schedules, to maximize the useful life of the assets.

Needs Assessment Criteria

The preceding section covered situations that warrant a strong Asset Lifecycle capability. Figure 5.2 provides a more synthesized guideline to define these needs further based on suggested thresholds.

We recommend that the factors in Figure 5.2 be considered as part of a larger, holistic picture, taking into account the unique characteristics of the organization. As an example, an organization with an average asset value of $1 million that only adds 250 assets per year would require much less sophisticated capabilities than one that adds 250,000 assets per year at an average value of $1,000. Although they both have the same value, an organization with 250,000 assets added per year requires a more advanced asset-tracking capability than one adding 250 (which can be handled quite effectively through less sophisticated means).

Factor	Strong Need	Moderate Need	Minimum Need
Annual Capital Expenditures	> $500m	$250m - $500m	< $250m
Capital Expenditures/Revenue	> 10%	5 - 10%	0 - 5%
Existing Asset Base Value	> $1.0bn	$500m -$1.0bn	< $500m
Average Asset Value	> $1,000	$500 - $1,000	< $500
Annual New Asset Volume	> 50,000	10,000 - 50,000	0 - 10,000
Asset Type–Ability to Track	Physical	Mixed	Soft Assets
Asset Movements/Total Assets	> 5%	2 - 5%	< 2%
Property Tax Reporting Entities	> 5	3 - 5	1 - 2
Asset Cost Data Sources	> 4	3 - 4	1 - 2

Figure 5.2 *Suggested thresholds for determining Asset Lifecycle needs*

ASSET LIFECYCLE MANAGEMENT BENEFITS

It is plain to see that managing capital and fixed assets is a basic cost of doing business. Our experience shows that most companies will realize many benefits by performing the process efficiently relative to competitors.

Capital Efficiency

Every organization needs to make the most of its capital to maximize performance and shareholder returns. Although this is often easier said than done, such efficiency can yield substantial benefits through capital investment optimization and expenditure avoidance.

Capital Investment Optimization

Capital investment optimization is the ability to identify, plan, prioritize, and manage the portfolio of capital investments, such that returns are maximized for a given risk level. This requires integrated strategic, capital, and operational planning, as well as the ability to monitor and measure investments across multiple evaluation criteria. All of this must be accomplished while one is maintaining business operations and working within any resource constraints.

Expenditure Avoidance

Expenditure avoidance comes in two forms. First, proactive asset maintenance, warranty management, and strong asset redeployment procedures can – if properly implemented with Oracle, PeopleSoft, or SAP – extend an asset's useful life. Second, portfolio management techniques can be used to avoid contributing more cash to nonperforming investments.

Operational Effectiveness

With any function that has a transaction processing component, we recommend a streamlined process to drive operational benefits by reducing redundancy and minimizing manual processing – both of which lead to fewer resources needed to administer the process.

Reduced Redundancy

With portions of the Asset Lifecycle typically distributed across the organization, duplicate activities are common. For example, the corporate finance group may have an Asset Lifecycle process defined around the ERP, and individual business units may develop "shadow systems" or databases. Such manual processes proliferate when the requirements of all stakeholders have not been addressed, when leadership is not enforcing the processes, or when a process/technology gap (either real or perceived) exists.

Minimized Manual Processing

As an asset moves through its lifecycle, it will often pass through many hands and systems. With each hand-off comes the possibility of duplicate data entry, errors in handling, or reconciliation issues. This can be avoided by having an integrated technology platform that eliminates unnecessary touch points and provides information transparency.

Risk Mitigation

Although Asset Lifecycle Management is often not as tangible as other benefits, it plays an integral role in the risk mitigation strategies of many organizations.

Enhanced Service Stability/Quality

Service issues, including outages and downtime, can often be linked directly to poor preventative maintenance programs, inferior asset quality, or a general asset failure. Although all service issues cannot be attributed to poor Asset Lifecycle Management processes, having the capability to track asset maintenance schedules and monitor them proactively, particularly at key failure points, can help minimize unexpected risks that often translate into unwanted results such as lawsuits, fines, or lost customers.

Improved Reporting Accuracy

Asset tracking becomes a difficult problem when "fixed assets" are more mobile than the name would imply (for example, laptop computers), when movement velocity is high, or when assets are frequently handled by contractors. Because this information directly feeds property tax filing and reporting, its accuracy is absolutely critical. Additionally, tax authorities learn which organizations can and which cannot easily defend their property tax records, and they will exploit this knowledge when they see a weakness. The more tax authorities there are requiring the organization to file returns, the more important reporting accuracy becomes.

BEGINNING THE IMPLEMENTATION JOURNEY

Virtually all organizations start with some degree of Asset Lifecycle Management capability in place. The question is whether the capability suffices to support the value and people involved in the process. Recognizing the need for improvements is just the beginning; the real work is planning and implementing the necessary changes.

Establish the Scope

Taking control of the Asset Lifecycle Management process may require extensive work; often organizations find it difficult to determine where to begin the series of improvement initiatives. The natural tendency is to begin such efforts with an objective of reporting all project-related costs or tracking all assets. In reality, these objectives can be quite hard to achieve. We recommend that organizations undertaking such initiatives be pragmatic when defining their scope, making certain to focus on capital expenditures for which detailed tracking will yield the greatest benefit. They need to begin defining their scope by asking several basic questions:

- What does the organization define as a project?
- What asset types comprise the majority of capital expenditures?
- Are all data sources integrated to the Project Accounting or Fixed Asset system?
- How feasible is it to track assets once they are placed in service?

Answers to these questions will focus efforts on the highest value assets and those most realistic to track. The organization can then establish and stabilize a business process that leverages leading Asset Lifecycle Management practices before adding incremental volume, lower value assets, and those that are more difficult to track.

Common Asset Lifecycle Implementation Challenges

Oracle and SAP have created flexible Asset Lifecycle capabilities to meet the varying business demands of their clients. This flexibility, however, causes its own share of implementation challenges and complexity. We find that beginning the implementation process with an understanding of the challenges and decisions that lie ahead can be invaluable. Figure 5.3 outlines some of the most common ERP implementation decisions and their implications.

Implementation Decisions	Implications
What constitutes a project/asset?	This decision drives transaction processing and ERP solution volumes. Definitions that produce many small assets/projects can add much work and little value. Using an example of an IT program, defining a specific "project" number for each unique work stream or phase will produce higher volumes than having a single code for the entire program.
At what level of detail will project/asset budget and actuals be tracked – Business Unit, Department, Employee #, etc?	This decision also drives volume, particularly as it relates to post-acquisition asset tracking, as greater detail will trigger more transfers than tracking at higher levels. Accuracy can also suffer if/when transfers are missed. Desktop/laptop computers provide an example of where this becomes a topic of discussion. If the computer is tracked to the employee level, people and processes must be in place to record each transfer of that computer in the Assets module, generating much activity. Some organizations elect to track only the computer purchase by entity and location (for tax purposes), eliminating the overhead required to track subsequent movements.
What are the capital allocation criteria and processes?	Failure to have strong capital allocation criteria and process control will allow spending to occur with minimal accountability for results. It will also diminish the value of capital budget-to-actual reporting from the ERP.
To what extent can project managers manually adjust project actuals?	Allowing project managers direct access to change asset/capital data can generate reconciliation issues and undermine data accuracy. Conversely, the preferred procedure is to require all changes to be made at the transaction source, but this can generate work volume in the source organizations.
What asset books will be maintained?	Carrying many tax books can multiply the volume of asset depreciation records in the system and produce maintenance challenges, particularly when handling very high asset volumes. A common solution, when many filings are required, is to maintain only the materially different asset books (e.g., Corporate, Federal Tax, State Tax) and then generate the filings for more minor jurisdictions with tax software that augments the ERP.
What is the asset tagging, maintenance and warranty strategy?	This decision will drive the functionality required (for example, barcode scanning) by those who generally use and handle assets and may also dictate whether third party software is required as part of the ERP implementation.
What set of capital reports are required to support the business?	Capital reporting requirements or preferences can diverge significantly across the organization. Coming to a standard definition can be very complex, but is necessary to achieve a common business language across the organization.

Figure 5.3 *Common implementation decisions and their implications*

ASSET LIFECYCLE ENABLED WITH ERP

"Implement a project management tool." "Implement a project accounting system." "Implement a barcode scanning and asset tracking tool." Organizations often launch point-solution initiatives such as these to address capital- and asset-related problems. As discussed in Chapter 1, leading with a tool implementation can result in an already faulty process being configured into the tool or, even worse, can neglect the process aspect altogether. The first order of business is to create and stabilize the process prior to or in conjunction with the application of the technology solution — preferably leveraging what is already in place.

In this section, we will discuss how organizations can effectively deliver each component of the Asset Lifecycle Management process, as previously illustrated in Figure 5.1, with the implementation or enhancement of an ERP solution.

1. Cross-Functional Collaboration: Integrating the Organization

A well-defined ERP implementation program must be organized in a way that ensures heavy involvement of all stakeholders in the design process. Omitting any of the critical stakeholder groups will invariably lead to a proliferation of solutions not well integrated with the ERP solution.

Business Unit Operations

Few large organizations operate only a single business. Those that manage several find that each separate business unit has its own unique capital project and asset needs. Take, for example, a global products company that manages its core product manufacturing, a distribution/logistics entity, and a services business. The first business will require significant property, plant, and equipment investments, as well as asset warranty tracking. The second entity will have substantial fleet management needs, as well as strict service schedule handling. The third business will require elements of fleet management, service schedule, information technology, and possibly the ability to issue assets from inventory. To ensure that all these needs are met with a new ERP implementation, the operations of each business unit must be represented during design.

Procurement/Supply Chain Management

Regardless of the capital project and asset types required to run the business, supply chain management (SCM) will be involved in procuring the necessary goods and services. SCM involvement from the beginning can help ensure that the item master file and procurement processes are properly aligned with downstream accounting and capital management. The SCM group will also help manage the long-term asset warranty, maintenance, and repair processes that are often enabled through the Fixed Asset module's tracking capabilities. Additionally, the capital management and SCM functions can partner to generate substantial value from assets late in their lifecycle through redeployment and sales. Failure to accommodate SCM requirements in the Asset Lifecycle design often results in the deployment of specific tracking solutions without integration into the ERP solution.

Information Technology

Today's IT function has responsibility for greater asset volumes and value than ever before. IT typically manages multiple capital projects, servers, desktops, laptops, mobile devices, and software across the entire organization. IT investments have also become increasingly complex and mobile, which makes accurate asset tracking and maintenance extremely important. Having the functionality to report these investments properly is critical to managing the often sizeable IT department budget. These IT requirements are commonly missed during ERP implementations, leaving the IT organization to deploy its own independent Asset Lifecycle solution.

Tax

Tax groups must be involved in defining ERP requirements for the number of tax books, filing requirements, and tax-reporting requirements. As discussed in further detail in Chapter 7, this group should be heavily engaged in any data conversion when the organization is moving from the legacy system to the new ERP.

Capital Committee/Capital Administrators

An organization's capital committee or capital process administrators will be key stakeholders for providing input into the design of capital allocation and reporting.

Stakeholder representation, as addressed in Chapter 1, should apply to the ERP implementation team as well. Our experience has taught us that those teams with the background and skills to understand different needs across the business and to ensure they are met will be more successful than teams that are built to focus on single process areas. Implementation teams that are fully integrated and collaborate across the entire enterprise will achieve greater synergy and accomplish economies of scale that will translate into substantial benefits. Figure 5.4 depicts the various functions that should be considered when one is formulating the stakeholder group for an Asset Lifecycle Management implementation.

2. Capital Planning and Budgeting

The Asset Lifecycle begins with capital planning and budgeting. In a traditional budgeting cycle, each business unit or department submits a budget request for the upcoming cycle. This does not provide either the level of detail or the update frequency necessary to handle capital budgets managed by project, project phase, or activity level. Organizations should consider using the planning functionality from an ERP vendor (for example, PeopleSoft Enterprise Performance Management) or a best-of-breed planning tool (for example, Hyperion Planning) to enable a rolling forecast. This functionality can efficiently capture detailed budgets from the distributed organization and then integrate the information with the budgeting functionality present in the Project Accounting and/or Fixed Asset modules.

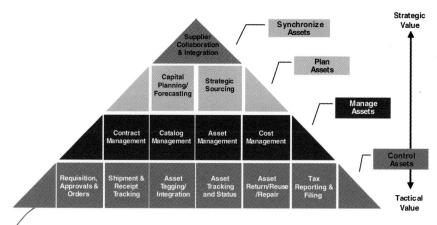

Figure 5.4 *Asset Management framework*

Organizations should also evaluate their budgeting processes. When budgets are based on prior year spending, budget holders have an incentive to spend all their money to protect their budget for the coming year. Although this type of gamesmanship is understandable and commonplace, generally it is detrimental to the organization's overall financial well-being. Regardless of the tools put in place, changing this mindset is a prerequisite to generating benefits through capital efficiency. Otherwise, expenditures will not be reduced and will continue to be made with little regard to overall return.

3. Capital Allocation and Approval

If asked how an organization should allocate its capital, most CFOs would answer that capital should go to those initiatives filling the greatest need for the organization or that generate the highest returns. Surprisingly, however, many companies still employ a process that involves a top-down allocation for individual business units or departments to spend as they choose. This process can leave the CFO with no real visibility into how the funds are actually used within the organization. In effect, it becomes virtually impossible to manage these investments for maximum value.

Consider the telecommunications industry: vast amounts of capital are deployed annually to complete capital projects and acquire millions of assets, as illustrated in Figure 5.5.[1] For the CFO of a capital-intensive organization such as one operating in this industry, the task of allocating and approving capital can be daunting or, at a minimum, very hard to control. In these situations, the sheer magnitude of the capital in play makes it imperative that the allocation and approval process be tightly integrated with the capital spending function to provide the necessary control and insight into how capital is deployed.

We recommend that the capital allocation and approval process, supported by the ERP solution, contain the following attributes:

- A cross-business unit/function committee that governs and approves large investments
- Timely approvals/denials made using a format comparable across investments
- A capital administration function responsible for managing/tracking investments
- Analysis of investments across multiple criteria using portfolio management techniques

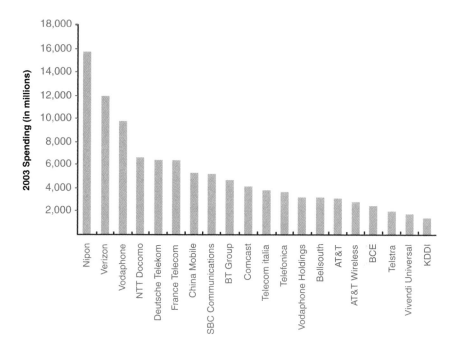

Figure 5.5   *Telecommunication services capital expenditures*

- A process for allocating and reallocating funds as appropriate in the ERP
- A rigorous process for periodically measuring investment benefits
- A periodic process for recapturing excess funds with incentives for the surrendering organization
- Budget limits that are automatically monitored or enforced in the ERP Procure to Pay modules.

The fundamental objective is to select and maintain the right investment mix over time. To make this happen, the capital allocation and approval processes should be controlled and also linked with the portfolio management and asset performance function discussed later in this chapter.

4. Asset Acquisition

The general goal of any ERP program is to integrate and automate basic transaction processing steps. When it comes to Asset Lifecycle Management, the ability to integrate and automate begins in Purchasing and Accounts Payable, where account coding is applied to newly acquired assets. This point is frequently missed during ERP implementations; we see from experience that organizations finding Asset Lifecycle automation difficult can often trace the problem to a disconnect between the Procure to Pay and Asset Lifecycle designs.

Avoiding this problem requires additional work, but the results can be well worth the time and effort. A solid design requires an early, careful mapping between item master categories, General Ledger accounts, and asset category/profiles, ideally resulting in a one-to-one mapping between the three. The outcome should be items purchased with a preassigned asset categorization that will carry through to the Fixed Assets sub-ledger and ultimately to the General Ledger.

Making this mapping work well requires simplicity. Even if tens of thousands of individual items are needed to run the business, these categories should be defined around a relatively small number of unique business classifications, taking into consideration the depreciable lives necessary to support property tax and internal reporting. A communications company, for example, may have 5,000 to 10,000 parts in its Oracle Item Master, but it should be able to map these parts into 30 to 50 asset categories in Oracle Fixed Assets.

5. Construction/Expenditure Tracking

The process for handling assets developed as construction or work in progress (constructed assets) must be tightly linked to asset acquisition processing, but this process does present separate challenges. Specifically, constructed assets typically involve an asset cost basis accumulated from many data sources (as highlighted in Figure 5.6), as well as some component of internal and/or contracted labor. Assets related to the utility infrastructure, the telecommunications network, or IT projects fall into this category.

A robust cost accumulation facility addresses these challenges by allowing the cost basis to be aggregated over a period of time. PeopleSoft, for example, provides this capability through the Project Costing module, which easily integrates data from other subsystems such as Purchasing, Accounts Payable, and Time and Labor. A proper project accounting design should also consider data sources from outside the ERP environment. However, the design should also balance the need to capture total project costs with the materiality of each source, as some inputs may not have a significant impact or could be more easily handled by applying a standard rate.

Figure 5.6   *Sources of total project costs (illustrative)*

A secondary design consideration is the method by which project adjusting entries will be made. Inevitably some project costs will be miscoded and need modification. If an Accounts Payable clerk incorrectly codes a capital transaction in Oracle, this could be fixed either by adjusting the entry directly in Oracle Assets or by requiring it to be made in Oracle Payables, which will allow the correction to flow through the system. Allowing direct adjustments, although easy and expeditious, does potentially leave the system open to mismatches between the Project Accounting module and its data sources. One remedy is to require that all adjusting entries be made directly in the source system. However, this solution introduces a layer of additional work and complexity to the process by forcing project managers to submit change requests to the appropriate parties. Although the answer to this problem is somewhat subjective, the important point is that the issue must be thoughtfully addressed during the design phase and the agreed-on solution consistently applied during implementation.

6. Capitalize and Depreciate

Once the asset cost has been established, whether through Procurement or Project Accounting, the asset must be capitalized and depreciated. Again, the underlying principle is to minimize manual intervention by automating the process. ERP solutions provide capitalization and depreciation as standard functionality, yet several design considerations affect its efficiency.

For acquired assets, the process is fairly straightforward, with predeveloped integration between the Procurement modules and Fixed Assets. The key consideration here, driven by accounting requirements, is whether to capitalize assets on receipt or as they are deployed. Assets that are for imminent use can be capitalized on receipt, whereas others may not. Understanding how each asset type will be treated will dictate the design of this integration, and the ERP implementation must map to the accounting flow to ensure that the automation works as planned.

For constructed assets, ERP solution functionality deserves more careful examination and can be a differentiator between vendors. All such assets have some level of automation between the Project Accounting and Fixed Asset modules; not all are equally effective. The design approach used by both Oracle and PeopleSoft requires users to establish the asset and then manually link project transactions to the asset before executing the automated interface. Although this model works for some organizations, others – particularly those with high volumes of constructed assets – may require customization to eliminate the manual steps. SAP, on the other hand, has a more automated process for integrating these modules but generally less flexibility for grouping individual assets into depreciable units. Often, organizations with high volumes of constructed assets and specific grouping criteria will find it necessary to customize this integration between the Project Accounting and Fixed Asset modules.

A final design consideration for this area concerns situations in which fixed assets get deployed through the inventory management process. Generally, ERP Inventory modules are designed with a bias toward manufacturing processes, yet some nonmanufacturing businesses need to handle capital items through their inventory network. This is commonly the case for organizations that have large infrastructures managed by a distributed set of technicians. In these cases, the organization must carefully map the accounting flow through Purchasing, Inventory, Project Accounting (if applicable), Fixed Assets, and General Ledger. During the design of this process, careful attention should also be paid to the inventory costing method and process for clearing variances between the asset purchase cost and the value placed on the item when it is issued from the warehouse.

7. Physical Asset Tracking and Maintenance

After capitalizing assets, organizations need to understand what they own, as well as where the assets reside once they are placed in service. Recording asset movements over time in the Fixed Assets module is not only required for tax reporting purposes but is also essential to support asset reuse and maintenance.

Our experience shows that a full asset tracking process can be onerous and expensive if not designed properly. The first step toward getting it right is not to overengineer the design and to determine which assets to track actively. Organizations should assess each asset classification's relative criticality, value, feasibility to track, and movement frequency. For example, assets with very low values or those that are completely stationary may not warrant a sophisticated solution.

For those assets that do require tracking, organizations must establish asset tagging and physical inventory procedures. ERP solutions support these processes by providing data fields to capture the necessary information when the asset is received. However, if the asset moves frequently, manual updates in the Fixed Asset module can become onerous. In these cases it may be necessary to integrate a scanning solution with the Fixed Asset module.

Beyond these immediate considerations, organizations must also manage assets for the long term to extend their useful life and increase their ultimate value. This goal requires that asset maintenance records and service schedules be actively monitored so the organization can take the right actions at the appropriate time. For example, consider an organization with a large fleet, each vehicle requiring periodic oil changes and maintenance. Without the ability to track and report maintenance schedules, the fleet manager will probably overlook key maintenance actions on individual vehicles, ultimately reducing the vehicle's useful life or increasing the total cost of ownership.

Some organizations with complex physical tracking and maintenance requirements will elect to integrate the ERP with a third-party solution (e.g., Datastream, Peregrine) designed specifically for this purpose.

Regardless of the tracking tool used, assets must be individually identifiable for any of the tracking processes to be feasible. Assets that have been summarized for financial purposes or during conversion (such that individual components cannot be uniquely identified with a barcode or other tracking mechanism) will be virtually impossible to integrate with a physical tracking tool. Organizations need to consider this point when they are defining the transaction flow and integration with each implementation.

8. Tax Reporting

Property tax reporting requirements are an extremely important but often underappreciated aspect of the Asset Lifecycle and ERP implementations. Tax management can generate savings, enhance internal controls, and avoid unplanned penalties assessed by taxing authorities. As Chapter 7 outlines, the first and foremost strategy for ensuring a solid tax reporting design is to have strong representation from the tax department during the ERP implementation.

The next tax-related decision for organizations implementing an ERP Fixed Asset module is the number of asset books to maintain in the system. As with other processes, automation and consolidation should be the goal. However, the organization should also give equal consideration to the system and maintenance overhead associated with each book kept within the system. Most organizations find it necessary to keep at least two books — one for corporate financial reporting and one for tax reporting. However, it may also need to report in many jurisdictions, some of which do not require different depreciation conventions. If these filings do not vary significantly from the existing books, it may be simpler for the organization to manage the filing process off-line or using a separate tax filing solution.

Finally, tracking assets by property location is a key tax input enabled by Oracle, PeopleSoft, or SAP software solutions. To make the most of this functionality, organizations should consider tax reporting requirements when they are designing the Location Master. Often, little attention is paid to Location Master configuration, and the values in the location table are allowed to evolve over time, creating tax reporting challenges. A strong design will align tax locations with reporting jurisdictions and follow a strict nomenclature that makes each location easy to identify when asset transactions are processed.

9. Capital Reporting: Developing a Meaningful Strategy

Keeping track of asset information does little good if the information cannot be extracted in a meaningful format to support decision making.

Definitions

Developing a solid reporting strategy starts with clearly defining what constitutes a "project" or "asset" and what level of detail is necessary for analysis and reporting. Those who start this process will often find that the answer varies across and within business units. Achieving clear and consistent definitions for projects and assets is absolutely critical for future comparability. Sample project definitions include:

- IT program (for example, ERP implementation)
- IT work phase (for example, development)
- Construction building site
- Multiple construction sites that combine to make a piece of infrastructure
- Initiatives over a certain value threshold
- Initiatives exceeding a certain work effort threshold.

Reporting from the General Ledger or Sub-Ledgers

The potential side effect of a robust capital reporting strategy is that it will probably require large data volumes and produce many report iterations. From the beginning, ERP programs considering such functionality must plan carefully to avoid what can become very visible system performance issues. Determining whether detailed capital reporting will be produced in the General Ledger or the Project Accounting/Fixed Asset sub-ledgers is one early design decision that has system performance and sizing implications.

Generally speaking, performing all capital reporting from the General Ledger (thick ledger) is appropriate when the organization has a relatively low number of projects/asset types and is attempting to report on a limited set of capital attributes. Companies with higher volumes and more data needs should consider a strategy that supplements General Ledger reporting with detailed capital reporting from the sub-ledgers (thin ledger). The relative merits of using a thick versus a thin ledger are discussed in more detail in Chapter 3.

Work/Cost Breakdown Structure Definition

Similarly, project details that are structured into work, cost, and asset breakdowns should be consistently defined to enable comparison. Although consistent definitions do not mean "one-size-fits-all" standardization, they do imply that common elements (for example, labor) will be handled in the same manner. An important design consideration here is the number of detailed coding elements to be captured, as each incremental level of detail will provide diminishing value and will place a burden on the organization to capture that data. A good design will systematically require the most critical information, provide a little flexibility for business unit/project-specific data elements, and generally avoid going into more detail than can reasonably be captured at the time of asset acquisition.

An illustrative IT project cost and work breakdown example is shown in Figure 5.7. This example is based on the hierarchy available to categorize project accounting transactions in PeopleSoft Projects: Project, Project Type, Activity Type, Resource Group, Resource Type, Resource Category, and Resource Sub-Category.

Reporting should be developed to support the information provided within the structure that is ultimately defined. These reports should give management a view of information starting from the summary level and drilling all the way down to transaction detail, to provide audit trail transparency. For example, based on Figure 5.7, one might expect to see the following set of reports:

- Budget/Actuals Summarized
- Activity Costs by Project Type
- Resource Costs by Project Type
- Activity Costs by Project
- Resource Costs by Project
- Project Transaction Detail.

Report Distribution

Each project should include a report generation and distribution plan in its Asset Lifecycle reporting strategy. Today's ERP solutions include many viable options, such as automated e-mail distribution, publishing to an intranet site, and ad hoc reporting through the ERP. The method selected should align with the company's overall reporting strategy but should also consider that capital reporting volumes may be significantly higher than one would normally envisage being produced from the General Ledger.

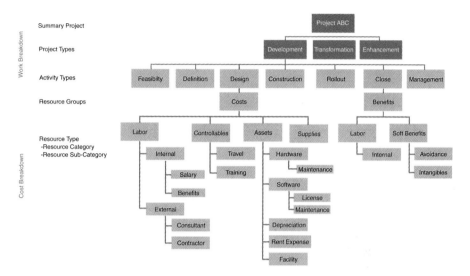

Figure 5.7 *Cost and work breakdown example*

10. Portfolio Management and Asset Performance

How many projects in the past five years have delivered their promised benefit in your organization? We find that few CFOs consistently have concrete information about the actual measured benefits generated by asset investments, rather, they more commonly have to evaluate success or failure based on measurements such as actual cost versus budget, completion to schedule, word of mouth, and perceptions. The implication is that vast amounts of capital are spent with very little oversight and minimal post-deployment benefit tracking. For an organization with significant annual capital expenditures across thousands of projects, it becomes virtually impossible to assess across the entire organization which investments will generate the greatest return.

Compare this approach with that of a mutual fund manager responsible for investment decisions across a large portfolio. The typical fund manager spends countless hours evaluating investments across numerous criteria and matching these investments with the fund's strategic intent. Once investments are made, the fund manager tracks performance constantly so subsequent adjustments can be made and profits returned periodically to shareholders. Fund investors would accept nothing less than this level of diligence and neither should shareholders, yet corporations do not apply the same rigor to their investment processes. Some companies have begun to share this view and adopt the portfolio management approach to the Asset Lifecycle, as reflected in the capital allocation paradigm in Figure 5.8.

Portfolio management discipline must start with the initial investment decisions and capital allocation. Investments must first pass financial scrutiny because no matter how much someone wants an investment to be made, it must add value to the organization. After financial considerations, the investment must meet other specific decision criteria, such as customer service improvements, people development, or quality enhancement. Finally, the organization must consider its own constraints when selecting the investments to fund including availability of investment funding and resources to execute.

The ERP solution can play a major role in this decision process. ERP solutions have long had the capability to address resource deployment and utilization through their Time and Labor functionality. Today, this functionality can be integrated with a more advanced project portfolio management capability that allows multiple criteria (for example, cost, value, and risk) and resource constraints to be modeled so that the optimum investment mix is selected. Additionally, fixed asset modules contain "what if" functionality to assess the depreciation outcomes of multiple investment scenarios. For example, SAP now provides Resource and

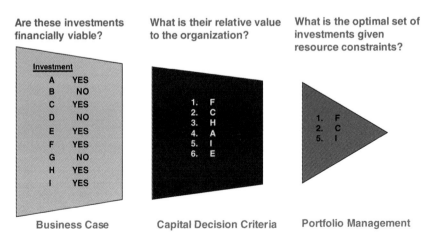

Figure 5.8 *Capital Allocation: portfolio approach*

Program Management functionality that combines financial and human resources data to provide this level of project analytics.

The chart in Figure 5.9 illustrates how a portfolio management tool may view the sample investment portfolio in Figure 5.8. In this case, investments B, D, and G do not clear the financial hurdles necessary to proceed. Investments F, C, and I provide the desired risk/reward tradeoff and have been selected as the portfolio to implement. Investments A, E, and H provide an acceptable risk/reward profile but are shown in yellow because resource constraints do not allow them to be completed at this time.

Underlying the concept of portfolio management is a basic prerequisite; the organization must have an inventory of its portfolio of investments and projects, regardless of where they sit in the development pipeline. Developing this inventory can be hard to put into practice if each individual business unit or department deploys its own capital. We find that one of the best solutions is to establish a project portfolio office to manage/monitor investments over a certain value threshold. Only by having a full picture of where an organization spends its money and the options it has available can any form of investment prioritization be effective.

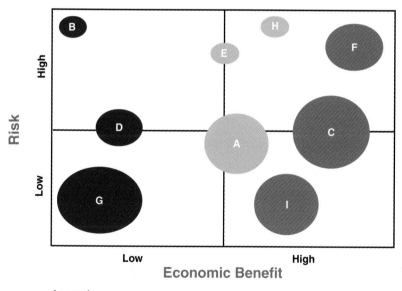

Legend:
Circle Size Represents Funding Required

Figure 5.9   *Portfolio analysis*

Industry	Usage
Cross-Industry	Information Technology, Marketing
Telecommunications	Network Construction/Upgrades, Network Asset Tracking
Utilities	Infrastructure Deployment, Meters, Poles
Consumer Products and Pharmaceuticals	Research & Development (single and multi-year)
Aerospace and Defense	Aircraft Construction, Defense Projects
Services	Billable Service Project Costs
Media & Entertainment	Film Accounting, Game Development
Construction	Client Construction Contract Handling
Gaming	Casino Construction

Figure 5.10   *Sample uses of Asset Lifecycle technology by industry*

INDUSTRY ADAPTABILITY

Facilitating the Asset Lifecycle Management process with technology requires capabilities that capture, process, and synthesize voluminous data into meaningful information that can be used to make better investment decisions. Although some solutions on the market target particular industries or business functions (for example, IT projects), Oracle, PeopleSoft, and SAP have focused on the benefits of a highly integrated solution supported by strong reporting tools.

These vendors offer capabilities that are extremely flexible and configurable, to accommodate business requirements as diverse as the companies they serve, as illustrated in Figure 5.10. Both Project Accounting and Fixed Asset modules are nearly 100 percent configurable, with predefined data being provided only when they are completely standard (for example, calendars) or are warranted by accounting regulations (for example, depreciation schedules).

CASE STUDY

Large Cable Services Provider

The case study in Figure 5.11 outlines how an organization in a capital-intensive industry deployed a leading practice Asset Lifecycle Management capability to improve operations and create value.

Large Cable Services Provider	
Organization Background	One of North America's largest multi-system operators of cable franchises was beginning a major network upgrade/expansion to deploy broadband and digital cable across its markets. To complete the upgrade, the company expected to spend approximately US$3 billion of capital over an 18-month period. These funds were to be jointly managed between corporate finance and six regional operations.
Vision/Belief	Previously, each regional finance operation managed its capital spending independently, using unique systems or offline spreadsheets. The organization believed that deriving the greatest possible value from its impending investment required an integrated view of capital spending and performance across the entire organization.
Implementation	The organization deployed a single PeopleSoft Financials instance to headquarters and each of the six regional operations. The solution included deployment of PeopleSoft Projects to track the cost, work and statistics associated with network construction projects. The Projects module was integrated with PeopleSoft Fixed Assets to automatically capitalize and track completed projects as assets. These modules were integrated with PeopleSoft Inventory, PeopleSoft Purchasing and PeopleSoft Accounts Payable to capture all network costs.
Implementation Challenges	The organization faced a number of challenges during its implementation, including: • Developing a common set of definitions so that information could be captured and reported in a comparable format. • Driving process consistency in a situation where each regional team previously had its own process. Managing the high transaction volumes generated by the new approach.
Value Realization	Despite the challenges, the organization realized significant benefits upon completion of their PeopleSoft Financials implementation, including: • Reduced transaction processing effort due to improved automation and integration with feeder modules. • Spending visibility at both the corporate and regional level for the first time in the company's history. • Capital management analysis, including cross-regional project comparisons, statistical reporting (for example, cost per home passed, cost per network mile), and property tax reporting by network location. • Reduced closing time to five days from previous eight days.

Figure 5.11 *Case Study: large cable services provider*

ROLE OF THIRD-PARTY SOFTWARE SOLUTIONS

Although this chapter has primarily focused on the functionality and flexibility of top-tier ERP vendors such as Oracle, PeopleSoft, and SAP, certain areas warrant the consideration of a third-party package. Regardless of the reason a third-party tool is considered, the decision to implement one can have far-reaching implications for the organization. In addition to the cost of maintaining multiple tools, the organization will need to work to integrate the third-party solution with the ERP Asset Management and Project Costing functions. Developing this integration becomes a challenge when it involves master data (for example, items, accounts, or projects) synchronization or differing levels of detail between systems. Additionally, systems that are linked via interfaces are subject to reporting mismatches, timing differences, and reconciliation problems that undermine the solution's credibility.

Physical Asset Tracking

Organizations that need to capture detailed physical attributes or location information for large asset volumes may consider using a third-party asset tracking solution, separating financial asset tracking from physical asset tracking. Often, this decision is driven by differing requirements between Finance and operations. The Finance organization needs to capture information supporting property tax reporting, including the cost basis, tax jurisdiction, movements, and disposals. Operations generally have less desire for financial details but will require significantly more physical information (such as pinpoint location details, size/weight, service schedule, and warrant). Additionally, some operations require detailed attributes that cannot be readily captured in the ERP. In either case, the physical information can produce significant transaction volumes that Finance does not want or require in the Fixed Asset system, which, in effect, forces Operations into building its own solution.

IT departments, as an example, will often track technology assets using a solution such as Peregrine, which has the ability to identify Windows- and Unix-based hardware and software automatically. This ability allows IT to capture detailed data on its assets that may not be relevant to Finance in a highly efficient fashion without manual data entry.

Project Management

The project functionality offered by ERP vendors tends to be dominated by Project Accounting, with less focus on basic project management or work-planning functions. Those organizations that complete hundreds or thousands of projects annually may find that the ERP solution project capabilities lack the functionality to support their needs. This scenario is particularly common in IT and construction-centric organizations. In these cases, separate project management tools such as Primavera or Microsoft Project may be considered to supplement and integrate with Oracle, PeopleSoft, or SAP Project Accounting functionality. Most ERP vendors have predeveloped integration between their Project Accounting modules and one or more third-party project management tools.

FUTURE TRENDS

As we look to the future, one thing is certain: CFOs feel the need to improve their current Asset Lifecycle Management capabilities and are planning to act (see Figure 5.12).[2]

Fortunately, as this chapter highlights, capital expenditures and the Asset Lifecycle offer many opportunities for leading organizations to create value − and the ability to create value undoubtedly will continue to grow as more advanced capabilities emerge and take hold. In this section, we take a brief look at some of these upcoming capabilities.

Radio Frequency Identification and Asset Self-Identification

The most rapidly evolving trend associated with Asset Lifecycle Management is the use of radio frequency identification (RFID) and/or asset self-identification. RFID offers the ability to capture detailed asset information and register asset movements without manual intervention. Over the past several years, this functionality has improved substantially and has become much more cost effective. Also, the adoption rate of RFID technology is growing quickly, with major companies requiring their suppliers to use it.

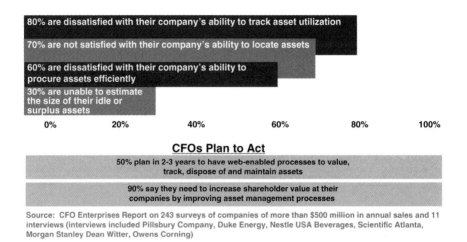

Figure 5.12 *CFO survey results*

The expectation is that in coming years, every device will have a computer chip and be plugged into a network. This advancement would allow assets to self-identify their characteristics, location, and status by registering over the network. In fact, this capability already exists for IT departments managing networked components.

Both RFID and asset self-identification capabilities will serve to decrease the manual effort needed to manage assets, while improving controls and enhancing property tax reporting accuracy.

Profitability Management

Another way future benefits will be achieved in the Asset Lifecycle is through asset profitability and project portfolio management – topics that have been previously addressed in this chapter. Although these concepts are not new, they have not been widely put into practice. With new ERP and reporting capabilities, the penetration and usage of these capabilities should increase significantly in coming years.

CFO INSIGHTS

- Organizations with effective Asset Lifecycle Management ensure that the process spans a greater scope than traditional Acquire to Retire activities. A full capability encompasses much more than the ERP Project Accounting and Fixed Asset modules and requires functionality that supports: capital planning and budgeting, capital allocation and approval, asset acquisition, expenditure tracking, capitalization, physical asset tracking and maintenance, tax reporting, capital reporting, and portfolio and asset performance management.

- Technical solutions alone are not enough to create a strong Asset Lifecycle capability. ERP implementations must first ensure that the process has been well defined in such a way that the technical solution streamlines and provides automation. ERP implementations configured around a poor Asset Lifecycle process are likely to result in manual transaction processing, the evolution of off-line/shadow tracking solutions, poor data and reporting accuracy, and requests to implement third-party tools.

- With a culture of continuous improvement and a strong ERP implementation team, organizations can use the Asset Lifecycle to drive substantial benefits measured through improved capital efficiency, operational effectiveness, and risk mitigation. The greatest benefits are available to those that maintain a large asset base, have multiple investment options, and require many resources to administer the process or process high transaction volumes.

- Financial benefits available through an enhanced Asset Lifecycle Management capability are unlikely to be maximized in organizations maintaining a traditional annual capital budgeting process that fosters negative "spend it all" behavior. Ultimately, the savings generated through increased capital visibility must be used for purposes that increase shareholder value.

- Leading organizations are adopting a portfolio approach to capital spending using multiple decision criteria and are moving away from investment evaluations based solely on net present value or internal rate of return. Each major ERP vendor has responded with project portfolio management capabilities that address this evolving practice.

FROM INSIGHT TO ACTION

FOCUS DETAILED TRACKING ON THE MOST MATERIAL ASSETS

For each asset type, weigh the costs and benefits of detailed physical tracking with the associated value, movement, and risks. When detailed physical asset tracking is employed, the integration between the physical tracking and financial asset management must be planned carefully to ensure that information can automatically and seamlessly flow throughout the process.

DESIGN A LEADING PRACTICE ASSET LIFECYCLE PROCESS

A process architecture centered on leading practices will serve as the foundation for an efficient Asset Lifecycle process. Each ERP implementation that includes Asset Lifecycle in its scope must involve the right stakeholders and understand the outputs and reporting objectives before defining the process. It then must focus on building a streamlined Asset Lifecycle process, rather than simply implementing the modules.

DEVELOP A ROBUST CAPITAL AND PROPERTY TAX REPORTING STRUCTURE

The ability to create value from the Asset Lifecycle depends on the capacity to unlock the decision support power provided by the information. Reporting should be architected with flexibility to support different constituencies across the Asset Lifecycle end-to-end process and levels of detail.

REFERENCES

1. Ronald Fink, "Capital Choices: The 2004 Capital-Spending Scorecard," *CFO* 20 (2004): 42–49, http://www.cfo.com.

2. CFO Enterprises Research Services Group, *Unlocking the Hidden Value in Fixed Assets – CFOs Look to the Internet for Help*, August 2000, http://www.fei.org.

CHAPTER 6

Order to Cash Management

ORDER TO CASH: AN OVERVIEW

"Cash is king." This infamous Wall Street saying continues to be true for all organizations. Every Finance executive understands the importance of cash not only in sustaining and building the operations of the organization, but also in providing the means for executing an organization's strategic objectives. In other words, cash is an enabler for an organization's success.

A frequent measure of a company's cash generation ability is free cash flow. Free cash flow is defined as operating cash flow minus capital expenditures. Free cash flow can be defined as cash that an organization generates after incurring costs to maintain/expand its asset base, and it is important because it allows an organization to pursue opportunities that enhance shareholder value. Diminished or even negative free cash flow is not necessarily a sign of trouble. For example, an organization may incur large capital expenditures that have the potential of providing superior returns. However, over the long term, positive cash generation is key.

Generating cash is about much more than selling goods and services. It involves all the steps necessary to collect the cash associated with the order. The Order to Cash (OTC) process starts with the receipt of an order and ends with applying the cash related to the sale. Figure 6.1 details the subprocesses that collectively comprise the OTC end-to-end process.

Figure 6.1 *Order to Cash process*

Effective Order to Cash Management

Traditionally, when Finance executives addressed OTC, they focused on managing the Accounts Receivable (AR) balance itself since AR usually represented a significant dollar amount. However, although AR is certainly important, it is only one element within the OTC process. Making changes based solely on AR management may not address other fundamental process issues.

Recent corporate fraud and new regulatory requirements have increased the importance of all subprocesses within OTC. For example, the bankruptcy of Enron Corporation highlighted deficiencies in the company's invoicing and revenue recognition process, among other items. As a result, leading organizations look at each step within the OTC process and incorporate a holistic OTC view to maximize effectiveness through people, subprocesses, and technology.

OTC and Revenue Assurance

A key goal of the OTC process is to collect the cash once an organization has billed for goods or services. However, our research has shown that fully 7 to 15 percent of orders taken fail to translate into cash collected (see Figure 6.2).[1]

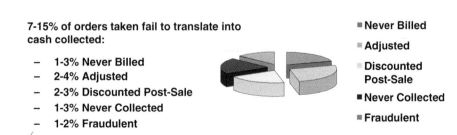

7-15% of orders taken fail to translate into cash collected:

- – 1-3% Never Billed
- – 2-4% Adjusted
- – 2-3% Discounted Post-Sale
- – 1-3% Never Collected
- – 1-2% Fraudulent

- ■ Never Billed
- ▧ Adjusted
- ░ Discounted Post-Sale
- ■ Never Collected
- ■ Fraudulent

Figure 6.2 *Revenue leakage*

Revenue assurance provides a core foundation to an effective OTC capability. Revenue assurance is the process of ensuring that all goods and services delivered are accurately billed and paid. Successful organizations include revenue assurance programs as an element within OTC, but first, an organization needs to determine whether it has a revenue assurance problem. In our view, determining whether the organization has revenue leakage and identifying the root causes should be part of every OTC capability.

OTC Benefits

Successful OTC programs not only maximize the effectiveness and efficiency of each subprocess within the OTC process but also link the subprocesses together to form one complete world-class end-to-end process. The result is an OTC process that produces benefits for the organization, its customers, its employees, and its shareholders, as outlined in Figure 6.3.

Dimension	Benefit
Organization	▪ Increased revenues ▪ Improved margins ▪ Improved working capital position ▪ Reduction in cost of capital ▪ Reduced bad debt ▪ Reduced operational costs ▪ Improved process management
Customer	▪ Improved customer service ▪ Differentiated service levels ▪ Value added services ▪ New customer offers
Employee	▪ Focus on value added activities ▪ Reduced "fire drills" ▪ Increased job satisfaction ▪ Increased ownership and accountability through process focus
Shareholder	▪ Improved long term growth ▪ Increase profitability ▪ Maximum return on invested capital ▪ Increased share price ▪ Increased dividends (as applicable)

Figure 6.3   *Order to Cash benefits*

ORDER TO CASH ENABLED WITH ERP

In this section, we will discuss how organizations can effectively deliver each component of the OTC process, as previously illustrated in Figure 6.1 with the implementation or enhancement of an ERP solution.

1. Receive Orders and 2. Process Orders

Receiving and processing an order are the first subprocesses in the OTC end-to-end process. They are defined as follows: sales orders are received from customers or prospects and processed by the customer service organization. Order receiving and processing are critical steps because they determine factors such as terms of delivery, terms of payments, carrier, pricing, products, product configuration, installation terms, and required prepayments. Furthermore, these steps define the hand-offs and communication points for the subprocesses that follow in the OTC end-to-end process, including credit and risk evaluation, pricing simulation and calculations, warehousing, post-shipment obligations (such as installations and training), invoicing, AR, revenue recognition, and final payments.

Many organizations suffer from long sales order receipt and processing times. Typical challenges in receiving sales orders include inadequate coordination:

- Among credit, risk management, and customer account management process owners
- Between credit approval and order entry process owners
- Between customer account management and order entry process owners
- Between export compliance and order entry process owner.

Issues contributing to extended processing time include coordination between various groups and order transparency. Lack of visibility or accessibility to pending orders for customers with potential credit exposure also leads to extended processing times. Additional delays can be experienced without order transparency in the following areas:

- Product pricing metrics
- Product catalog
- Special promotion
- Deal sheet
- Product availability

- Foreign currency exchange rates
- Freight and carrier management information.

Other challenges include missing paperwork or inaccurately completed order forms; inconsistencies in customer purchase orders in relation to payment terms, shipping information, return terms, or preferred carrier; and inadequate or no clear definition of hand-offs and communication points.

As a result of these shortcomings, organizations lose revenue and cash flow, overpay sales commissions because of order overstatement and cancelled orders, and incur high costs for acquiring sales in manual order processing, exception processing, rework, and fixing billing errors. Organizations also experience an increase in customer dissatisfaction and suboptimal decision making. All these consequences could adversely affect an organization's ability to compete in the marketplace.

We believe it is imperative to strive for continuous process improvements by simplifying and standardizing processes. By leveraging the technology benefits of ERP solutions, organizations can overcome their problems in receiving orders, prevent them from recurring, and transform the order receipt and processing subprocess into a competitive advantage for cross-selling and optimizing customer satisfaction.

Oracle, PeopleSoft, and SAP software solutions provide integration among the order processing, AR, and associated modules to ensure that the appropriate information hand-off takes place between each subprocess work-stream. For example, the orders generated out of SAP's Sales and Distribution (SD) module passes the order and billing information to the AR module. A user in AR then has the ability to view the sales order document via the generated invoice.

Samples of leading practices driving improvements in receiving and processing orders include:

- Product Information Management
  - Clearly convey terms of the sale and any information regarding interest or other fees for late payment on the credit application, sales order, sales order acknowledgment, and other transaction documentation.
  - Publish the full terms of the sale (including shipping and return processes as well as payment expectations and late fees) in product catalogs, sales sheets, and other communications.

- Ensure that all program information (for example, advertising for new promotions) is delivered prior to the campaign to front-line staff.
- Information Technology Management
  - Use ERP solutions to build visibility and accessibility for the order entry process owner into current, available inventory information; to determine availability of product on the customer requested delivery date; and to view foreign currency exchange rates (fixed or floated) and restricted party/product/destination lists for export compliance. For example, an organization can implement an ERP solution that integrates the SAP Customer Relationship Management (CRM), SD, and AR modules, sharing the same customer information contained in a single repository.
  - Define a systematic workflow to specify hand-offs and communication points clearly for each sales order type.
  - Extend the distribution pipeline into the customer's procurement cycle and promote the customer's view of the organization as "easy to do business with."
  - Provide on-line information on bundles, special promotions, and substitution suggestions; fully automating eligibility, application, and compliance with existing contracts and promotions; and streamlining customer orientation pricing and payment functionality to address credit card and cash on delivery (COD) orders.
  - Use advanced systems to provide customers with self-service information on more complex transactions (such as payment deferrals or delivery confirmations, for example).
  - Implement best-in-class contact center operations, which are able to support telephone, Internet, and mobile sales and service.

The distributor and sales representative workbenches of the major ERP and Customer Relationship Management (CRM) vendors provide full CRM lifecycle support, from lead qualification through opportunity management, quotation management, credit and risk management, order entry, order fulfillment, and after-sales activities that lead to new opportunities. The user-centric applications support mobile, Internet, or telesales and provide consistent, up-to-date information and a real-time interactive feedback loop. They also seamlessly integrate with financial and supply chain management modules.

ERP solutions, such as Oracle, PeopleSoft, and SAP, provide high levels of integration that organizations can leverage as soon as orders are received. For example, Oracle AR allows for a customer's credit history to be checked automatically, so organizations can manage their credit risk more efficiently. Additionally, ERP solutions centrally store and maintain information such as product master data. This enables organizations to ensure that accurate product information, including pricing and item availability, is obtained at the time of order entry. This functionality dramatically decreases order processing time and allows organizations to service their customers more effectively and more efficiently.

Figure 6.4 describes sample ERP functionality that an organization can use to improve the order receipt and processing steps of OTC.

3. Fulfill Orders

After the sales order has been received and processed, order fulfillment is the next subprocess. Based on the committed delivery date at the time of order entry, availability of inventory, and changes in customer's creditworthiness on the delivery date, the order will be fulfilled or held back.

As with sales order receipt and processing time, many organizations also suffer from extended sales order fulfillment processing time. Typical challenges in fulfilling the sales orders for the right products or services, at the right time, at the right place, and with the right quantity include inadequate or no coordination between:

- Order entry and order fulfillment process owners
- Customer service and order fulfillment process owners
- Export compliance and order fulfillment process owners
- Financial accounting and order fulfillment process owners
- Freight calculation and order fulfillment.

Other challenges include the following:

- Little or no real-time visibility or accessibility for the order fulfillment subprocess owner to the inventory on hand and of customer purchase orders and return policy information
- Manual or only semiautomated inventory replenishment processes
- Inadequate definition of hand-offs and communication points.

OTC Process Area	ERP Functionality
Credit and risk management	▪ Multiple credit and risk management matrices, tightly integrated with internal and external databases, such as customer account maintenance, order management, shipments, AR sub-ledger and credit bureaus. ▪ Real-time credit and risk evaluation at the time of order entry and shipment. ▪ Real-time order blocking based on internal and external credit rating of the customer at the time of order entry or shipment. ▪ Multiple types of payment terms based on customer credit evaluation and creditworthiness.
Product prices and discount matrices	▪ Tightly integrated with internal and external databases, such as products, customers, engineering, order management, billing/invoicing and business to business (B2B) marketplaces. ▪ Multiple prices and discounts matrices based on multiple functions such as product, product group, product configuration, inter-organization, geography, special promotions or deal sheets. ▪ Multiple price and discount simulations to process "what if" analyses. ▪ Integrated with internal and external databases, such as credit and risk management, products, customers, pricing, engineering, manufacturing, shipping and warehousing, freight and carrier management, installation management, training, after-sales service, billing, finance, credit bureaus and B2B marketplaces.
Order receipt and processing	▪ Web based, electronic data interchange (EDI) or bar-coded imaging order receipt interfaces with real-time default information checks from other internal and external databases, such as customer, product, pricing, terms of payment and geography. ▪ Real-time prices and discount updates based on customer contracts. ▪ Real-time probable delivery date calculations based on pending orders and available inventory. ▪ Real-time estimated freight amount calculations, based on shipment weight, special features and destination. ▪ Real-time automated hand-offs of the order, with the shipping instructions, to the warehousing/logistics function.

Figure 6.4   *Sample ERP functionality: 1. Receive Orders and 2. Process Orders*

Again, we recommend that organizations strive for continuous process improvements by simplifying and standardizing the processes and leveraging IT to overcome the challenges in fulfilling orders, to prevent them from recurring, and to transform the order fulfillment process into a competitive advantage that optimizes customer satisfaction.

Key leading practices for improving the order fulfillment process include:

- Provide real-time visibility into pending orders to monitor cycle times.
- Provide real-time inventory data to reduce backorders and prevent substitution issues.
- Review customer purchase orders to ensure that terms of delivery and other information are accurately reflected and in agreement with published standards.
- Provide visibility into shipment information for the financial accounting department to account for or verify the financial transaction for inventory movement.

ERP solutions also enable simpler order fulfillment because of the tight integration with the purchasing module. This integration allows organizations to forecast and source raw materials and finished goods more efficiently. ERP solutions also help organizations to realize their procurement strategies by providing flexibility in setting up the procurement organizational structure, which enables a more efficient and effective supply chain operation. For example, an organization can implement the SAP inventory management application integrated with SD and manage raw material and finished goods quantities by monitoring the demand forecasts generated in SD.

Figure 6.5 describes sample ERP functionalities that an organization can use to improve the order fulfillment subprocess of OTC.

OTC Process Area	ERP Functionality
Order Fulfillment	▫ Integrated with internal and external databases such as credit and risk management, products, customers, pricing, engineering, manufacturing, order management, EDI, freight and carrier management, installation management, training, after-sales service, billing, finance, credit bureaus and B2B marketplaces.
	▫ Real-time visibility into pending orders and inventory data to monitor cycle times.
	▫ Automatic prioritization of orders based on certain norms, such as committed delivery dates of pending orders, existing backlog and customer priority.
	▫ Real-time shipment information updates in the freight and carrier management system for accurate freight calculation.
	▫ Real-time updates of shipment information to the financial accounting department to account for/verify the financial transaction and track inventory movement.

Figure 6.5 *Sample ERP functionality: 3. Fulfill Orders*

4. Invoice Customer

Once the sales order is shipped and all applicable post-shipment obligations are met, the invoice or billing step occurs. Many organizations have used an ERP solution, such as the PeopleSoft AR module, to automate the invoice generation and mailing process in an effort to minimize human error and to make the billing process more efficient.

Typical challenges in the sales invoice generation process include:

- Multiple paper documents with no imaging performed
- Billing error rates greater than 2 percent
- Multiple invoice format styles *→ Use submenus instead*
- Inaccuracies created during the customer maintenance, order entry, or order fulfillment process, which are carried forward to the sales invoice generation process
- No multilingual invoice generation
- Inconsistencies in updating the General Ledger, customer sub-ledger, and tax records after invoice generation.

To deal with these challenges in the drive to transform the sales invoice generation process into a competitive advantage, some examples of leading practices include:

- Use an ERP solution to integrate customer account management, credit and risk management, order management, distribution, billing, General Ledger, AR, and other financial modules to avoid subsystem reconciliation and hand-off points.
- Give customers their choice of billing, for example, EDI invoicing, faxing, imaging, e-mailing, and self-service options.
- Consolidate invoice printing and mass mailing when e-invoicing is not acceptable.
- Use imaging so that the original copy of the invoice is available with fax capability.

In any organization with disparate IT solutions performing one or many processes independently, the challenges just described are inherent and unavoidable. Compounding the challenge is the fact that there is often very little or no technical interface between these islands of systems.

Our experience shows that invoicing customers and accounting for the process no longer requires two steps, rather, the customer invoice itself triggers accounting of the business process automatically. In some instances, the order fulfillment transaction initiates the invoicing process. This simplifies the complex relationship between billing and accounting and provides tighter internal control between operations and accounting. Later in the chapter we will discuss how ERP solutions enhance AR through integration with the sales operation, especially in the revenue recognition area.

The order and credit management relationship has tightened because of ERP-integrated modules. For example, in the PeopleSoft AR module, once cash is applied to invoices, customer credit will be automatically adjusted to reflect the true credit limit. Orders may be blocked owing to insufficient credit, and a dunning letter can also be automatically generated to advise customers on overdue payments.

Figure 6.6 describes sample ERP functionality that an organization can use to improve the invoicing step of OTC.

5. Record Revenue

Revenue recognition and reporting have been under severe scrutiny in recent years. The fact that these items are the leading cause of public financial restatements highlights the inadequacy of internal controls with regard to revenue recognition in the OTC process.

Why is revenue so important – in particular with regard to an organization's OTC operation? Many feel that revenue is a key measure of growth and a key measure for comparative analysis. The Committee for Improved Corporate Reporting (CICR) conducted a survey on issues such

OTC Process Area	ERP Functionality
Invoice Customer	• Integration with internal and external databases such as credit and risk management, products, customers, pricing, engineering, manufacturing, order management, EDI, freight and carrier management, shipping/logistic installation management, training, after-sales service, finance, credit bureaus and B2B marketplaces.
	• Multilingual invoice generation to accommodate global requirements.
	• Instant cycle time metrics to track process from receipt to invoice issued.
	• Customer choice for billing and payment due dates, i.e. EDI, e-billing, fax, or self serve options.
	• Real-time updates of order and invoice information to the General Ledger for Revenue and Cost of Sales, AR Sub-Ledger, Credit and Risk Management and Tax Management.

Figure 6.6   *Sample ERP functionality: 4. Invoice Customer*

as the importance of revenue versus other income statement items and discovered that 38 percent of respondents said that revenue is the most important line in the income statement, whereas 41 percent considered it the second most important.[2]

When Can Revenue Be Recognized?

Revenue recognition is a difficult and pressing problem facing the accounting profession. Although the profession has established general guidelines and principles for revenue recognition, accounting practitioners are required to use their professional judgment to identify and include the right accounting information to validate and recognize revenues at the appropriate time. Staff Accounting Bulletin No. 101 states that revenue is generally realized, realizable, and earned when all the following criteria are met[3]:

- Persuasive evidence of an arrangement exists.[4] Within an ERP solution, the signing of a contract or the completion of an order or contract could suggest that an arrangement exists.
- Delivery has occurred or services have been rendered.[5] This could be interpreted as software made available, license key being sent, and products being shipped that can be supported in most ERP solutions by a goods issue and/or delivery document.
- The seller's price to the buyer is fixed or determinable.[6] Pricing in most ERP solutions can be predetermined based on materials and/or services set up in the product master record.
- Collectibility is reasonably assured.[7] ERP solutions provide integration among functional modules and on-line reporting capabilities to execute a payment history report and an aging report and to conduct a financial analysis.

Many studies have been conducted to assess whether organizations have a sufficient level of control in the revenue recognition process. In this section, we will review how components of the proper revenue recognition process can enhance the efficiency of the OTC end-to-end process and discuss how ERP solutions further that goal.

Accuracy

Sophisticated order entry solutions or ERP solutions provide a complete audit trail of all activities entered into the solutions. These solutions provide an electronic data feed, which avoids human data-entry error and ensures accurate data entry of all contract and/or order information. ERP solutions predefine revenue recognition rules to support various components of revenue such as hardware, services, and maintenance. This functionality ensures that revenues are properly categorized at the time of order entry to reduce the amount of revenue-related manual processing in general accounting.

Pricing

Recognizing revenue accurately depends on pricing; it is a key component of a seamless OTC operation. Controls have to be established to ensure that appropriate pricing is applied to each revenue component. ERP solutions maintain a single price book for revenue recognition and recognize revenue automatically based on this price book. These ERP solutions also help to reduce unnecessary manual steps in gathering product prices and obtaining proper approval to complete the order or contract.

Timing

Timing is critical in accounting for revenue recognition. For the nondelivered component of a contract, revenue recognition schedules should be established within an ERP solution, independent of billing terms and based on predefined revenue recognition rules. Typically, for the delivered components of an order such as physical goods and products, orders should not be released for invoicing and revenue recognition until shipment is confirmed. The ERP solution should support the delivery-dependent component of the revenue recognition process, and a revenue recognition solution should be established at the time of order entry.

For orders or contracts with complex terms such as milestone billing, an organization needs to create, review, and sign off these terms at the time of order entry. ERP solutions can automatically generate invoices based on these terms; the system will not release any invoices tied to an event until the completion of the event is confirmed.

An integrated ERP solution, such as SAP CRM combined with SD and AR, provides organizations with nimble access to information throughout the organization – from order entry clerks to decision makers – with no delay. In the sections that follow, we briefly describe how the strong integration between submodules provided by ERP solutions reduces manual reconciliation time and enhances stronger system control.

Reconciliation and Integration

Oracle, PeopleSoft, and SAP solutions have strong integration between sub-ledgers and the General Ledger, providing tighter system control over data and reducing the amount of manual reconciliation required. In fact, to maintain accounting integrity, SAP will not allow manual entries to the General Ledger accounts affected by the sub-ledgers. Sub-ledger postings are made either in real time or through a batch process into the General Ledger, which reduces manual intervention and minimizes reconciliation between ledgers. ERP solutions maintain complete end-to-end audit trails from the point of order entry to the General Ledger. Proper security controls can also be put in place at various functional process access points to limit user access and provide the necessary segregation of duties.

Finally, as shown in Figure 6.7, timely and accurate information allows controllers and chief accounting or financial officers to work toward a seamless OTC operation, which means they contribute to the overall success of the organization. A well-planned ERP OTC solution will certainly ease the process of retrieving the critical and timely information that decision makers need to manage a world-class organization.

The following case study highlights how one telecommunications company used readily available technology to improve its revenue recognition process for substantial savings.

Figure 6.8 describes sample ERP functionalities that an organization can use to improve the record revenue step of OTC.

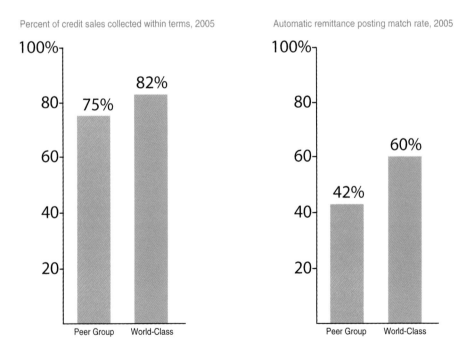

Source: The Hackett Group

Figure 6.7 *KPIs for a world-class OTC cycle*

OTC Process Area	ERP Functionality
Record Revenue	• It enables revenues to be calculated and established easily and flexibly using set rules.
	• Revenue can be recorded: i) at the time of billing, ii) between specific sets of dates in equal proportion, iii) on the basis of specific events (e.g., Delivery).
	• Revenue can be recorded on the basis of the criteria which have been established for the contract or order item; it can be recognized before, during and after billing. The restriction of recording Sales revenues indirectly credited after invoicing in the GL can be removed.
	• Real-time updates of revenue information to the GL and AR sub-ledger.

Figure 6.8 *Sample ERP functionality: 5. Record Revenue*

CASE STUDY

Leading Telecommunications Organization

A leading telecommunications organization recently launched its nation-wide mobile virtual network operation. The airtime Revenue Recognition functional area was experiencing operational challenges. In certain scenarios, the existing prepaid billing system was not rating minutes of use that an organization's customers were consuming on their prepaid service. Consequently, some costs that were incurred on the mobile virtual network were not matched with their associated revenue for these nonrated minutes of use.

The organization created a project team that reviewed as-is processes and the system capabilities of the organization's Finance/Revenue Assurance function. Their goal was to enhance or develop new processes and controls to support and manage airtime revenue assurance across the organization. The organization used Telecordia to support the airtime rating of minute usage and JD Edwards to support the Revenue Assurance function.

The project team documented airtime transactions from inception to recording in the General Ledger to assess the integrity of the data feeds and determine whether the organization was both correctly recording these transactions and measuring/monitoring the results to provide effective revenue assurance. In addition, the team instituted financial control points to enable risk management; identified daily, weekly, and monthly metrics to manage financial performance effectively; and developed processes for the Finance/Revenue Assurance team to review and approve all changes made by the IT organization to any systems that would have an impact on revenue recognition and recording.

The effort contributed to the validation of network cost savings of approximately U.S.$70,000 per month, which would scale with subscriber growth. The team also determined that unmatched usage records could provide further cost reductions. The Current Call Detail Record usage match rate is 95 percent.

---

6. Collect Cash

Cash collection is defined not only as the initial act of receiving cash, but also the Collections activities that are initiated when a customer account becomes past due. The process can include internal Collections, external Collections, and legal action. Typical challenges in Collections include:

- Long collection cycle
- Bad debt inflation
- High collections cost
- Reduced customer satisfaction.

Organizations can significantly improve Collections effectiveness by adopting leading practices. The most common areas for improvement in Collections include:

- Segmented Collections treatment
- Bad debt write-off management
- Days Sales Outstanding (DSO) management
- Improved dispute management.

Segmented Collections Treatment

We see leading organizations improve Collection effectiveness and in turn lower uncollectible accounts by designing Collection services to target specific customer segments. They segment customers based on various factors, such as account history, payment behavior, demographics, value, lifestyle, risk, size, historical behavior, and psychometrics. They model the relationship between changes in Collections strategy and financial impact and systematically test and fine-tune their Collection strategies for relative effectiveness on a regular basis. Thus, different customer segments receive tailored Collection treatments, as Figure 6.9 illustrates.

Examples of these differentiated treatments include:

- Proactively contacting customers with large invoices or customers who are habitually late
- Assigning dedicated and trained collectors for bankruptcy, legal, and fraud cases
- Grouping collectors by skills
- Using caller identification and computer telephony integration to automatically retrieve customer information and route calls based on customer segmentation and history
- Using collection agencies or external legal services for applicable accounts.

Although much of this capability is beyond current ERP functionality, niche software providers have developed solutions that are complementary to the major ERP solutions and can be integrated for a complete solution.

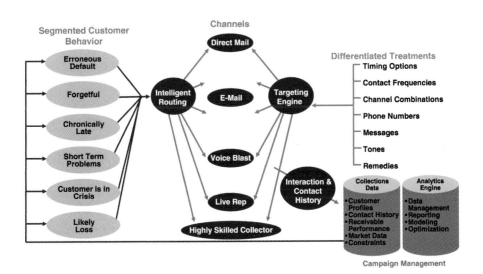

Figure 6.9   *Collection treatment by customer segment*

Bad Debt Write-Off Management

Leading organizations focus on return on Collections efforts instead of mere debt recovery; thus they automatically write off uncollectible accounts up to a certain predetermined level, if treatment is unsuccessful. However, technology has allowed us to treat a larger percentage of delinquent balances because it is now cost effective whereas historically it was not. Leading organizations also design and maintain their bad debt provisioning policy based on charge-off experience. They maintain bad debt data, such as service and write-off accounts. They review accounts regularly and automatically. When activating an inactive customer account, leading organizations can use partial matches and "fuzzy logic" algorithms to identify and transfer prior written-off balances.

The following case study highlights how one international shipping organization, facilitated by technology, completely redesigned its Collections processes to reduce its delinquent AR balances dramatically.

CASE STUDY

Leading Shipping Company

A leading shipping company faced significant challenges in the performance of its AR portfolio, with increasing levels of seriously delinquent receivables and pressure to reduce operating expenses while maintaining acceptable levels of DSO. In early 2003, the organization signed a multiyear agreement with an outside service provider to consolidate and manage globally major back-office Finance and Accounting functions, including AR and Collections.

The organization and the service provider jointly defined service-level objectives to reduce DSO. Then, the project team transitioned centralized Collections functions and undertook a portfolio of initiatives to improve Credit and Collections capabilities including the following:

- *The project team employed a data-centric diagnostic of the Credit and Collections processes to identify and pinpoint distinct root causes and form the basis for action plans to correct the problems and prevent them from recurring.*
- *A comprehensive ledger clean-up effort was performed.*
- *The project team resegmented its customer base and reengineered Collections processes that reflect business and transaction differences.*

- *I-many, a best-of-breed Collections application, was implemented to help collectors better prioritize Collections efforts, track actions taken, and assign treatment activities directly linked to the likelihood of eventual payment. The company leveraged debt collection agencies and enhanced compliance with write-off policies and schedules. The organization's management proactively monitored credit policy compliance, mitigating the risk of overextending credit limits to high-risk customers, and implemented more disciplined credit line management, including proactive periodic credit limit reviews as well as clear accountability and ownership of credit policy/credit decision.*
- *The workforce was realigned to leverage specialized skill sets, and metrics were redesigned to increase overall risk manageability.*

As a result, the organization achieved a 35 percent reduction in AR balances more than 120 days past due in certain business segments and a sizeable reduction in delinquent AR dollars overall during a focused six-month transformation period. In addition, the organization improved customer service as a result of the reduction in billing and payment processing errors and related disputes.

DSO Management

DSO shows both the age in terms of days of an organization's AR and the average time it takes to turn the receivables into cash. It provides a clear measure of an organization's efficiency in collecting cash. Improving DSO can significantly increase an organization's cash position as well as its working capital efficiency. We see that two simple but effective actions can drastically improve an organization's DSO:

1. Identify and quantify the root cause of DSO inflation
2. Secure accountability or clear responsibility of the managing/mitigating root causes of DSO inflation in each OTC process.

To identify and quantify the root causes of inflated DSOs, an organization should first calculate and measure select key OTC performance metrics – either by leveraging the reporting capabilities of the AR module or by doing further analysis with the reporting functionality offered by a solution such as SAP Business Warehouse (BW).

Once these OTC performance metrics have been calculated, organizations must take additional steps to validate the Key Performance Indictors (KPI) and their applicability by:

- Comparing their metrics with external and industry benchmarks to understand adequately where they stand
- Validating that the problem areas identified in fact correlate with DSO inflation
- Quantifying the impact of each KPI on DSO to begin to prioritize based on opportunity size and complexity.

The following case study highlights how one international telecommunications company used ERP functionality to drive down its DSO aggressively.

CASE STUDY

Leading Telecommunications Organization

The Collections organization at a leading international telecommunications organization had over £2 billion of receivables with DSO at an all-time high (80 days). The Collections organization was particularly inefficient; the Collections staff faced a high level of low-value delinquent accounts and had to deal with fragmented systems, including eight different AR ledgers and seven different billing systems. The organization lacked the in-house skills, systems, and structured business processes needed to run an effective Collections organization.

In 2001, the organization entered an agreement with an outside service provider to outsource several Finance functions and implemented a new Finance system, SAP Revenue Management and Contract Accounting module. The new solution provided a single AR ledger that replaced eight legacy ledgers. It also included a fully integrated specialist collections add-on tool called Telecredit Management.

The outsourcing provider worked with the company to design and configure the Telecredit tool. The Telecredit tool was at the center of a Collections transformation effort intended to improve the efficiency of the Collections organization, with the ultimate goal of shrinking DSO. The organization implemented the Telecredit tool, resulting in structured Collections processes and additional functionality that allowed the new Collections organization to:

- *Align collectors to customer accounts*
- *Define treatment strategies for different customer types*
- *Establish and manage collector workflow*
- *Establish call lists*
- *Document call notes via diary functions*
- *Assign a dispute code to each AR balance in order to document why the receivable remained uncollected*
- *Report on dispute codes.*

Through strict use of predefined treatment strategies, routine customer calls, thorough documentation of call outcomes, and coding of the AR base, the Collections organization was able to drive down DSO consistently in excess of 30 percent.

Improved Dispute Management

Implementing a dispute management tool and process is also an effective approach to improve Collections effectiveness. A Collections tool that enables a Collection team to code (e.g., assign a classification to a delinquent account) the receivables and generate reports showing the amount of past-due receivables assigned to each code is critical to a successful dispute management process.

Implementing a successful dispute management program involves technology in conjunction with a well-defined process that drives accountability. Technology enables identification, monitoring, and reporting of disputes, while the process assigns accountability for timely resolution of disputes.

When an organization is selecting and implementing a dispute management tool, it can choose between a third-party solution, such as I-many, or a "bolt-on" solution provided by an ERP vendor, such as Oracle iCollections. The dispute management tool should include workflow, call management, and treatment strategy functionality and should provide a mutually exclusive, collectively exhaustive list of dispute codes within the dispute management tool. A robust solution will generate meaningful reports out of the dispute management tool that can provide visibility to areas of dispute and allow organizations to address them.

One of the most important factors in a successful dispute management process is the consistent coding of receivables by the Collections staff. Dispute management software enables Collections' management to view coded versus uncoded AR by collector. The percentage of coded receivables, by collector, should be viewed as a critical performance metric.

Figure 6.10 describes sample ERP functionality that an organization can use to improve the order receipt and processing steps of OTC.

One of the major trends is that ERP vendors are now providing integrated products to span a large part of the OTC process. Oracle has two tightly integrated components for their Oracle eBusiness Suite: Receivables Management and Revenue Management. SAP has always had advanced credit and Collection capabilities, but a company must enable them. In an attempt to address this need, Optura has developed RapidFlow A/R Optimization, which provides Credit, Collection, and deduction management capabilities within SAP's architecture. Because it is a "bolt-in"

OTC Process Area	ERP Functionality
Collect Cash	▫ Payment reminder or a dunning notice to remind business partner of their outstanding debts can be automatically issued, when business partners fall behind on payments.
	▫ Collection functionality selects the overdue open items, determines the severity/dunning level of the account in question, and creates a payment/dunning notice. It then saves the collection/dunning data determined for the items and accounts affected.
	▫ Collection functionality may be used for both customers and vendors. It may be necessary to send out payment notice to vendor if he/she has a debit balance as a result of a credit memo.

Figure 6.10   *Sample ERP functionality: 6. Collect Cash*

not a "bolt-on" solution, RapidFlow operates in real time with one click access to SAP screens, such as blocked orders. It also benefits from easy access to SAP's integrated document warehouse and uses SAP reason codes, which ensures consistency throughout the enterprise.[8]

7. Apply Cash

Cash application is defined as the activities required to associate and assign cash receipts to the appropriate customer invoices. What may appear to be a relatively simple activity is a time-consuming, error-prone exercise for many organizations.

Cash application can be performed either manually or automatically. Typically, manual cash application involves going through batches of paper and/or electronic cash receipts and matching them with open invoices in the AR system by customer and invoice line description. The disadvantages of the manual approach include the reliance on AR clerks for processing and entering remittance information and the lack of sufficient control over human errors and fraud in the cash receipting process. Because of these issues, we find most organizations prefer to use manual cash application for processing only the exceptions and to employ an automated cash application process for the majority of cash receipts.

To enhance operational efficiency and reduce human errors, most ERP solutions have features to automate the process of cash application on open items associated with customer accounts. The automation allows one to apply cash receipts without manually entering remittance information. Cash receipts can be identified by using a magnetic ink character recognition (MICR) number to locate customers; the MICR number holds the unique bank account number of the customer, used as a unique identifier. In other instances, customer invoice number and/or customer number can be used as key identifier(s) to locate open items for application of cash receipts.

Automatic cash application is slightly different from exact posting since it is a less precise process that relies on defined rules, which mostly yield proper results. It can improve the processing of both direct and lockbox cash receipts, and the benefits of not manually entering remittance detail can reduce the overall amount of clerical labor required to complete the cash application process and its resulting human errors. Only exception items that cannot be processed by the system require clerical, manual intervention.

A predetermined set of rules or algorithm is required to establish automatic cash application to assign the cash receipt amount to the open items. The most popular rules include exact match of amount and the match of a split amount. The major ERP packages allow for configuration to handle duplicate receipt identification whereby the same customer, receipt, and amount are applied to an open item in a current or future accounting period. Additionally, the packages also handle automatic over- and underpayment of cash to open items. In the case of overpayments, the ERP packages handle this situation with slight variations. PeopleSoft and SAP allow the overpayment to be applied to another item or placed on the customer's account, whereas Oracle only allows for the overpayment to be "unapplied" or "on account." Additionally, most ERP solutions handle discounts applied to partial payments. Oracle and PeopleSoft allow for discounts on partial payments as long as the system is configured in advance. Instead, SAP applies the discount upon the final payment. No pro rata discount is applied at the time of partial payment receipt.

In addition to using standard features provided by most ERP packages, we suggest that organizations evaluate their current practice in the cash application area by leveraging leading practices to yield significant automation. Most productive AR environments involve no manual review and application of cash receipts. Instead, the system automatically posts each cash receipt to the proper invoice(s) based on information provided either in batch or lockbox files. When this is completely automated, it can be considered more of a posting process than a cash application process. By then, organizations can realize benefits such as reduced processing costs, availability of real-time data for reporting, reduced error levels, and decreased cycle times as well as strengthened internal controls. SAP provides more "real-time" posting versus Oracle and PeopleSoft, which utilize a sub-ledger batch posting process to move accounting transactions between AR and the General Ledger.

Additional benefits of automating cash application include impacts on cash and treasury management. The ability to forecast future cash flow accurately adds value to an enterprise by enabling the cash management function to manage its liquid assets effectively. Reliable estimates of the amount and timing of cash receipts and payments help to reduce the cost of debts and increase the revenue from investments. Furthermore, the visibility of customer transaction and accurate payment history/habits can also influence the Collection effort. This information can be analyzed by the cash manager in making decisions about what receivable will be more beneficial to factor or discount for immediate cash. The ERP packages handle cash forecasting differently. Oracle does not provide predictive forecasting per se, rather, the Cash Management module has a cash forecasting tool that collects data from other modules to provide cash forecast spreadsheets including customer invoices, noncleared receipts, and cleared receipts. The forecasting is based on current data and an estimated payment date based on payment terms and is predictive only in this manner. PeopleSoft generates a cash forecast report based on open balances versus customer payment patterns Similarly, SAP generates a cash forecast report displaying incoming and outgoing cash based on existing payment patterns but does not use payment patterns or history.

Figure 6.11 describes sample ERP functionality that an organization can use to improve the apply cash step of OTC.

OTC Process Area	ERP Functionality
Apply Cash	▪ Tight integration with various modules, such as Treasury and Cash Management which enhances the ability to accurately forecast future cashflow.
	▪ Real-time clearing of open items can be performed to provide visibility of customer transaction, balance and payment history.
	▪ Cash application functionality includes: creating automated cash application algorithms, linking lockbox report transmissions directly to AR records through automated feed, using EDI interfaces with banks for cash-application processing, duplicate receipt detection, automatically creating memos and entries for customer returns and refunds, and providing cash tolerance levels to automatically write-off under-payments within limits, and reviewing these levels formally every six months.
	▪ Accepted payment methods include lockbox, checks, bank transfers, wires, EFT and credit card.
	▪ Updates to the GL, AR , and Credit Management.

Figure 6.11   *Sample ERP functionality: 7. Apply Cash*

THE HACKETT GROUP ON ORDER TO CASH

A key measurement of the revenue cycle is Days Sales Outstanding (DSO), which affects an organization's ability to generate cash flow more quickly. The peer group organization performers are at 48 days, whereas the world-class companies perform 50 percent better, with a DSO of 22 days. Assuming a 10 percent cost of capital, every day outstanding on a billion dollars of sales represents roughly $275,000 in capital costs.

The Hackett Group data show that the key to generating cash more quickly (lower DSO) is by effectively leveraging electronic transmission of invoices. Not only do these world-class companies generate more cash, but they also have less staff assigned to these processes. It is interesting that they also staff these processes quite differently, with a greater proportion of their staff in the front of the process — in billing — and less staff in the back end of the process. Because their emphasis is on aligning customer expectations with billing, these world-class organizations experience fewer problems in the back end, resulting in lower processing costs, reduced cycle time for Collections, and improved cash flow.

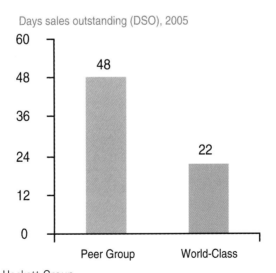

Days sales outstanding (DSO), 2005

Source: The Hackett Group

continued

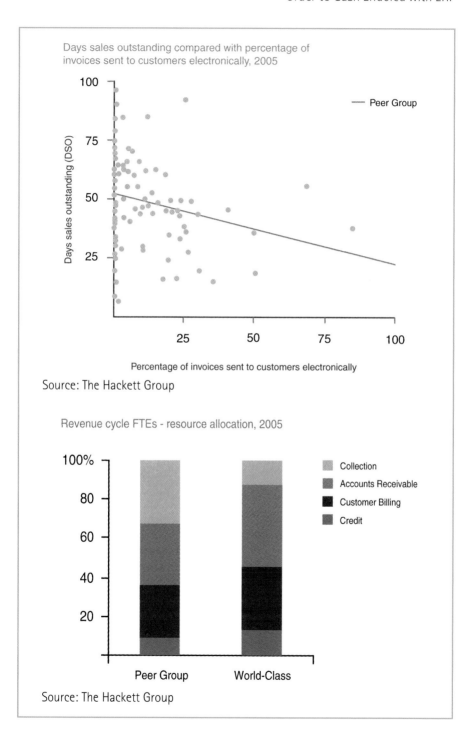

Days sales outstanding compared with percentage of invoices sent to customers electronically, 2005

—— Peer Group

Days sales outstanding (DSO)

Percentage of invoices sent to customers electronically

Source: The Hackett Group

Revenue cycle FTEs - resource allocation, 2005

Collection
Accounts Receivable
Customer Billing
Credit

Peer Group   World-Class

Source: The Hackett Group

CFO INSIGHTS

- Organizations with a strict focus on a single measure such as Days Sales Outstanding (DSO) or the size of the receivables balance fall short of expectations. It is important to develop and adhere to leading processes and to leverage technology fully to create transparency throughout the entire Order to Cash (OTC) cycle.

- Organizations need to develop credit policies, standardized payment terms, and payment default conditions, but they also need to establish the degree of flexibility they are willing to extend. Over time, organizations develop a reputation with customers for shorter payment terms, rigid credit denials, or extended terms and lax payment default consequences. As a result, the organizational approach directly affects customer expectations and behavior.

- Leading organizations create alignment throughout the entire end-to-end process: from sales all the way to payment and Collection responsibilities. Without sufficient alignment, sales teams can generate significant Collections activities and substantial write-offs, whereas the credit teams are perceived to be restricting selling activities and ultimately company revenue. Shared goals and aligned team and individual performance measures contribute significantly to optimal balance between revenue and risk.

- DSO or receivables tend to be addressed only when they become severe issues. Without a focus on continuous improvement throughout the process, organizations are leaving money on the table until it becomes a significant enough issue that it demands organizational attention. Even relatively minor OTC improvements can produce significant paybacks over time.

FROM INSIGHT TO ACTION

LEVERAGE TECHNOLOGY THROUGHOUT THE ORDER TO CASH PROCESS

There may be untapped functionality within the organization's existing technology applications and platform. For example, technology can help organizations overcome problems in receiving orders, prevent future order issues from occurring, and transform order receipt and processing.

continued

These improvements provide competitive advantage through cross-selling opportunities and optimizing customer satisfaction.

ENSURE PROPER REVENUE RECOGNITION

To avoid embarrassing and costly financial restatements, ensure that revenue is appropriately recognized. The ERP solution predefines revenue recognition rules to ensure proper categorization at the time of order entry. This approach not only improves accuracy but reduces manual processing and decreases financial reporting cycles.

DESIGN COLLECTION SERVICES TO TARGET SPECIFIC CUSTOMER SEGMENTS

Segment customers based on factors such as account history, payment behavior, risk, and historical behavior to improve Collection effectiveness. Model relationships between changes in Collection strategy and financial impact in order to test and fine-tune Collection strategies. Apply tailored Collection treatments (e.g., proactively contact habitually late customers, assign and group collectors by skill, use collections agencies) by customer segment.

REFERENCES

1. David J. Santoro, Jr., *Stop Leaking Cash! Ensuring your Earnings Reach the Bottom Line,* AsiaPac Economist CFO Roundtable, Shanghai, March 23, 2005.

2. New York Society of Security Analysts, *CICR Revenue Recognition Survey,* August 16, 2005, http://www.nyssa.com.

3. Securities and Exchange Commission, *SEC Staff Accounting Bulletin No. 101 – Revenue Recognition in Accounting Statements,* http://www.sec.gov.

4. Financial Accounting Standards Board (FASB), Statements of Financial Accounting Concepts *SFAC No. 2, Qualitative Characteristics of Accounting Information,* ¶63, http://www.fasb.org.

5. FASB, *SFAC No. 5, Recognition and Measurement in Financial Statements of Business Enterprises,* ¶84 (a), (b), and (c), http://www.fasb.org.

6. FASB, *SFAC No. 5,* ¶83(a), http://www.fasb.org; Statements of Financial Accounting Standards *SFAS No. 48,* ¶6(a), http://www.fasb.org; Statement of Position *SOP 97-2,* ¶8. *SOP 97-2,* http://www.aicpa.org.

7. Accounting Research Bulletin *ARB No. 43,* Chapter 1A, ¶1, http://www.fasb.org; Accounting Principles Board *APB Opinion No. 10,* ¶12, http://www.fasb.org. See also *SFAC No. 5,* ¶84(g), http://www.fasb.org and *SOP 97-2,* ¶8, http://www.aicpa.org.

8. David Schmidt, "2003 Credit and Collection Software Overview: New Products + Tools = More Options for Credit Pros," *Business Credit* 105 (Sept 2003): 38 (11), http://www.nacm.org.

CHAPTER 7

Tax Management

TAX MANAGEMENT: AN OVERVIEW

The New World

"Accounting and reporting of income taxes has received increased scrutiny by investors, analysts, Congress and others. Your auditors will be asking for more information, and you may have noticed an increased level of scrutiny from the SEC staff. That spotlight is likely to continue. Welcome to the new world."[1]

The need to meet tax-compliance obligations is at the core of most Tax function responsibilities. One challenge always exists; there are never sufficient data in finance systems to meet Tax's reporting needs. To be more effective, Tax functions must take matters into their own hands and actively influence data capture in their organization's systems.

Although tax is a statutory obligation of commerce, organizations focus on managing the tax burden and regularly report their effective tax rate as part of the external reporting process. The effective tax rate is typically a key priority for executives – with good reason. According to The Hackett Group research, companies with world-class Finance functions show dramatically lower effective tax rates than their peers (3 percent less on an average of 32 percent) and, in doing so, contribute $4.5 million per billion in revenue to their companies' bottom lines.[2]

The Tax Data Supply Chain and the Role of the ERP Solution

Those in charge of leading Tax functions understand the importance of managing their data supply chain. They ensure that data are captured efficiently, can be used effectively in tax-compliance activities, and, perhaps more important, can support value-creating tax-planning opportunities.

Few organizations view capturing tax information as an end-to-end process. For organizations that do, the focus is typically limited to support of the compliance process. We find this is the wrong approach. Organizations should instead focus on ensuring that the supply chain is optimized to capture tax information at all appropriate points, as depicted in Figure 7.1.

The traditional emphasis on Tax and Enterprise Resource Planning (ERP) solutions has been to ensure that the organization has appropriately accounted for transactional (indirect) taxes. Although this role is still valid, we recommend that the scope of ERP solutions for Tax ideally should take into account four areas: direct tax, indirect tax, tax reporting, and tax data archiving.

The Elements of a Comprehensive Tax Function

The importance of the ERP solution to the Tax function, through its role in data collection and information integration, forms the foundation for the development of a successful Tax function. This relationship is depicted in Figure 7.2.

The ERP solution forms the data foundation from which Tax collects its data needs. This is the fundamental building block for the tax processes and ultimately the enablement of the successful Tax function.

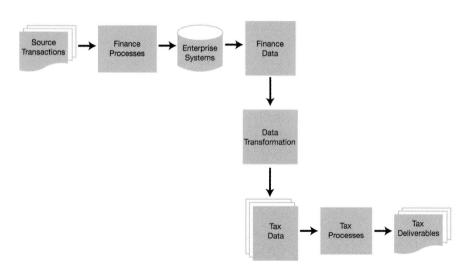

Figure 7.1 *Tax data supply chain*

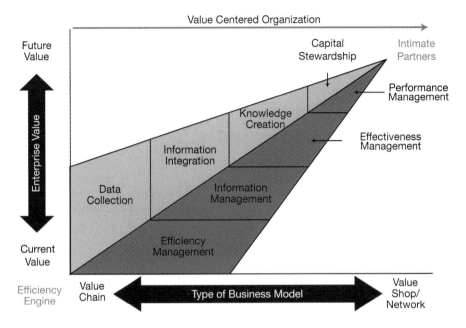

Figure 7.2   *Foundation of a successful Tax function*

Data Collection and Efficiency Management

Traditional tax-compliance activities require data across business and finance systems, leaving the Tax function with a myriad of detailed transactional analyses and time-consuming information requests, all to provide underlying information to support basic tax-compliance activities. Organizations that recognize the value of tax information address the underlying data problem by sensitizing the data at their source.

Information Integration and Management

ERP solutions typically do not have tax-specific modules for taxes, which creates a reliance on third-party tax compliance and determination solutions. Data from ERP solutions feed these solutions and enable the transformation of Finance data into tax information.

Knowledge Creation and Effectiveness Management

The Tax function is the unique combination of both a Finance and Legal function. This combination requires both structured and unstructured information. Tax requires supporting tools and processes to enable the management of both forms of information, as well as the ability to retrieve, analyze, and archive this information for planning, compliance, and defense.

Performance Management through Tax Insight

A successful Tax function uses the information delivered through the underlying finance solution and integrated tax applications in identifying tax value-creation opportunities or in monitoring and managing the tax risk associated with current strategies.

A Seat at the Table

An organization's business model is usually founded on strategies that have Tax as a major driver of operations. Although Tax produces no revenue, it has significant influence over a large part of the organization's cost structure and earnings.

We see that if Tax is not properly engaged, the implementation of an ERP solution can represent significant risk for Tax, and, by extension, the organization as a whole. Too often tax requirements are ignored, which results in difficulties accessing critical information or in the elimination of key data altogether. In fact, a survey by the Tax Executive Institute indicated that 80 percent of Tax functions had partial or no involvement in the design of the organization's financial system.[3]

Not engaging Tax in the design of the ERP solution may cost the organization millions of dollars and may expose the enterprise to substantial tax risk. Establishing a firm foundation of tax information within an organization's ERP solution is critical to developing a successful Tax function.

Tax-Centric Approach to ERP Solution Design and Implementations

Achieving a step change improvement in ERP solutions requires that Tax be actively involved in technology initiatives. A passive approach to data management is no longer a viable option for Tax. Figure 7.3 highlights the problems and consequences related to tax data and the tax processes when Tax is not involved in ERP design.

To effect a significant improvement, Tax must:

- **Actively participate in ERP solution design, take the lead in defining its requirements,** and commit the appropriate level of resource to the ERP design team. Furthermore, Tax leadership must be willing to provide

Common Problems	Consequences
▪ Significant differences between management and legal structure are not reflected in ERP solution.	▪ Potential inability to comply with statutory and tax reporting requirements.
▪ Organization of accounts does not reflect the information capture required for Tax.	▪ Inordinate amount of data manipulation and scrubbing required to meet tax-reporting requirements.
▪ ERP solution is not "tax-sensitized."	▪ High level of chasing and reworking data for tax professionals —resulting in loss of focus on core tax-planning opportunities.
▪ Multiple, disintegrated instances of ERP solution and other financial and operating technologies exist.	▪ Tax impact of major business events is guessed at, or worse, not considered at all.
▪ Limited capability to access data within ERP solution impedes ability to respond quickly and accurately with tax impact of proposed business event.	▪ Tax is incapable of providing more than a basic reporting service.
▪ Geographical spread of Tax and Finance results in difficulties in the sourcing of information.	▪ Significant audit assessments, fines and penalties.
▪ No standardization: Different data collection packs are used for tax returns and financial statement provision.	▪ Earnings volatility and cash-flow inefficiencies.
▪ No record-retention strategy for financial and tax data.	

Figure 7.3   *Tax data management challenges and consequences*

the sponsorship to see that the tax requirements are given the support they deserve in decision-making processes.

- **Have IT, project management, and change management representation** that allow Tax to interact with the ERP design team. These skills are in addition to traditional compliance and tax-planning skills sets.

Designing Common Solutions to Support Local Reporting Requirements

When Tax is involved in ERP solution design for multiple tax jurisdictions or multiple countries, the traditional approach has been to provide solutions on a per jurisdiction basis – the rationale being that differing tax laws require different solutions.

The leading practice systems design approach, however, dictates the use of a common design (for example, an Oracle or SAP global Chart of Accounts) with enhancements to support local regulatory requirements. Organizations that are successful in embedding tax requirements into their ERP solution designs are cognizant of this practice and develop solutions that are functionally and technically common but that also allow localization for each jurisdiction's requirements. This common approach gives Tax a platform to develop solutions for the downstream components of the tax data supply chain.

What Tax Requirements Should Be Addressed in the ERP Solution Design?

The reality is that every business transaction has a tax impact, even if it does not result in a taxable transaction. Tax pervades business operations and system processes. However, from the perspective of ERP solution design, we find that Tax can be segregated into two components.

Direct Tax

ERP solutions are implemented to support an organization's business operations. At the center is the need to support financial reporting, in the form of management and fiscal and tax-regulatory reporting.

Indirect Tax

Although the reporting requirements are at the heart of the organization's need, the ERP solution must also encapsulate the tax information for fundamental business operations, transactions, and processes that it supports for both the Order to Cash and Procure to Pay processes.

The remainder of this chapter covers the issues and challenges involved in implementing tax solutions and meeting data requirements for both direct and indirect tax activities.

DIRECT TAXATION

Tax reporting can be seen as an annual event that requires Finance to provide data. However, for organizations reporting to the financial markets on a quarterly basis, the ability to communicate the tax component of results with a high level of confidence is essential. When the financial reporting cycle is different from the tax statutory compliance timeline in each of the tax jurisdictions the organization operates, the process of generating the tax submission can be fraught with challenges.

Direct Tax: An End-to-End Perspective

For organizations that are focused on improving their tax processes, we recommend the emphasis should be on ensuring that the components of the tax processes are integrated. Start with the direct tax process in mind and develop solutions that support the leading practices for this process.

The core of this approach is the "cumulative or continuous build," which builds the final annual tax submission based on interim submissions made during the year (monthly or quarterly). The traditional approach to the end-of-year filing has been to start with the entire year's data set, thereby compressing the annual compliance effort into a single, extremely intense resource effort. By following the cumulative build, an organization can smooth out the resource effort and in doing so allow time to focus on sensitive elements of the tax return. Figure 7.4 shows this new approach.

Following the cumulative build process requires a "rethink" of how Tax addresses the compliance process. Although the computation or provision can be enhanced by tax calculation solutions, the essence of the concept is to think about tax compliance as an end-to-end process, starting with the provision and finishing with the true-up (actual taxes calculated and paid to the authorities). From an ERP solution perspective, what is essential is that the process and activities be documented and adhered to. Too often organizations are not able to reconcile estimated taxes, actual taxes, and

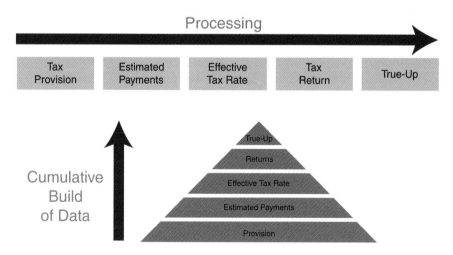

Figure 7.4 *Direct tax compliance: end-to-end process*

associated payments in the financial systems without intense scrutiny of the underlying detail.

By following this leading practice, Tax builds a provision for improving accuracy over the period of analysis and in so doing creates a repository of information that is invaluable for other planning and reporting needs.

The cumulative build concept, although simple to comprehend, can be enhanced by utilizing tax applications that support these practices, working in an integrated manner with an ERP solution and other systems. Tax service providers are able to provide applications that support this process for a specific tax jurisdiction; other organizations have developed custom solutions to support the global provisioning process.

Challenges of Designing Solutions for the Direct Tax Process

ERP solutions have the capabilities to support elements of direct tax reporting but do not provide a comprehensive solution for direct tax data management. Nevertheless, ERP solutions can be tailored to deliver a solution that works in unison with applications that have been developed specifically to support the concepts associated with tax reporting (e.g., providing a database for managing and tracking Schedule 'M's and other book-to-tax adjustments in the United States). Some of the challenges associated with obtaining data that are usable for tax are identified in the following sections.

Legal Entity and Statutory Accounts Data

Statutory accounts data constitute the basic starting point for the tax-compliance process, as Tax has to show the reconciliation between the auditor-approved accounts and the end tax computation clearly. We have seen that the challenge for many large organizations is to comply with group reporting, (e.g., U.S. 10K – Generally Accepted Accounting Principles [GAAP]) while providing a solution for local GAAP. Few organizations succeed in supporting multiple reporting requirements without some manual intervention.

The quest for financial data by legal entity is nothing new; in fact, it is the fundamental principle by which accounts and tax returns are filed and the basis by which data structures are defined within an ERP solution. For example, in SAP, the company code is typically related to the legal entity structure. The challenge is that many large organizations operate at a transnational level and are managed by global functions rather than country divisions. The fundamental principle of using the company code as the legal entity can result in unwieldy transaction processes.

For those organizations that are able to establish the relationship between company code and legal entity, we find it often proves difficult to maintain this as a one-to-one relationship over time. The result is that Tax may be forced to perform off-line, often extensive, manual analysis to produce the needed legal entity level reporting.

Most ERP solutions support journal entries, but the challenge for organizations is to instill a discipline of updating the General Ledger so that it captures the financial position in accord with the account filings. Although the ERP solution captures the transactions of an organization, accounting entries relating to corporate-level transactions and other year-end adjustments (e.g., cost allocations, dividend receivables, and payables) are often outside the solution and are managed in other tools or spreadsheets. These data are used in preparing the accounts but seldom make it back to the ERP solution.

It is therefore important to develop guiding principles from which the ERP design teams can develop solutions. Tax must champion the need to capture statutory accounts by legal entity in the ERP solution design and must work to enforce this capture so that the accounting entries are entered into the ERP solution within the required timeframes and that these principles are maintained over time.

Data Sensitization and the Chart of Accounts

Tax relies on the trial balance as the starting point for its processes, but often the Chart of Accounts (CoA) is not fit for Tax's purposes. The principles that guide the CoA design are typically an infusion of different needs. In implementations that adopt a global CoA approach, this characteristic can be especially challenging.

Although the CoA design is usually an optimal solution for group financial accounting and management reporting, it typically is not optimal for corporation tax purposes. The reason is that tax focuses on the purpose rather than the nature of transactions.

The ability to capture tax information of this nature can greatly influence an organization's filing position. For example, an organization with $100 million promotional spend may have a permanent 10 percent (or $10 million) disallowance due because of an inability to substantiate tax audit queries related to nondeductible business entertaining. The result would be an increase of $10 million in taxable profits or a tax charge of $3 million, assuming a 30 percent tax rate. Moving to an actual basis or even reduction, reducing the disallowance by 1 percent could contribute to a $300,000 saving. Clearly, being able to provide information on components of disallowance spend is sufficient reason to justify the participation of Tax in ERP solutions design for most large organizations.

For example, a global products organization embarked on a tax data sensitization effort within their SAP solution to improve the quality of the information to support the tax-compliance process and to demonstrate to the tax authorities its ability to substantiate its returns. The organization data-sensitized both the purchasing and financial components of the SAP R/3 application to ensure that users were prompted to make a distinction between certain types of expenditure for tax purposes. The organization was able to show it had systematic solutions that prompted users for the relevant inputs. Apart from the opportunity to move from estimated to actual numbers in its tax charge, the benefit of instilling tax authority confidence in its technology and processes was a key consideration for the organization in starting the initiative.

Although data are captured in the General Ledger, data flow from many different modules. It is therefore important that the information required by Tax be captured as far upstream in the process as possible (for example, in the requisition and not the invoice, or in the asset record and not in the General Ledger posting).

An obvious solution would be to expand the CoA. However, this may not always be the right answer, as the result may be an incomprehensible CoA. A preferred approach is to work with the rest of the ERP solution design team to develop an optimal CoA that suits the needs of Tax and the rest of the reporting stakeholders, while leveraging all aspects of the financial codeblock. Figure 7.5 proposes a potential decision-making process for determining the suitability of a CoA for tax purposes.

ERP solution implementers should also educate their tax counterparts. An ERP solution captures useful data in multiple dimensions beyond the traditional financial trial balance.

For example, although the financial codeblock segments for Oracle Financials may seem long, they provide an excellent opportunity to create the most appropriate structure for supporting an organization's multitude of reporting requirements through a globally agreed-on segmental

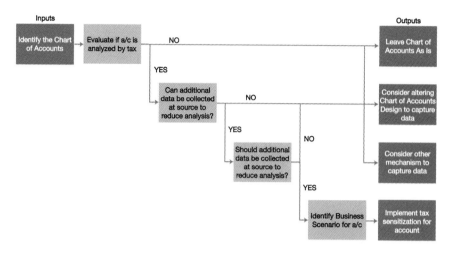

Figure 7.5 *Systematic approach to determining a suitable CoA for tax reporting*

reporting structure. Each segment can be targeted for a specific need, for example, management, statutory, or tax entity reporting and transaction type of segregation.

Oracle also provides accounting flexfields to allow organizations to extend the delivered codeblock to suit their needs. These can be adopted by Tax or other parts of the organization to capture reporting needs specifically for their purposes. Key flexfields enable the organization to control the data entered, whereas descriptive flexfields provide a means to allow users to enter free-form narrative.

Other ERP solutions, such as SAP R/3, may be more restrictive owing to their predefined reporting structures. However, these structures can equally be used to support tax reporting as long as the use is agreed on in the design. For example, cost center can be used to specify the deductibility of a transaction. When other data elements cannot be used, organizations may choose to extend the delivered codeblock to capture additional information to support tax reporting requirements.

Other areas of consideration also exist for how ERP solutions can best be used for tax reporting or tax data sensitization; this largely depends on what Tax deems to be weaknesses in the reporting process and prioritizing these to develop solutions. Some potential considerations follow.

Use of the ERP Solution to Provide a Tax Solution for Fixed Assets

Analysis of Fixed Assets can be one of the most time-intensive areas in the tax computation process, yet the simple task of assigning tax-relevant location indicators to vendor master records can significantly reduce this effort.

Solution to Support the Reconciliation of Book to Tax Differences

Tax must ensure that solutions exist to support its reporting and reconciliation requirements. This is not a stand-alone activity and requires cooperation with Finance to:

- Identify statutory accounts using local accounting standards
- Reconcile results of local with group accounting standards
- Identify tax accounts using tax accounting standards
- Reconcile results of tax with local accounting standards (for example, Local Effective Tax Rate reconciliation)
- Reconcile results of tax with group accounting standards (for example, Group Effective Tax Rate reconciliation).

Solutions to these requirements may rely on a mixture of ERP solutions functionality and interfacing third-party tax tools (e.g., consolidation applications, tax-compliance tools).

Intercompany Transactions Requiring Account Process Discipline

When creating intercompany journals, avoid summarizing the journal. The opportunity to claim deductions in the receiving organization is diminished when the cost details are not available. Not surprisingly, the area of intercompany cost allocations is typically an area of tremendous scrutiny.

Other System Interfaces to the General Ledger

It is important to ensure that the correct level of granularity is transferred from interfacing systems to the General Ledger to avoid additional follow-up analysis.

Tax Provisions and Returns Applications

In many of the large tax jurisdictions, tax service providers and the authorities offer applications (e.g., Abacus or CORPTAX) that support organizations in preparing their tax returns. The capabilities of these solutions vary from supporting the booking of book to tax adjustments to providing an interface from which the tax authorities can gather data to feed their computation applications. These solutions are generally jurisdiction specific and have no use outside the tax codes for which they were intended.

Solutions from the tax service providers and specialist tax technology providers recognize the challenges global organizations have in meeting their tax provisioning requirements. Often they are custom-developed solutions. At their core is recognition of the need to provide a platform that manages and automates book to tax differences, gathers data from multiple technology solutions to generate legal entity data, manages and automates book to tax differences, and provides an audit trail from the systems accounting data to the final tax computation.

The benefits of these applications cannot be underestimated, as they provide a solution to the challenges of tax data management efficiency. They can drastically cut the time required to provide provision data and can thus compress the organization's reporting cycle. However, although many such specialized solutions do exist, sensitizing the core ERP solution for tax purposes is still a valuable exercise. It forces organizations to assess the quality of data in the ERP solution and to ensure that data capture to support the tax processes is at the right level of detail to support reporting needs.

INDIRECT TAXATION

CASE STUDY

John Doolittle, Vice-President Taxation, Nortel Networks

"Nortel is a recognized leader in delivering communications capabilities, serving both service provider and enterprise customers in more than 100 countries. It delivers innovative technology solutions encompassing end-to-end broadband, Voice over IP, multimedia services and applications, as well as wireless broadband designed to help people solve the world's greatest challenges. In 2004, its revenues were over US$9.8BN.

Nortel in North America annually files more than 1,500 indirect tax returns, representing hundreds of thousand of invoices and over one million distinct line items. The environment at Nortel is very complex, due to the number of products and services that we buy and sell and the fact that it is a truly global company operating in almost every country around the world.

Given the number of transactions and dollars that are involved, it is imperative that our transaction tax systems 'get it right' the first time. We cannot afford the dollars or the time to deal with problems in this area. As well, the relationships that we have with our suppliers and customers are put at risk if our systems are not reliable.

We must have a tax determination solution that can match our footprint and deal with the complexity of the business. A system that matches our needs will result in significant benefits, both in savings in tax as well as savings in design time."

Organizations that have significant transaction turnover flows benefit from improvements in tax determination accuracy. Using an automated rules-based solution to ensure proper treatment of transactions proactively takes a fraction of the effort that it takes to audit and correct a massive volume of transactions after the fact. In addition to the reduction in effort, there is considerable value in having a well-controlled process that gives internal management and external auditors greater confidence in the ERP solution's output.

However, we see that most organizations are still a long way from having such smooth and reliable outcomes. A European Commission survey of companies across the European Union revealed that although 64 percent of respondents indicated they had no difficulties in applying tax requirements for invoicing domestically, less than 24 percent reported no difficulties for operations abroad.[4]

Transaction tax determination requirements in ERP solution implementations traditionally have been segregated by process, as follows:

- **Record to Report:** defining tax codes for receivables and payables and determining how transactions map and post to the ledger accounts.
- **Order to Cash:** determining the output tax for sales transactions, ensuring that the parameters that drive tax determination are integrated into the process design and that statutory reporting is supported.
- **Procure to Pay:** determining input tax on purchase orders and invoices and ensuring that the correct tax is applied to support compliance requirements and enable accurate cash forecasting, while enabling input tax reporting requirements.

This end-to-end process-based approach may result in a disjointed view of the tax determination process:

- Requirements for each jurisdiction are often developed on a piecemeal basis, leading to an unmanaged evolution of the tax design.
- The Tax function is not able to understand how the tax determination process has been designed.
- As the organization develops new business models, it is uncertain how these developments impact the existing business tax parameters.

A leading practice is to develop a common understanding and approach for the design, so that the tax determination process can be deployed in a consistent manner. Typically, the tax configuration is complex, requiring process configuration and specific master data setups that need to be thoroughly understood. The knowledge needed to integrate the entire transaction tax determination process resides across multiple teams, and the silo approach results in a suboptimal tax solution.

In adopting a proactive tax-centric approach, Tax personnel are able to understand and own the ERP solution. In doing so, they can build their knowledge of and confidence in the design. They can also add value by supporting the business in assessing the impact of new channels, customers, or products to market.

A Comprehensive Transaction Tax Determination Approach

At its simplest, transaction tax determination is about ensuring that the organization complies with the tax obligations arising from its business operations. The ERP solution must support determination of output taxes, entry or self-assessment of input taxes, and any restrictions related to the validity of customers' and suppliers' clearance to operate. The business flow is depicted in Figure 7.6.

We recommend that design teams also give consideration to the reporting and payment of these taxes. Although ERP software packages provide solutions to how the taxes are recognized and posted to the financial ledgers, the sophistication of the reporting solutions vary, and the design teams must understand how the configuration can be controlled and what reports are available. Then they can determine an optimal solution to meet the organization's need. However, back-end processes for making payments to tax authorities typically are missed during the system design, as these

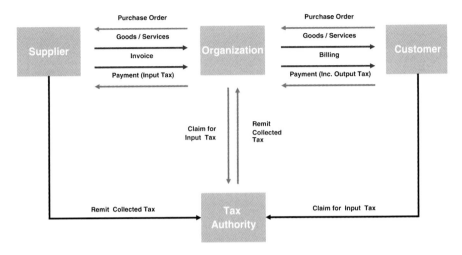

Figure 7.6 *Transaction taxes process summary*

occur infrequently. Their omission from the design process subsequently results in inefficient processes.

Design Approach: Defining the Application Tax Rates

For ERP solution implementers new to transaction taxes, the simplest approach is to develop ERP solution configuration for tax rates and codification based on legacy solution settings. Soliciting input from indirect tax specialists will invariably uncover organization or reporting issues for which the solutions have not been able to provide a solution. Examples of these include:

- **Not accommodating restricted expenses.** For example, business entertainment may carry a tax at the standard rate but be disallowed for indirect tax purposes.
- **Not recognizing cross-border transactions.** For example, non-European Economic Community (EEC) or intra-EEC transactions may have a neutral tax impact but still must be tagged accurately so they can be reported.
- **Failing to determine Use Tax for suppliers.** At times it may not be clear under what circumstances Use Tax should be determined for suppliers or when it is supplier/product exempt.

A comprehensive approach involves defining the business requirements for tax reporting from the bottom up, ensuring that the elements of the tax authorities' returns are incorporated. Once the requirements are known, determining how they can be achieved in the ERP solution is simplified. The table in Figure 7.7 shows an example of Value-Added Tax (VAT) codes configured for PeopleSoft Financials.

Design Approach: Identify the Business Scenarios

Defining how transaction tax determination should operate is more complex than defining tax codes. Globalization has resulted in business models that transcend national boundaries, and although business practices may have evolved to take advantage of the situation, ERP solutions and the configuration rules that govern them may not. As a result, transaction processes may be more cumbersome than envisaged, requiring multiple transactions to replicate even the simplest of physical or title movements.

SetID (key)	Tax Code	%	Description	Authority
SHARE	UK17.5	17.5	UK 17.5% Domestic G&S	UK1
SHARE	UK5.0	5	UK 5.0% Domestic G&S	UK2
SHARE	UK0	0	UNITED KINGDOM 0%	UK3
SHARE	IR21.0	21	IRELAND 21.0% Domestic G&S	IRL1
SHARE	IR12.5	12.5	IRELAND 12.5% Domestic G&S	IRL2
SHARE	IR0	0	IRELAND 0%	IRL3
SHARE	GE16.0	16	GERMANY 16.0% Domestic G&S	GER1
SHARE	GE0	0	GERMANY 0%	GER2
SHARE	FR19.6	19.6	FRANCE 19.6% Domestic G&S	FRA1
SHARE	FR0	0	FRANCE 0%	FRA2
SHARE	NL19.0	20	NETHERLANDS 19% Domestic G&S	NLD1
SHARE	NL6.0	6	NETHERLANDS 6% Domestic G&S	NLD2
SHARE	NL0	0	NETHERLANDS 0%	NLD3

Figure 7.7 *PeopleSoft: illustrative tax codes for VAT*

In some instances, some scenarios are not supported by the standard process configuration and require enhancements to resolve.

A tax-focused approach considers all the business scenarios that result in the multitude of tax output conditions. Documenting these scenarios helps the system design team architect a tax-centric solution and avoid a situation in which the design does not fit the purpose. The structured output, together with the knowledge of how the ERP solution models tax determination, enables the design team to map the requirements into the application successfully and determine the processes or activities that must be followed to achieve the right result.

When to Consider Third-Party Transaction Tax Determination Tools

Our discussion of the design for transaction-tax determination has so far focused on harnessing the functionality of the ERP solution. However, choosing whether to adopt an alternate solution is often one of the first considerations for indirect taxes. The use of third-party tax determination applications (e.g., Sabrix, Taxware, and Vertex) depends on a number of parameters, ranging from the number of jurisdictions in which the organization operates to the range of products, locations, and partners with which it interacts and the variation in tax rates necessary to support tax reporting and auditing.

Using third-party solutions brings many data administration benefits. For example, Vertex Inc. provides the ability to automate address validation for both SAP and Oracle order management; Oracle also provides interfaces to upload rates information provided by Vertex. The power of the tax determination solutions lies in their ability to determine the taxability of a transaction based on the rules embedded in the solution; their ability to configure rules based on unique circumstances; and their provision of all this in a central location for Tax to administer rather than across complex configuration settings in the ERP solution.

Figure 7.8 outlines the components of transaction tax determination automation and the role of third-party applications.

Marketplace trends suggest that third-party tax solutions are most prevalent in North America, where the number of jurisdictions and rates that need to be maintained are immense and the effort to maintain them manually in the ERP solution is unrealistic. There is also increasing interest in solutions that focus on global transaction tax determination. The business case for these applications is built on:

- Reducing tax error rates
- Enabling cost-effective tax processing
- Reducing compliance costs through automation
- Reducing tax audit exposure
- Increasing control of tax liabilities.

Although most third-party transaction tax providers (e.g., Sabrix, Taxware, and Vertex) have developed global indirect tax solutions, take-up of these solutions varies considerably. That said, a standardized third-party bolt-on tax application has many advantages, including comprehensive reporting capabilities. Organizations must therefore determine their criteria for adopting these toolsets. Figure 7.9 gives an example of a selection process.

When transaction tax requirements are considered on a jurisdiction-by-jurisdiction basis, the effort required to implement these solutions may be considered too discrete to utilize a comprehensive third-party solution. However, consideration of the organization's entire transaction tax determination requirements from the outset of the ERP solution design may result in a different answer.

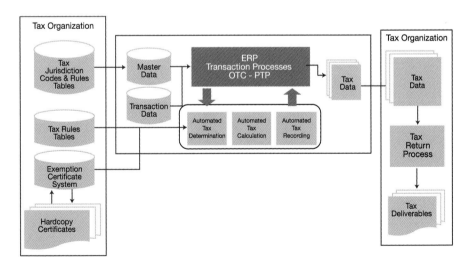

Figure 7.8   *Transaction tax determination*

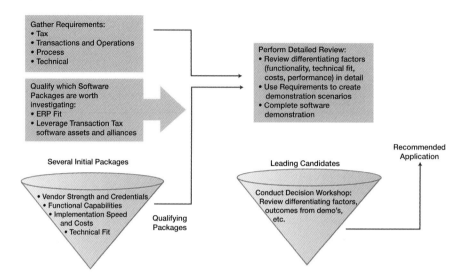

Figure 7.9 *Tax application selection approach*

TAX INSIGHT

CASE STUDY

David Boege, Tax Information Specialist, BP

"BP is one of the world's largest energy companies, with more than 100,000 employees and operating in more than 100 countries. BP's main activities involve exploration and production of crude oil and natural gas; refining, marketing, supply and transportation; and the manufacture and marketing of petrochemicals, as well as a presence in gas and power. The company is organized into three business segments: Exploration and Production; Refining and Marketing; and Gas, Power and Renewables.

The number of accounting systems across segments and geographies has always posed many issues in terms of ensuring data consistency and accuracy. There are many projects under way to consolidate these systems and define new, more efficient Finance processes. A constant challenge for the tax department is keeping abreast of these implementation projects. The Tax Technology team works across BP to ensure that tax requirements are adequately incorporated into systems designs, and that tax is involved with testing, migration and change management.

Another requirement is for Tax to have continued access to data in legacy systems, and moreover, to tax-relevant data over a period of time. The remit of Finance does not typically require access to historic data more than a few years old. Thus, archiving normally occurs earlier than tax would like, and such archives do not usually allow quick, easy access. However, an efficient response to tax auditors' queries is of high importance.

Data warehouses can provide an interim solution – serving as a central repository of information over a period of time. If configured correctly, these can allow data from different source systems to be populated, helping to provide a consolidated view: for example, to see a legal-entity perspective. However, the sheer size of data warehouses makes them less efficient to use.

A tax-specific data archiving and retention tool, such as SAP's DaRT (Data Archiving and Retention Tool), is a more efficient solution and provides BP with an easily configurable, flexible solution that meets tax requirements. BP took the opportunity as part of new systems implementations to implement data retention solutions that extracted tax relevant data (derived from tax scenarios identified by local country tax users).

In addition to data, there is often a regulatory requirement to retain images (such as invoices), reports and even emails. Use of optical storage solutions can meet these requirements."

Tax Data Warehouses, Archiving, and Retention

Regulatory requirements often mandate the archiving and retention of data. An organization's approach to meeting these requirements can vary dramatically, depending on the organization's view of the risk to cost-benefit associated with these initiatives. However, an organization should segregate data archiving and retention as two distinct activities and apply a comprehensive approach to ensure that the lifecycle of the tax process, from planning through compliance to audit, is not compromised.

Most organizations will adopt archiving policies as a means to manage financial data volumes and to support retention requirements. Data retention, however, also includes ensuring that the archived data can be readily accessible after archiving, so that the organization can reconstruct the data as necessary to support audit and fiscal queries. Here, ERP solutions are valuable because they provide functionality to support these requirements.

For example, a global pharmaceutical company embarked on a data-archiving initiative from their SAP R/3 application, not only as a means to manage technology performance, but also as a way for the Tax to readily access the data and report on it for audit and general query purposes. This solution was readily accessible to Tax with minimal support from the IT function. The organization used the available SAP DaRT functionality and integrated it with a flexible end-user reporting tool. Compare this with another organization that had archived its financial transaction to a proprietary legacy format. It had to retain the legacy application to restore transactional detail.

Although retention methodologies vary, we find successful initiatives involve integrating regulatory requirements with the desire to create value from tax data. In the past, data warehouse initiatives evolved as discrete initiatives. In today's ERP solutions implementations, data warehouse initiatives typically are considered along with the management information delivery platform (for example, SAP R/3 with SAP-BW). Figure 7.10 outlines the organizational benefit gained from adopting a strategic approach to providing reporting and retention solutions.

Organizations that are successful at delivering a comprehensive tax data-archiving and retention solution begin with a view of their information needs and integrate this with their data archive and retention requirements. The result is an integrated application architecture, depicted in Figure 7.11.

Tactical Approach	Strategic Approach
▪ Almost exclusive use of request and respond tools—separate data requests for provision, tax return, audit information and planning	▪ Automated interfaces to multiple sources of data, increasing the accuracy and timeliness of data access
▪ Financial and operational data maintained on a decentralized basis with no standardization, including manual creation of archive files for compliance and record retention	▪ A central source of tax data stored in a consistent format and structure
	▪ Reporting and analysis tools that provide support for and enhance tax compliance, tax audit defense and tax analysis and planning capabilities

Figure 7.10 *Reporting and analysis approach for Tax*

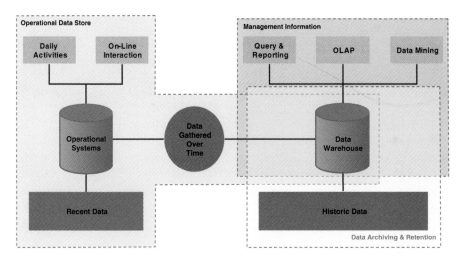

Figure 7.11 *Integrated Tax reporting and retention*

Tax Data Archiving

Many organizations rely on the IT function and/or Finance to generate and store historical tax information. Any changes to technology, storage protocols, or responsibilities result in a separation between Tax and the historical information required to substantiate audits and close off returns.

In many cases, the cost and effort required to access tax data from updated or replaced sources can be substantial; often, they can prevent information from being accessed at all. Such risks are significant and constitute one of the primary efforts to substantiate and document tax controls in relation to the Sarbanes-Oxley Act.

Data archiving and retention capabilities are often only considered after the ERP solution has been implemented, even though they are among Tax's priority areas. These considerations must be embedded into the design principles. An optimal solution will integrate the archiving, retention, and reporting requirements within the ERP solution design.

To be successful in embedding data archiving and retention into the ERP solution priorities, Tax personnel must develop and drive requirements, emphasizing their regulatory needs and strategic intent. Examples of regulatory requirements from a tax and statutory accounting perspective are shown in Figure 7.12.

How long must accounting records be stored for?	Can accounting/tax records and returns be stored/maintained electronically?
Netherlands Seven years, according to Article 394(2) Civil Law Code and Article 52(4) GTA. Records relating to immovable property must be stored for a period of 9 years (Art. 34a VAT Code).	Accounting • There is no restriction on the media of retention, providing the accounting trail remains accurately and completely available within a reasonable time. Tax • There are no restrictions, as long as the relevant records remain accurate and complete and can be made available to the authorities within a reasonable time of approximately 4-6 weeks.
United States Statement on Auditing Standards-41 provides that accounting records should be maintained as long as the auditor is legally liable. Auditors generally are liable for the opinions given and representations made by them on the financial statements they audit.	Accounting • Yes Tax • Yes. Revenue Procedure 97-22, pursuant to section 6001 of the Internal Revenue Code, provides that taxpayers may maintain books and records by using an electronic storage system that either images hardcopy books and records, or transfers computerized books and records, to an electronic storage media.

Figure 7.12 *Illustrative data retention requirements by country*

Some ERP vendors will provide tools to support data archiving and data purge. Examples include PeopleSoft Data Archiving Tool or SAP DaRT. Other ERP vendors may not possess specific data archiving capabilities but may have reporting and analysis solutions that can be used to support a tax retention strategy.

An important aspect of data archiving and retention to consider is what the ERP software package supports, what data elements are archived and what tools, if any, are available to analyze the data. Furthermore, Tax's reporting requirements will also help determine whether the analysis tools are sufficient. For example, although SAP-DaRT facilitates data archiving and retention, the views that users are able to create from the query tool may not be sufficient to satisfy all of Tax's reporting requirements. Standard views may not be adequate to join the data across application areas or provide a full view of the transaction (in other words, linking purchase order to invoice and payment information). In this scenario, custom views will be required to support the reporting requirement.

The Need for Tax Data Warehouses

The 2004–2005 Corporate Tax Department Survey by the Tax Executive Institute indicates that 36 percent of all open tax audits were from four years prior to the current tax year. Another 31 percent of open audits were older than four years.[5] More than 50 percent of information requests from the tax authorities required more than 20 days[6] to develop a response. As these numbers illustrate, having quick access to the system's accounting transactions and a mechanism by which the information can be analyzed to support audit responses cannot be overemphasized.

The data access challenge requires getting the right access to the right data at the right time without increasing labor costs or headcount. The goal is to reduce tax compliance and audit cycle time, as well as the associated effort, so that the tax function can refocus its resources on tax planning and analysis. The solutions for getting this data effectively will largely depend on the business requirements and the processes that need to be supported. Several examples are listed in Figure 7.13.

When data reporting requirements are considered as part of an ERP solution implementation, our experience demonstrates that Tax must drive the business case to support the requirements for its own data reporting solutions and identify the best solution to meet its needs.

FUTURE TRENDS

The Need for Transparency

The critical importance of engaging the Tax function in ERP solution design has been emphasized throughout this chapter; in fact, the role of

	Compliance & Tax Accounting	Audit	Planning & Business Support
Standard	Typical, recurring data needs	Respond to audit requests	Basic statutory reporting
Ad Hoc	Required when standard reporting does not provide answer	Required when standard reporting does not provide answer	Primary data gathering method
Analytics	Monitoring tools can be used to look for new cost elements (companies, accounts)	Conduct "mock audit" looking for trends	Predict consequences of business and tax decisions

Figure 7.13 *Tax data use*

Tax in ERP solution implementations will only increase as organizations strive to create new business models to bolster their value-creation agenda. As processes become embedded in customer-facing and back-office applications or modules, Tax will no longer be considered a Finance solution issue alone.

Tax must ensure that the organization retains its historic data to support its filing positions with the tax authorities and therefore must champion the need for financial data archiving and retention solutions. Organizations are beginning to explore the use of tax data warehouses, not only as a means to access archived data easily, but also as a way to provide a solution for addressing legal entity reporting issues and analysis of accounts and details. For Tax, the justification for any technology initiatives is not only about savings from efficiencies, but also about managing risk and, ultimately, creating value.

Beyond Business Transactions

Organizations have also begun to see the importance of managing knowledge and processes beyond the transactional business activities. User-centric solutions for managing knowledge and content have existed for some time. Organizations are starting to embrace these solutions, especially within the internal support functions, such as Finance. Tax functions also benefit from these solutions.

CASE STUDY

John Borgeson, Senior Director, Global Reporting and Analysis, Pfizer Inc.

"Pfizer Inc. discovers, develops, manufactures and markets leading prescription medicines for humans and animals and many of the world's best-known consumer brands. Pfizer sells its products in 150 countries. Its 2004 revenues were $52.5 billion.

Pfizer doubled its size in the early years of this decade after acquiring two other global companies: Warner-Lambert in 2000 and Pharmacia in 2003. Pfizer's *annual revenues had skyrocketed to $50 billion, making it the world's leading research-based pharmaceutical company. But along with bigger operations came a far more challenging workload for Pfizer's Corporate Tax Division. In light of the company's new scale, the tax team faced a critical decision: hire more people or radically change the way the work was done.*

We really needed to reinvent the tax organization and chose to initiate an innovative transformation of the people, processes and technology supporting the entire Tax function, which resulted in a 40 percent process improvement in the function's performance within 12 months. Today the division is successfully completing its work with roughly the same team of tax professionals it employed when the company was half its current size.

The team effort resulted in a new strategic vision for Pfizer Corporate Tax, with a totally new suite of solutions, all integrated in the Corporate Tax Portal (a 'virtual desktop' for every Pfizer tax professional). Now, the Corporate Tax Portal is the common starting place for every Pfizer tax professional each working day, enabling them to get the latest divisional news, see projects at a glance, access shared templates and work processes, and reach all the data they need, in the most efficient and effective way possible.

Our innovative thinking led to a solution that fully integrated standard business processes with document management, tax data warehousing, balanced scorecard reporting and all other major information processes, for a corporate tax function in a single, portal-accessed platform.

At the end of the day we needed a real-world solution to meet unprecedented demands for greater capability and efficiency. As a global leader in pharmaceuticals operating a highly complex business in heavily regulated marketplaces, Pfizer must maximize its statutory compliance and minimize its exposure to risk. These capabilities help us do just that. When Pfizer Corporate Tax does its job well, it reduces the company's tax liabilities; these savings can then be redirected into research and development of new drugs, more advertising and promotion and other valuable business uses."

The success of integrating traditional tax requirements in ERP design will be judged by those who rely on the information from the ERP solutions – from the internal tax information user to the tax-compliance partner and the tax authorities. Our experience shows Tax can create and sustain immense value for the organization, but first supporting Tax with the right tools and capabilities will be a critical element to creating and sustaining a leading Tax function.

THE HACKETT GROUP ON TAX MANAGEMENT

World-class tax organizations have the best of both worlds: lower tax management costs and lower effective tax rates. World-class Finance leaders do an exemplary job of increasing cash flow through a variety of channels. One of these is tax management, as measured by effective tax rate. The leaders manage an effective tax rate of 28 percent. For the peer group, the average is 31 percent.

Consider that a one percent tax on every hundred million dollars of pretax earnings equals $1 million in taxes. Assuming that a company had pretax earnings of 15 percent, every 1 percent reduction in effective tax rate would equate to 0.15 percent of revenue, or $1.5 million per billion of revenue.

The concept that world-class Finance executives have mastered is that effective tax rate is an efficiency-versus-effectiveness tradeoff: efficiency is still important for certain activities, such as collection and compilation of tax information, whereas effectiveness is primarily driven by decisions made as a result of investments in tax planning.

continued

Tax management costs as a percent of revenue, 2005

Source: The Hackett Group

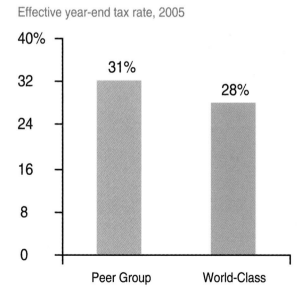

Effective year-end tax rate, 2005

Source: The Hackett Group

CFO INSIGHTS

- The ERP solution forms the data foundation from which Tax collects its data needs. If Tax is not properly engaged, the implementation of an ERP solution can represent significant risk for Tax and the organization as a whole.
- The traditional emphasis on Tax and ERP solutions has been to ensure that the organization has appropriately accounted for transactional (indirect) taxes. Leading organizations develop ERP solutions for Tax that take into account four areas: direct tax, indirect tax, tax reporting, and tax data archiving.
- Leading organizations are managing tax knowledge and processes beyond the transactional business activities. These organizations support Tax with the right tools and capabilities to create and sustain a world-class Tax function.

FROM INSIGHT TO ACTION

DEVELOP THE TAX BUSINESS CASE FOR AN ERP SOLUTION
The need to meet tax reporting obligations is well understood; however, it is important to identify the individual components of the business case for Tax. This will help drive the scope and budgetary considerations for the ERP solution.

DESIGN THE CHART OF ACCOUNTS WITH TAX IN MIND
Ensure that Tax is part of the Chart of Accounts design, not only in the section specific to Tax, but also in areas in which Tax relies on detailed information to support reporting and disclosure.

CREATE COMMON SOLUTIONS FOR TAX
Although Tax requirements may vary across each tax jurisdiction, the underlying capabilities in the ERP solution may be largely the same. Success in integrating Tax requirements in the design will come from ensuring that the capabilities in the ERP solution are utilized to their fullest extent. Solutions should be developed with scalability and multi-jurisdictional use in mind.

REFERENCES

1. Donald T. Nicolaisen, Remarks at the Tax Council Institute Conference on The Corporate Tax Practice: *Responding to the New Challenges of a Changing Landscape*, Washington, D.C., February 11, 2004, http://www.sec.gov/news.

2. The Hackett Group, *World-Class Finance Executives Deliver Benefits Equal to 60 Percent of the Total Cost of Typical Finance Operations by Cutting Effective Tax Rates and Days Sales Outstanding*, November 1, 2004, http://www.thehackettgroup.com.

3. Schulman Ronca and Bucuvalas Inc., *Corporate Tax Department Survey*, Tax Executive Institute Survey, 2004–2005, Figure 43, http://www.tei.org.

4. European Commission (Directorate-General Tax and Customs Union), *European Tax Survey*, November 2004, http://europa.eu.int/comm/taxation.

5. Schulman Ronca and Bucuvalas Inc., *Corporate Tax Department Survey*, Tax Executive Institute Survey, 2004–2005, Figure 29, http://www.tei.org.

6. Ibid., Figure 33.

CHAPTER 8

Implications of Regulatory Compliance

COMPLIANCE: AN OVERVIEW

Finance organizations today are under constant pressure to deliver increased levels of business unit support. Organizations are looking for Finance to become a value-added partner with the business units – to help improve their performance – which means the Finance organization is now becoming more involved in the core managerial and strategic business processes and major corporate projects of the business units.

Finance's traditional focus on transaction processing has left little time to spend on more strategic, value-added services. These changes, which include Finance process improvements, better information technology, and increasing utilization of business process outsourcing, have led to a major reduction in time allocated to transaction processing and reporting activities and more time for the Finance organization to focus on this desired partnering. Additionally, Finance is developing people who have the skills and tools to play this broader role in managing the business.

Yet even as Finance organizations focus on better business partnering, they must still flawlessly execute their primary roles: ensuring Generally Accepted Accounting Principles (GAAP) and Securities and Exchange Commission (SEC) compliance, producing accurate external forecasts and explaining any fluctuations from expectations, providing timely and relevant management reporting to the business units, ensuring consistent adherence to internal controls at all levels, and assessing and proactively managing operational risk. Add to that mix new responsibility for supporting compliance with recent and complicated regulations, and the criticality of sophisticated technological tools to help manage the complexity becomes apparent.

In this chapter we discuss two of the most significant recent developments, the Sarbanes-Oxley Act and International Financial Reporting Standards. These regulations will add considerable impetus to an organization's drive for a value-adding ERP solution. Although ERP solutions are still in their infancy in meeting compliance for these specific regulations, their demonstrated ability to consolidate and streamline reporting has executives clamoring for significant enhancements to these products.

THE LEAD-UP TO SARBANES-OXLEY

Throughout its history, the accounting profession has weathered its fair share of infamy. For example, McKesson & Robbins, Penn Central Railroad, Equity Funding, the Savings and Loan industry and, of course, Enron, have all taken center stage on television and radio, while making headlines on the front page of every major newspaper and magazine.

Recent accounting scandals began a snowball effect; gradually more and more fraud became exposed. Beginning with Xerox in 2000 through Krispy Kreme in 2005, no industry, it seemed, was spared from the taint.

These accounting scandals have resulted in an increase in financial restatements. In fact, other than a small decline in 2003, financial restatements have grown steadily since 1998 (see Figure 8.1).

Following each major incident, numerous changes in GAAP, Generally Accepted Auditing Standards (GAAS), professional standards, and government regulations were implemented with varying degrees of success (see Figure 8.2).

On July 19, 2002, WorldCom, with $107 billion in assets, became the largest company ever to file for bankruptcy. This filing came on the heels of Enron's bankruptcy filing in late 2001, which involved $63 billion in assets. The financial woes of these and other corporations hit the larger economy hard. Between March 2000 and July 2002, the Wilshire Total Market Index declined over $7 trillion − a 42% decline.[1] This loss in value impacted on thousands of jobs, destroyed life savings, and caused large declines in 401(k) funds and pension balances.

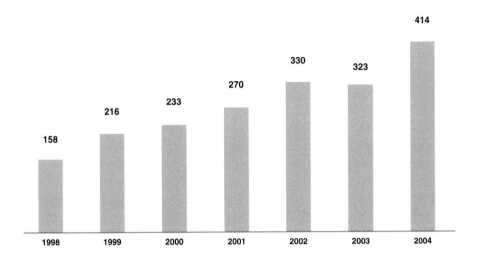

Source: Huron Consulting Group Analysis, January 2005; Edgar database of 10K and 10Q revised filings

Figure 8.1 *Number of financial restatements by year filed*

These reporting irregularities and improprieties, although devastating to so many, did have one positive outcome – far greater public awareness. Constant scrutiny by the media has placed corporations under the microscope, which has led institutional investors, employees, and the public to have higher standards for corporate behavior. In addition, rating agencies have increased their vigilance, which has resulted in both an increase and faster downgrades in credit. Perhaps most importantly, governmental agencies have now become quite concerned about corporate governance.

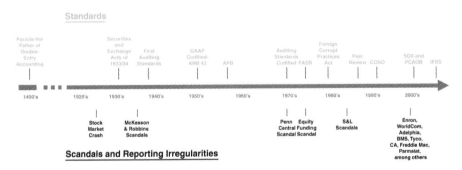

Figure 8.2 *History of major accounting scandals, reporting irregularities, and resulting standards*

SARBANES-OXLEY: AN OVERVIEW

On July 30, 2002, in response to the unprecedented financial reporting irregularities and corporate improprieties, President George W. Bush signed the Sarbanes-Oxley Act into U.S. law. In addition to U.S.-based companies, the Act also covers non-U.S. companies that are listed and trade their American Depositary Receipts (ADRs) on a U.S. exchange.

Sarbanes-Oxley is the most significant legislation to affect the accounting profession and corporate accountability since the Securities Act of 1933 and the Exchange Act of 1934. It enforces governance and fiduciary responsibility and establishes a number of provisions, including the establishment of an independent, not-for-profit Public Company Accounting Oversight Board (PCAOB), enhanced rules for auditor independence and responsibility, and stricter accountability for senior management. As President Bush declared, "The era of low standards and false profits is over; no boardroom in America is above or beyond the law."

Figure 8.3 provides a brief overview of the 11 titles of the Sarbanes-Oxley Act, covering new requirements for an independent oversight board, auditor independence, corporate governance, additional financial disclosures, corporate and criminal fraud, white-collar crime, and corporate tax returns.

Compliance is no longer optional. Even those companies not specifically affected by the legislation are finding that compliance with Sarbanes-Oxley has become a de facto requirement for doing business. For example, privately held companies, as well as many foreign publicly held companies, are complying on a voluntary basis. They feel that the Act demonstrates better governance and has created stronger partnering with both vendors and customers. Many high-growth electronics and technology companies are adapting to Sarbanes-Oxley voluntarily in anticipation of a future Initial Public Offering (IPO). Sarbanes-Oxley has become part of everyday life, and everyone within a corporation needs to understand the criticality and importance of accurate financial reporting, ethics, and business principles.

Many CFOs are now realizing that they should have started their compliance initiatives sooner. Although they may not yet have been discovered, the longer these companies go without being compliant, the greater their future risk of exposure.

Although the discussion of The Sarbanes-Oxley Act in this section is considered accurate, it is not presented in enough detail to be relied on

Title	Summary
Title I Public Company Accounting Oversight Board	• Establishes an independent, nongovernmental board to oversee the audit of public companies to protect the interests of investors and further public confidence in independent audit reports. • Defines the major responsibilities of this board. • Requires public accounting firms to register with the board and take certain actions in order to perform audits of public companies.
Title II Auditor Independence	• Sets forth required actions by registered public accounting firms ("external auditors"), audit committees and companies that are intended to strengthen auditor independence. • Legislates certain services, generally consistent with current independence rules, as unlawful if performed by the external auditor.
Title III Corporate Responsibility	• Requires audit committees to be independent and undertake specified oversight responsibilities. • Requires CEOs and CFOs to certify quarterly and annual reports to the SEC, including making representations about the effectiveness of specified controls. • Provides rules of conduct for companies and their officers regarding pension blackout periods and certain other matters. • Requires the SEC to issue rules requiring attorneys in certain roles to report violations of securities laws to a company's CEO or chief legal counsel and, if no action is taken, to the audit committee.
Title IV Enhanced Financial Disclosures	• Requires companies to provide enhanced disclosures, including a report on the effectiveness of internal controls and procedures for financial reporting (along with external auditor attestation of that report) and disclosures covering off-balance sheet transactions and pro forma financial information. • Requires disclosures regarding code of ethics for senior financial officers and reporting of certain waivers. • Requires accelerated disclosures by management, directors and principal stockholders concerning certain transactions involving company securities.
Title V Analyst Conflicts of Interest	• Requires the SEC to adopt rules to address conflicts of interest that can arise when securities analysts recommend equity securities in research reports and public appearances.
Title VI Commission Resources and Authority	• Provides additional funding to the SEC. • Gives the SEC and federal courts more authority to censure and impose certain prohibitions on persons and entities.
Title VII Studies and Reports	• Directs federal regulatory bodies to conduct studies regarding consolidation of accounting firms; credit rating agencies; violators, violations; and enforcement actions involving securities laws; certain roles of investment banks and financial advisors; and certain other matters.
Title VIII Corporate and Criminal Fraud Accountability	• Provides tougher criminal penalties for altering documents, defrauding shareholders and certain other forms of obstruction of justice and securities fraud. • Makes debt non-dischargeable if incurred in violation of securities fraud laws. • Protects employees of companies who provide evidence of fraud.
Title IX White-Collar Crime Penalty Enhancements	• Provides that any person who attempts to commit white-collar crime shall be treated under the law as if the person had committed the crime. • Enhances penalties and sentencing guidelines for certain white-collar crimes, such as mail and wire fraud and ERISA violations. • Requires CEOs and CFOs to certify in their periodic reports to the SEC that their financial statements fully comply with the requirements of the Securities Exchange Act of 1934, and imposes penalties for certifying a misleading or fraudulent report.
Title X Corporate Tax Returns	• Conveys sense of the Senate (the opinion of the Senate) that the CEO should sign a company's federal income tax return.
Title XI Corporate Fraud and Accountability	• Provides additional authority to regulatory bodies and courts to take various actions, including fines or imprisonment, with regard to tampering with records, impeding official proceedings, taking extraordinary payments, retaliating against corporate whistleblowers and certain other matters involving corporate fraud.

Figure 8.3 *Summary of Sarbanes-Oxley provisions*

exclusively for compliance. Readers should consult the Sarbanes-Oxley Act itself, along with counsel from financial and legal advisors, to understand all the Act's implications more fully.

Key Provisions of Sarbanes–Oxley

As organizations grapple with the intricacies of compliance with these provisions, they are desperately looking for the technology tools that will help them solve the compliance problem.

A number of these provisions should have particular relevance and provide additional impetus to companies' drives to implement or enhance ERP solutions. In the sections that follow, we discuss these specific provisions and how ERPs should fit into the picture in the near future.

Title III, Section 302: Corporate Responsibility for Financial Reports

Section 302 was one of the first sections of Sarbanes-Oxley to become effective. It clearly assigns responsibility to the CEO and CFO for establishing and maintaining disclosure controls. Furthermore, their certification indicates that they have performed an evaluation of such controls and procedures within 90 days of the filing date.

As companies looked at their financial reporting systems with an eye to compliance with Section 302, it quickly became obvious that their systems were too complex and did not provide the reporting transparency needed. Now, many companies are simplifying their financial close and reporting process through tighter integration with legacy systems, simplified interfaces, and greater integration with the budgeting and forecasting process, as discussed in Chapter 2. They are also using scorecards and key performance indicators that are more focused on both financial and nonfinancial data and enhanced drill-down capability through the use of data warehouses, as discussed in Chapter 3. Now that these top-level executives are on line, all data are being strictly reviewed. Companies are reviewing and simplifying or eliminating journal entries and reclassification entries; standardizing Charts of Accounts and rationalizing the number of accounts; questioning allocations across business units as to their business purpose; and rationalizing reports to ensure data integrity and reporting consistency.

Title IV, Section 404: Management Assessment of Internal Controls

After a number of postponed effective dates, Section 404 became effective for most filers for their first fiscal period ending after November 15, 2004. Section 404 requires each annual report of the issuer to contain an internal control report that:

- States management's responsibility for establishing and maintaining an adequate internal control structure and procedures for financial reporting.
- Contains an assessment, as of the end of the issuer's fiscal year, of the effectiveness of the internal control structure and procedures of the issuer for financial reporting.
- Requires the company's external auditor to attest to and report on the assessment made by the management of the issuer.

Individuals, corporations, and major auditing firms alike assumed that when Sarbanes-Oxley was passed into law, it would include a definitive and prescriptive approach to complying with Section 404. When the effective date for Section 404 was postponed numerous times, many assumed it was because this formalized approach was being deliberated in great detail. Finally, on March 9, 2004, the PCAOB provided additional guidance for Section 404(b) in its Auditing Standard No. 2: *An Audit of Internal Controls over Financial Reporting Performed in Conjunction with an Audit of Financials.* However, although this standard provides guidance for companies in developing their approach, it is not the definitive solution expected. Companies now realize there is no single approach for compliance, nor should there be. Larger, complex, and multinational companies must have a more extensive and advanced internal control system than smaller companies.

Most companies are using the Committee of Sponsoring Organizations (COSO) framework as a basis for their 404 compliance. The COSO framework allows a company to customize its approach for the effectiveness and efficiency of operations, safeguarding of assets, reliability of financial and management reports, and compliance with various laws and regulations – depending on its own unique situation.

The COSO framework was jointly developed in 1992 by the American Institute of Certified Public Accountants, the Institute of Internal Auditors, the American Accounting Association, the Institute of Management Accountants, and the Financial Executives Institute (FEI). The COSO framework is titled Internal Control – An Integrated Framework.

In addition to the COSO framework for general guidelines, most companies are using the Control Objective for Information and Related Technology (CobiT) framework for their IT guidance. CobiT provides guidance for implementing effective IT practices to ensure that an organization has sound controls in place, is reducing risks, and has implemented cost-effective processes. It works within the COSO framework as well as with numerous other related standards.

Section 404 has probably required as much, if not more, effort as Y2K compliance did a few years ago. The first-year cost for most companies, as reported by the FEI, is averaging $1 million per billion dollars of revenue.[2] For smaller companies, this ratio is even higher. Many groups, including AeA (the United States' largest high-tech trade association), have estimated that this first-year cost, for all compliance-related activities, could be between $30 and 35 billion when all the books are closed.[3] Part of that first-year cost stemmed from the expectation that the delays in 404 were related to the development of absolute compliance rules by the SEC. When what the SEC actually released was merely guidelines, many companies took an extremely conservative approach to compliance to avoid becoming the next major headline.

It is not surprising, then, that many C-level executives have been very vocal that the cost of their 404 compliance to date has exceeded its benefits. However, most will also agree that financial reports are now more accurate and reliable and that the process has helped to detect and prevent fraud. In addition, there has been an increase in investor confidence. Fortunately, future costs of compliance will probably be significantly less. Most companies now have all the necessary documentation in place, and for them, future compliance will just be a matter of updates. AMR Research has estimated that the cost for the period 2005 to 2009 will be $80 billion or, on average, $20 billion per year.[4] A recent FEI study echoes this assertion; 85 percent of executives expect a 40 percent decrease in cost.[5]

Six percent of the companies that initially were required to comply with Section 404 (for the most part, those with fiscal years ending on November 30, 2004) failed to do so. This number quickly grew to almost 8 percent for all companies that had fiscal years ending through December 31, 2004. Virtually all industries have had some difficulties, with very few achieving 100 percent compliance initially. The primary weaknesses that were cited in annual filings included the inability to close the books properly, inventory accounting, revenue recognition, taxes, accruals and reserves, and organizational deficiencies (skills, number of qualified professionals, and so on). According to a report by *Compliance Week* in early April 2005, 94 percent of those that failed reported that "they did not maintain effective internal controls over financial reporting."[6]

These failures have caused a significant amount of remediation effort in ERP solutions; virtually no module has escaped. In fact, according to AMR Research, 32 percent of the remediation cost for companies is technology related.[7] The focus of investment will be on compliance management software and continuous controls for monitoring software. In addition to software functionality that needs to be remediated, companies are simultaneously reviewing and strengthening access rights, user authentication, segregation of duties, and delegation of authority.

Title IV, Section 409: Real-Time Disclosure

Prior to Sarbanes-Oxley, the timelines for reporting events were longer and allowed a company to delay disclosure of many significant events. These events (including changes in control, acquisition, or disposition of a significant amount of assets, bankruptcy or receivership, changes in certifying accountant, resignation of directors, and changes in the corporate Code of Ethics) could be reported on Form 8-K 5 business days or 15 calendar days later, depending on the event. As a result, investors could not make up-to-the-minute evaluations of a company.

As part of Section 409, in August 2004 the SEC added eight additional events that need to be reported on an 8-K:

- Entry into a material agreement that is not in the ordinary course of business
- Termination of such a material nonordinary course agreement
- Creation of a material direct financial obligation or a material obligation under an off-balance sheet arrangement
- Triggering events that accelerate or decrease a material direct financial obligation or a material obligation under an off-balance sheet arrangement
- Material costs associated with exit or disposal activities
- Costs incurred during an exit from a business or disposal of an asset
- Notice of a delisting
- A decision stating that previously issued financial statements or audit reports can no longer be relied on.

A number of events that were reported to the SEC in other periodic reports now also will trigger an 8-K filing; these include disclosures of the sale of unregistered securities, modifications of shareholder's rights, departure or the election of directors or principal officers, and amendments to the corporate charter or by-laws.

Not only have new events been added, but the reporting deadlines have changed as well. Because of the complexity of some of these events, as well as the computations that were required, the SEC finally settled on four business days for reporting these Section 404 events – quite an aggressive timetable.

HOW ERP VENDORS WILL ASSIST WITH SARBANES-OXLEY COMPLIANCE

With the Sarbanes-Oxley Act so new and with so many critical compliance requirements to meet, those companies that needed to comply first had a very immature software market to provide assistance. Many companies struggled with their first year of compliance, and the majority did not implement specialized software to assist them in the process.

In 2004 and early 2005, virtually no critical mass of any one software tool for compliance existed. In fact, most companies used a combination of various collaboration tools and spreadsheets, such as Microsoft Sharepoint, Microsoft Word, and Microsoft Excel. Vendors such as Certus, HandySoft, SAS, and Stellent, among others, also offered various point solutions. In addition, many public accounting firms had tools that they created themselves. However, as companies complete their first year of compliance, the time has come for them to review the market again and decide whether their current solution needs to be replaced with a product that is beginning to mature.

While development of compliance tools continues, the two major ERP vendors, Oracle and SAP, have tools currently within their solutions that will foster compliance with various aspects of Sarbanes-Oxley. These tools should be tailored to meet each individual company's compliance program.

For example, Oracle offers its Internal Controls Manager (OICM) to assist with the documenting and testing of internal controls (for Section 404 compliance) along with monitoring for ongoing compliance. Other functionality of OICM that should assist with Sarbanes-Oxley compliance includes:

- Defining and managing business processes by using a familiar spreadsheet interface, which ensures controls through flexible workflow
- Defining and managing risks and controls in a risk library
- Managing audit operations through the creation of risk assessment surveys
- Enabling the certification process through a tool that allows the user to deliver a list of processes, risks, and controls that were added, modified, or deleted within the system.

These capabilities foster compliance with the sections of Sarbanes-Oxley emphasized earlier in the chapter, by mitigating the risks of certification for corporate executives and by helping to manage internal controls.

PeopleSoft offers the Internal Controls Enforcer (IC Enforcer). IC Enforcer helps companies comply with Section 404 of Sarbanes-Oxley by moving beyond simple documentation of internal control processes to enabling companies to monitor key controls, proactively alert management to changes, and enforce accountability across all levels of the organization. IC Enforcer has prebuilt diagnostics that continuously monitor controls and alert management to changes in transaction systems;

comprehensive survey tools built into its data model to measure compliance on both automated and manual controls; a document repository and process automation to strengthen controls and streamline ongoing costs; and rules-based dashboards that drive accountability for compliance and enforce security throughout the organization.

SAP's mySAP ERP Financials includes Management of Internal Controls (MIC), which can assist with the annual and quarterly certifications that are required under Section 302, as well as with the disclosures required by Section 409. It allows the user to design, establish, and maintain disclosure controls and procedures; evaluate and report on the effectiveness of those controls and procedures (per Section 404); and indicate any significant changes, including any deficiencies and material weaknesses that have occurred since the most recent evaluation.

The Management of the Audit Information System (AIS) component of mySAP ERP Financials includes an auditor's toolbox to help comply with corporate governance requirements, such as sections 302 and 404. The solution delivers comprehensive functionality for system and business audits, enables drill-down audit trails to the document level for exception analysis, tests financial system security controls, and provides structure reports for better auditing.

Finally, the SAP Compliance Calibrator allows immediate and extensive checking of ERP authorization compliance; automated segregation of duties analysis and monitoring of critical transactions; instant assessment of authorization risk for business users, auditors, and IT security staff; blocking of violations before committing to production; fast remediation, with direct drill-down to root causes; and avoidance of manual analysis and false positives. These capabilities all can have a decided impact on the level of comfort corporate executives should have in certifying their corporate financial results.

In summary, Oracle and SAP have not yet fully matured.

INTERNATIONAL FINANCIAL REPORTING STANDARDS

Like Sarbanes-Oxley compliance, International Financial Reporting Standards (IFRS) present another significant challenge to the management of many companies. The information required for various IFRS disclosures requires far more flexibility and multidimensional transaction handling than before. Major ERP software solutions such as Oracle, PeopleSoft, and SAP have different technical approaches to address IFRS requirements; however, they commonly advocate a single global ERP instance and harmonized local accounting processes. To support more efficient and timely financial reporting that provides management with the maximum time to review and understand their financials under IFRS presentation, ERP solutions must be updated. Furthermore, since IFRS is a European Union (EU) strategy to bolster its capital markets, ERP solutions will also need to be focused on providing enhanced performance management capabilities.

In the remaining sections, we will provide a background of IFRS, an overview of its impact, and a discussion of how the three major ERP solutions can assist with IFRS adoption.

IFRS: AN OVERVIEW

IFRS constitutes a set of accounting standards currently issued by the International Accounting Standards Board (IASB). In 2002, the European Council of Ministers passed a regulation that requires publicly listed EU companies to comply with IFRS for the financial years beginning during 2005. It is estimated that 7,000 listed companies in the European Union are affected by this change.

IFRS does not change any local EU statutory reporting requirements; furthermore, IFRS adoption can be deferred to 2007 if an EU company trades its stock on a U.S. stock exchange and uses U.S. GAAP.

Although there are significant initial adoption costs, the single and comparable cross-border GAAP will ultimately benefit investors by reducing the administrative costs of companies that have to maintain financial statements for multiple statutory reporting jurisdictions. Even before mandated adoption by the European Union, many large listed companies from Switzerland and Germany had already adopted IFRS. In addition, IFRS has been adopted (or will soon be adopted) as the national GAAP in Russia, Australia, Malaysia, Singapore, and the Caribbean.

The Impact of IFRS

Initial Adoption

The initial adoption of IFRS requires a restatement of historical data so that there are at least two years of comparable data in the IFRS financial statements. In addition, initial adoption of IFRS will probably increase the volatility of the company, as both the company management and the capital markets need more than several quarters to acclimate to the new way of presenting financial performance to their various stakeholders and analysts. To mitigate the typically slow start, some EU companies have been proactive and already implemented IFRS upgrades to their systems – in some cases, years ahead of the EU compliance deadline – to improve their competitive position and reputation in the marketplace. For example, DekaBank, one of Germany's top financial services organizations, implemented a state-of-the-art financial management system and statutory accounting system based on IFRS. Its custom SAP R/3 solution was up and running by 2003 – well ahead of the EU compliance deadline – and became a lever for competitive advantage.

Europe and the United States

Despite the cross-border agreement on accounting standards, within each country, local (national) tax requirements, laws, and regulations still apply. Therefore, affected companies may still have to prepare at least two sets of financial statements, which will continue to require resource time and expense to prepare. Additionally, until January 2005, many European companies listed on both U.S. and European stock exchanges were able to use U.S. GAAP financial statements exclusively. However, with the adoption of IFRS, that option is no longer available for EU capital markets. Practically speaking, even nonlisted EU companies may still be forced to comply with IFRS, as the capital market increases its demand for comparable company information to make its investment decisions.

IFRS is not exclusively an EU issue. It could also impact on U.S. companies, if:

- A U.S. company's international parent uses IFRS
- A U.S. company's foreign subsidiary uses IFRS
- A U.S. company has foreign operations
- A U.S. company issues debt or equity in a foreign capital market
- A U.S. company's foreign customers, vendors, or lessors require IFRS statements
- A significant foreign investor in a U.S. company uses IFRS.[8]

The Benefits of IFRS

Despite the initial costs of implementation, IFRS has a variety of significant benefits. First, it should improve access to capital for many companies. For example, companies that adopt this standard (which is often higher than local standards) will probably present a more attractive risk to a bank. Adhering to the dominant GAAP, then, becomes a means for a competitive edge. The second benefit is that globalization of GAAP leads to better comparison between companies and across borders, which in turn improves relations with investors and analysts, who have greater confidence in reported financial data. Finally, adoption of IFRS provides the impetus to standardize global business practices to increase the efficiency of financial reporting.

IFRS should be viewed as more than a change in accounting standards or another regulation requirement. It is also an opportunity for a company to enhance its performance management capabilities significantly through improved information to management for strategic decision making and more timely delivery of management information through streamlined reporting systems and faster publication of period-end results. Some companies also have concluded that IFRS adoption is an opportunity to rationalize subconsolidations and reengineer Order to Cash and Supply Chain transaction data to capture enhanced segment and geographical information.

Ultimately, providing IFRS disclosures requires complete visibility into all aspects of a company's businesses and operations, with continuous monitoring for changes and proactive management of disclosure obligations. In other words, adhering to IFRS increases the overall attention and focus management must give to performance management.

Key Differences between IFRS and U.S. GAAP

IFRS and U.S. GAAP are based on different frameworks of accounting standards. U.S. GAAP, established by the Financial Accounting Standards Board (FASB), is a "rules-based" framework, whereas IFRS, developed by the IASB, are principles based. The U.S. rules-based system is based on conservatism and a legal form guided by very specific requirements that result in a "letter-of-the-law" compliance approach; the foundation of IFRS is fundamentally based on "fair-value" measurement principles for assets and liabilities.

Critics of U.S. GAAP argue that the rules-based approach can distort the economic substance of financial statements. In contrast, the economics underlying each transaction or material event are the foundation of IFRS, along with the broader concept of exercising prudence in preparing financial statements. As a result, IFRS requires a higher level of professional judgment than U.S. GAAP. (This is one reason the U.S. SEC remains concerned about IFRS enforcement.)

Figure 8.4 outlines some key differences between U.S. GAAP and IFRS in three main categories, namely: definitions and explanations, accounting and measurement principles, and disclosure requirements.[9]

Although Figure 8.4 outlines some of the key differences between IFRS and U.S. GAAP and is considered accurate, it is not a complete list of differences or presented in enough detail to be exclusively relied on for compliance.

Global Convergence

The FASB and IASB have been in discussions to converge accounting principles and since 2002 have agreed to coordinate their project agendas to eliminate differences between their respective standards. Progress has been made in a number of areas; however, full convergence is a long-term target significantly influenced by a variety of factors, namely, the SEC and its oversight of the dominant capital market in the United States.

Topic	IFRS Treatment	US GAAP Treatment
Scope of Group Consolidation	IAS 27 looks at governance risk and benefits for control to determine consolidation.	US GAAP consolidation is determined by a majority of voting rights.
Asset Impairment	In IAS 36, asset impairment is triggered if an asset's carrying amount exceeds the higher of the asset's carrying amount or exceeds the discounted present value of expected future cash flows and net selling price. If certain tests are met, impairment can be reversed.	In US GAAP, an asset is impaired if the carrying amount exceeds the asset's undiscounted expected future cash flows. US GAAP is more conservative in that it does not allow impairment reversals.
Basis of Property, Plant and Equipment.	IAS 16 allows either historical cost or fair value.	US GAAP requires historical cost.
Provisions	IAS 37 allows "best" estimate to settle obligation, generally using the expected-value method.	US GAAP mandates the low range of possible amounts.
Goodwill	IAS 22 defines that goodwill is capitalized and amortized over its estimated useful life, which is presumed to be 20 years or less, subject to an impairment test.	In US GAAP, goodwill must be capitalized, but only subject to an impairment test.
Fair-Value Accounting	IAS 39 has the option to measure at fair value any financial asset or liability through the income statement.	US GAAP does not allow this.
Hedging	IAS 39 requires that hedges are specifically matched to measure effectiveness.	US GAAP does not if certain conditions are met.
Stock Options	IAS 19 does not provide guidance on recognition and measurement.	US GAAP requires that stock options are expensed, however does not provide guidance on which valuation method to use.
Limitation on Recognizing Pension Assets	IAS 19 limits the recognition of pension assets in excess of unrecognized past-service cost and actuarial losses plus the present value of benefits available from refunds or reduction of future contributions to the plan.	US GAAP provides no such limitations.
Financial Instruments	IAS 32 defines financial instruments as liabilities or equity in accordance with the substance of their contractual agreement on initial recognition.	US GAAP classifies financial instruments based on legal form.
Segment Reporting	IAS 14 requires disclosures for "primary" and "secondary" segments and by business line and geographic area. IAS 1 requires segments to be reported on IFRS GAAP measures.	US GAAP requires only one basis of segmentation as reported internally to top management. US GAAP segments are based on whatever measurements are used for internal reporting purposes.

Source: Deloitte. IAS Plus, June 2004, Special Edition, www.iasplus.com

Figure 8.4 *Key differences between IFRS and U.S. GAAP*

Apart from U.S. GAAP, Japan remains the only other G7 market with divergent accounting standards. One possible scenario is that IFRS, U.S. GAAP, and Japanese GAAP never completely converge but are mutually accepted by all global markets.

Addressing IFRS Implementation Challenges with ERP Solutions

Adapting technology solutions to produce the required information for IFRS is a challenge for most companies. Fortunately, the inherent flexibility and multidimensionality of leading ERP solutions position them well to help companies adopt IFRS.

Preparing financial statements under IFRS requires that ERP solutions extract more operational data from the organization than any demand of local GAAP. For example, according to IFRS, a segment is any business unit that accounts for more than 10 percent of revenue.[10] IFRS requires that each segment externally disclose a full balance sheet, income statement, and cash flow with comparable prior year data. Since management, discussion, and analysis (MD&A) may be required for this external disclosure, the ERP solution will need to support year-on-year variance analyses at a level of comprehensive detail not currently available to most companies internally.

IFRS will also require new account lines, General Ledgers, and consolidation solutions, changes to existing operational solutions, and changes to report systems and interfaces. Sub-ledgers will be critical for heavily impacted accounts, including:

- **Financial Instruments.** Per IAS 39, the audit trail of specific hedges matched to specific underlying transactions needs to be available. This requirement will ultimately mean that Treasury, Accounts Payable, and Accounts Receivable systems will have to be far more integrated.
- **Fixed Assets.** Per IAS 16, the basis of assets could be either fair value or historical cost. The basis should also include major inspection and overhaul costs as part of the asset.
- **Inventory.** Inventory needs to account for the reversals of write-downs permitted under IFRS.

Comparison of IFRS Handling by Major ERP Solutions

All three of the leading ERP software packages, Oracle, PeopleSoft, and SAP, have functionality that will help companies adopt IFRS.

Oracle advocates the Common Data Model as its approach to IFRS, so that all accounting from any country is performed in a single database to produce a single source of financial data. Worldwide consistency is a fundamental part of the design philosophy of the Oracle E-Business Suite. Oracle's approach enables companies to maintain a common basis (or definition) for global data and to report data in any format required. Furthermore, Oracle's financial software is designed to accommodate a global single instance.

Oracle Financials supports multiple languages, major international currencies, and local regulations. With its integrated architecture, single data model, and analytic tools, companies can roll up, view, and report global financial performance at a corporate level in the desired accounting standard, language, and currency, while adhering to local requirements.

Multinational companies typically use multiple ERP solutions, which makes it difficult to extract and collate data into a consolidated company-wide report. Therefore, in addition to harmonizing local business practices, consolidating and centralizing accounting systems is another option. Consolidated Oracle accounting systems avoid manual reconciliation of intercompany balances and are better positioned to achieve much faster and higher quality reporting.

PeopleSoft Enterprise General Ledger efficiently manages the multi-GAAP entries required to provide a unified, consistent data source for reporting and analysis. It is based on a flexible accounting structure that allows companies to define how they want to capture and access their financial information based on IFRS and local GAAP requirements. In addition, PeopleSoft Global Consolidations enables companies to consolidate financial information for fast and accurate IFRS financial reporting requirements.

SAP addresses the demands of IFRS with parallel accounting in the enhanced General Ledger functionality of mySAP. Parallel accounting allows for a complete, separate ledger environment within the General Ledger module for each different accounting treatment. In addition, each additional ledger can be viewed in a variety of currency options.

Once parallel ledgers are created, all postings for accounts that do not have any valuation differences are posted to the main General Ledger and, at a summary level, to the additional ledger. Valuation differences create alternative valuation postings only to specifically defined accounts in the additional ledger. To the extent there are other corporate GAAP adjustments, they are posted only to the additional/special ledgers.

Parallel accounting is advantageous if there are not a large number of General Ledger accounts and companies require a complete and separate set of books. The downside, in addition to the increased volume of data, is that any special account required in the additional ledger has to be in the main General Ledger, which means the General Ledger is not simplified.

THE HACKETT GROUP ON COMPLIANCE IMPACTS

With the recent trend toward increased regulatory controls and reporting, it should come as no surprise that compliance management costs have increased for all companies. The intricacies of complying with the Sarbanes-Oxley Act have created an enormous burden for all publicly held corporations, compounded by an across-the-board increase of external audit fees.

However, CFOs at world-class organizations have been able to, if not stem the tide, at least slow the growth of this cost area. Peer group companies have seen compliance management costs go up over the past two years from 0.074 percent as a percent of revenue to 0.094 percent. World-class organizations, on the other hand, experienced an increase of just 0.043 percent to 0.060 percent — a lower proportional cost today than what peer groups managed to achieve two years ago. The difference is the use of best practices at world-class corporations.

It is worth noting that although the raison d'être for Sarbanes-Oxley is consistent with the way that world-class organizations view controls and risk management, the aggressive deadlines that came with Sarbanes-Oxley caused many executives to implement procedures that can be at odds with Hackett-Certified™ Practices, such as simplification and statistical process control. However, despite an overall slowdown in improvement, the fact remains that world-class companies continue to widen the gap between themselves and the average company.

continued

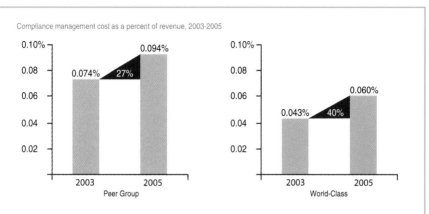

Compliance management cost as a percent of revenue, 2003-2005

Source: The Hackett Group

Looking ahead, The Hackett Group believes that, depending on their position relative to world-class organizations, Finance organizations will either choose to remain on course in their goal to be a strategic business partner, or they will readopt the "corporate cop" role common in the early 1990s. This means that the existing gap between world-class Finance organizations and others will widen even more.

CFO INSIGHTS

- Compliance with the Sarbanes-Oxley Act is no longer optional. Everyone within a corporation needs to understand the criticality and importance of accurate financial reporting, ethics, and business principles. Corporate training programs are being created and enhanced to communicate the importance of Sarbanes-Oxley.
- IFRS adoption is a challenge to most organizations, because of both the increased scope of disclosure and the increased volatility of the company. Company management and capital markets need more than several quarters to acclimate to the new way of presenting financial performance to their various stakeholders and analysts.

- IFRS should be seen as an opportunity for a company to enhance its performance management capabilities significantly, improve information to management for strategic decision making, and provide more timely delivery of management information by streamlining reporting systems and publishing period-end results faster.
- Flexibility and multidimensionality are critical performance factors for ERP solutions. Preparing financial statements under IFRS requires that ERP solutions extract more operational data from the organization than any demand of local GAAP.

FROM INSIGHT TO ACTION

LEVERAGE EXISTING ERP FUNCTIONALITY TO MEET SARBANES-OXLEY COMPLIANCE

Although ERP solutions regarding compliance are not yet fully mature, organizations can still make use of the existing vendor capabilities. This positions them to upgrade more efficiently and quickly to the future improved compliance applications, when available from the ERP vendors.

PREPARE AND PLAN FOR COMPLEXITY AND TIME REQUIRED TO IMPLEMENT IFRS

The new standards involve changes in presentation, new valuation rules, and additional disclosure requirements. A successful conversion must plan and manage change across business processes, technologies, and the organization, affecting both the group and business unit levels. The length of time needed to complete an IFRS implementation depends on several factors, such as the complexity of the business, size and geographic diversity of the company, and familiarity among accounting staff with IFRS and how it differs from local GAAP.

continued

EXPECT CONFIGURATION CHANGES ACROSS MULTIPLE MODULES FOR IFRS

Assessing the impact on existing ERP configurations requires that the IFRS standards be mapped to the applicable ERP module(s). For most organizations, several ERP modules will require configuration changes to meet the new compliance criteria.

CONSIDER OTHER REPORTING EFFORTS AND PROCESS CHANGES IN CONJUNCTION WITH THE ADOPTION OF IFRS

Group-wide harmonization is achieved by integration of legal and management-reporting entities. Reporting speed is improved by reduction of manual activities, prompt provision of actual financial information, and shortening of reporting cycles through automation. Management is better supported by consistent reports for all legal entities and business units.

REFERENCES

1. CNN Money, July 11, 2002, http://www.money.cnn.com.

2. Bruce Bartlett, "Other Comments: Sandbagging the Market," *Forbes* 176 (2005): 134, http://www.forbes.com.

3. AccountingWeb.com, *Internal Control Compliance Cost Could Top $35 Billion*, February 14, 2005, http://wwwaccountingweb.com.

4. AMR Research, *Spending in an Age of Compliance 2005*, March 14, 2005, http://www.armresearch.com.

5. Financial Executives International, *Survey on SOX Section 404 Implementation*, March 2005, http://www.fei.org.

6. Compliance Week and Raisch Financial Information Services, *Internal Control Report Scorecard*, April 4, 2005, http://www.complianceweek.com.

7. John Hagerty and Fenella Scott, *SOX Spending for 2006 to Exceed $6B*, AMR Research, November 29, 2005, http://www.amrresearch.com.

8. D. Gannon and Alex Ashwel, "Financial Reporting Goes Global," *Journal of Accountancy* 198 (2004): 43–47, http://www.aicpa.org.

9. Norlin Rueschhoff, *Perspective*, August 2002.

10. International Accounting Standards Board, *IAS 14*, http://www .iasb.org.

CHAPTER 9

Implementation and Operational Imperatives for ERP

INTRODUCTION

The previous chapters of this book explored how Enterprise Resource Planning (ERP) solutions support Finance end-to-end processes. This chapter will discuss other important topics related to ERP, including:

- Shared Services
- Enterprise Performance Management
- Total Cost of Ownership.

Why are these topics important to consider in relation to your Finance ERP program?

Shared Services

We find that ERP and Shared Services go hand in hand. Shared Services drives the end-to-end process and organization redesign that requires the standardization, automation, and leading practices built into today's ERP solutions. ERP solutions from the top-tier vendors such as Oracle and SAP can be a key enabler of highly efficient Shared Services operations.

Enterprise Performance Management

Enterprise Performance Management (EPM) is concerned with the analysis and management of the aspects of an organization's performance that drives current and future value. Much of the data required by EPM solutions comes from the core ERP transaction processing solutions. In fact, the top-tier ERP vendors (Oracle and SAP) have EPM components in the latest release of their product offerings. We see EPM solutions as the next step in the journey to high performance.

Total Cost of Ownership

The implementation of an ERP solution is likely to be the single most expensive IT acquisition an organization will make, especially considering the hardware, software, and services required to implement the ERP solution successfully. Total Cost of Ownership (TCO) is an important measure of the entire cost of an investment over its expected lifecycle. Critical TCO analysis should consider all up-front costs associated with implementing an ERP solution, as well as ongoing operating costs.

I. TRANSFORMING FINANCE THROUGH ERP-ENABLED SHARED SERVICES

SHARED SERVICES DEFINED

Shared Services has been around for well over a decade and is now an integral part of many progressive organizations. Shared Services involves consolidating and redesigning end-to-end processes into major service centers to deliver the optimum balance in cost-effective, high-quality services. When designed, implemented, and executed properly, Shared Services creates a highly effective Finance organization that performs as a stand-alone utility to serve the specific needs of the entire organization efficiently.

Shared Services should not be confused with centralization. In fact, depending on the services provided, Shared Services may have components that are centralized or distributed. Shared Services is not primarily about where the service is provided – although that is a consideration – but rather about how services are provided (see Figure 9.1). Shared Services has a critical emphasis on the "shared" responsibility for end results and on "service" for extremely high stakeholder satisfaction.

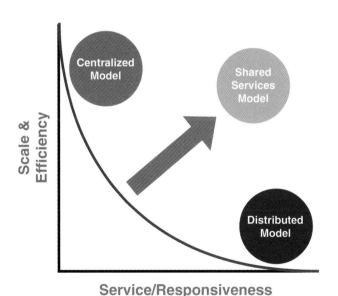

Figure 9.1 *Shared Services, centralized and distributed*

Successful Finance Shared Services solutions share some common characteristics, including:

- Reengineered processes
- A committed, empowered organization
- Low-cost infrastructure
- Highly integrated technology platforms
- Value-based strategic intent.

SHARED SERVICES AND ERP

ERP and Shared Services are perfect together. ERP programs can be notorious for achieving suboptimal benefits by simply automating the status quo. Shared Services drives an end-to-end process and Finance organization redesign that requires the standardization, automation, and leading practices built into today's ERP solutions. The end result can be a combined business case that pays for the ERP program and builds the foundation for future benefits. Technology, especially applications from top-tier ERP vendors such as Oracle and SAP, can be a key enabler of highly efficient Shared Services.

For example, Boise Cascade, a forest products company, implemented a Shared Services organization using PeopleSoft. The result was millions of dollars of savings each year. Boise Cascade's Shared Services Center (SSC) involved reengineered processes, new technology, and lower cost and was based on clear strategic intent, all of which demonstrated Boise Cascade's commitment to improving performance.[1]

Our experience has identified the most common services, enabling technologies, and success factors for Shared Services (shown in Figure 9.2).[2]

ERP solutions (Oracle, PeopleSoft, and SAP) can help transform Finance and serve as the technology platform to enable Shared Services. In conjunction with leading practices, ERP solutions can also help reengineer end-to-end processes. For example, the Carrefour Shared Services case study provides an excellent example of how Shared Services and ERP solutions can deliver value and create a high-performance Finance organization.

Top 10 Services in Initial Shared Services Scope		Top 10 Business / Technology Enablers	Top 10 Shared Services Success Factors
Accounts Payable	83%	ERP	Executive management and sponsorship
General Accounting	65%	Data analysis and reporting tools	Quality of shared services leadership
Fixed Assets	57%	Workflow	Standardized processes
Accounts Receivable	56%	Document imaging	Clearly defined scope of services
Payroll	55%	Data warehouse	Quality of shared services personnel
Travel & Expense	50%	ePayment	Well defined business strategy and objectives
Financial Reporting	48%	Employee self-service	Communications and training
Human Resources	44%	EDI	Solid technology platform
Credit & Collections	43%	Manager self-service	Change and journey management
Help Desk	39%	Financial consolidation tool	Well defined mission and vision

Figure 9.2 *Top ten services, technologies, and success factors in shared services*

CASE STUDY

Carrefour

With more than 9,000 outlets in 27 countries, Carrefour is the world's second largest retailer. It operates a variety of store formats, including hypermarkets, supermarkets, and convenience stores. Carrefour wanted to increase the size of the business quickly, but its Finance processes and systems were disparate and inconsistent, and it had a Finance organization characterized by lost productivity, increased errors, and inefficient use of time.

When Carrefour adopted a new global vision, it called for systems that were consistent across the entire organization. The Carrefour team designed, built, deployed, and installed a fully integrated financial system to support effective accounting and financial activities. The project team implemented PeopleSoft Financials General Ledger, Purchasing, Accounts Payable, and Asset Management modules, with additional modules to be added later.

This program was Carrefour's first global system deployment initiative, but its implementation partner had experience in designing and implementing integrated global IT and management systems and shared services organizations, as well as a global reach and ability to provide on-the-ground worldwide support. Local teams were involved at each step of the design and implementation process to ensure that the solution addressed local needs and was being used in a similar manner across boundaries.

The benefits Carrefour achieved have been substantially in excess of predictions. The Shared Service accounting centers enabled streamlined processes, lowered costs, and introduced standard processes, a standard system, and standard data for a global company. The new infrastructure can support rapid expansion and can add new stores with the flip of a switch. From a systems point of view, Carrefour now has a "factory" in place to deliver high-efficiency systems, tools, processes, and training.

ERP SOLUTIONS CAN HELP REENGINEER PROCESSES WITH LEADING PRACTICES

ERP, Leading Practices, and Shared Services

ERP technology, leading practices, and Shared Services should be tightly linked. In fact, The Hackett Group argues that "maximum impact is obtained from ERP investments [when] one's focus can instead be on properly implementing leading practice processes and organization optimization" – in this case, Shared Services.[3] Similarly, other Shared Services experts have found that "the major advantages of modern ERP solutions include the consolidation of data from diverse business processes into a single information repository, the incorporation of best practices and other features that allow organizations to reengineer their business processes for greater efficiency, and the ability to disseminate information through all levels of an organization."[4]

When The Hackett Group certified PeopleSoft's Financial Management solutions for embedding leading end-to-end process support, they performed a detailed analysis of PeopleSoft solutions across key financial management end-to-end processes.[5] They identified built-in support for leading practices in the ERP solution, including:

- Early warning and proactive controls throughout end-to-end processes
- A paperless procurement process with electronic settlement
- Automated financial consolidations and closes
- Business analysis based on financial and non-financial key business drivers using enterprise scorecards.

By using the various Finance ERP application modules and the inherent leading practices on which they are based, our experience shows that organizations can reengineer existing processes to support the high efficiency required by the Shared Services model.

Finance Shared Services programs, in conjunction with ERP solution programs, should be approached as holistic change initiatives to achieve the full cost benefits possible; that means incorporating leading practice processes to provide significant productivity gains and reduce operating costs.[6]

Shared Services, Leading Practices, and ERP in Action

The case study that follows shows how Marriott International significantly decreased operating costs by implementing Shared Services in conjunction with leading practices across multiple Finance end-to-end processes and a new PeopleSoft technology platform.

CASE STUDY
Marriott International

Marriott is the world's leading hotelier by revenue, with 2,700 operated or franchised properties in more than 65 countries. Over the past several years, Marriott's business model has changed from property owner to hotel management company and franchiser. This has unleashed a new level of growth and profitability for the enterprise and precipitated the need to retool its Finance capabilities to match its new business model better.

Marriott is not just a lodging company. It is a service company that excels in the Finance domain. It is a leader in exploring creative ways to add value to its enterprise, stakeholders, and shareholders. Marriott was the first lodging company to sell its properties and charge others fees for managing them. It was the first lodging company to expand into timeshares and make it a legitimate business. These capabilities demonstrate how Finance supports the business focus on owner and franchisee service and value delivery excellence.

Beginning in 2000, Marriott consolidated a large portion of its Finance function into a shared services model. The program to create shared services capability was designed to reduce costly, redundant processes in individual hotels and to streamline information systems support and business process integration procedures.

"We had a number of obstacles slowing us down," recalls Marriott's president and chief operating officer, Bill Shaw, who was the executive sponsor of the shared services program.

"All around us the new economy was taking hold, and the business environment was speeding up. We needed to leverage our operations to provide consistent, cost-effective service, achieve economies of scale, and make our organization quicker and more flexible."

The shared services operating model appealed to Shaw not just because it provided the opportunity to cut costs dramatically — the typical benefit of shared services — but also because it could reposition Marriott's support organization as a service provider to the core business. For instance, 75 percent of hotel controllers' time had been spent managing processes like Accounts Payable and Accounts Receivable. Marriott wanted to use technology to streamline processes and free up controllers to work more actively with line managers to improve profitability. Bill explains: "We have never thought of ourselves as a hotel company. Anybody can provide a room and a bed. Marriott is a service company. With the capabilities we could gain through this transformation, we would be well positioned to provide our global workforce with the tools and information they needed to better serve our customers. And we would be better able to do business the way our customers, owners, and franchisees want us to."

One small example of how Marriott improved was within Accounts Payable. The company created a new process that automated the workflow from invoicing through payment and provided a single point of contact for the entire payment cycle. Some of the leading practices employed in the Finance Shared Services and ERP transformation included:

- *Consolidation and rationalization of more than 200,000 suppliers across 185+ vendor files to fewer than 50,000 suppliers in one master vendor database*
- *Automated routing of electronic vouchers/invoices through workflow for payment approval*
- *Imaging of paper invoices and electronic linking to payment vouchers*
- *Electronic Funds Transfer (EFT) payments*
- *Implementation of a Purchasing Card program to reduce paper invoices*
- *Vendor Purchasing Compliance Reporting*

- *Minority/Women-Owned Business Reporting*
- *Accounts Payable Metrics Reporting.*

Improving Accounts Payable

A global company provides an excellent example of how an ERP solution can become the foundation for implementing Finance Shared Services, with leading practices end-to-end processes as a priority.

This company initiated a program to create Finance Shared Services capabilities to reduce costly, redundant processes in individual operating units and to streamline information systems support. The back-office function is now "shared" between the Shared Services Center and each operating unit, with responsibilities clearly established in service level agreements.

The PeopleSoft Financials modules served as the processing backbone for this global company's new Finance Shared Services organization and a series of reengineered business processes. An example of one of their reengineered processes included the Accounts Payable process. In the old model, invoices were sent through the mail, opened in the Accounts Payable department, reviewed and sent out to the appropriate department via interoffice mail, manually passed around within the department for approval, signed by the appropriate department person, sent back to the Accounts Payable department for an approval stamp, entered into the system for payment, and then stored in a file cabinet for later retrieval if needed. Other Accounts Payable processes, such as adding new vendors and rush check requests, were similarly burdensome and not capable of providing a high level of service to customers in a Shared Services environment.

This mostly manual process was not merely an opportunity for improvement, but a required overhaul. The company integrated the PeopleSoft Accounts Payable application with a fax and image-scanning application to allow paper-based suppliers to fax or send invoices directly to the Shared Service Center rather than to the various operating units (where they were prone to getting buried in someone's in-box). At point of entry, the paper invoice is immediately turned into an electronic indexed document, attached to the PeopleSoft Voucher as entered by the Accounts Payable person, and then routed for payment approval through automated workflow. The PeopleSoft Accounts Payable module and the integrated imaging solution also use workflow to route requests for new vendors and rush check requests and standard vouchers to the correct personnel within the Shared Services Center organization. These documents are scanned into the imaging tool and are routed to the appropriate user, based on document type as well as on business priority through the use of a bar coding technique. These workflow-based tools have been central to the successful implementation of revised business processes to support the Shared Services model.

In addition, the company introduced a Purchasing Card (P-Card) program that included an interface to load automatically approved vouchers that represent the P-Card purchasing activity into the PeopleSoft Accounts Payable system. Several operational systems with purchasing capabilities have also been integrated with the PeopleSoft Accounts Payable system to pass approved voucher data to the Accounts Payable system. For example, a PeopleSoft-based custom eSupplier web site was created to enable suppliers to enter their own vouchers for automated approval as well as to perform basic payment and invoice inquiry functions.

To support its new Shared Services model, the company had to reengineer its Accounts Payable business processes completely. That exercise delivered significant business value, including:

- Centralized invoice and payment processing, resulting in consolidation of payments and improved timeliness of payments
- A centralized vendor setup, resulting in elimination of duplicate vendors, improved national contract leverage, and the ability to perform consolidated spend analysis
- A P-Card program that eliminated Accounts Payable checks and introduced cash rebates on volume purchases
- Electronic invoice approval and payment, resulting in a reduction in the number of paper invoices as well as improved supplier-payment options
- Centralized Accounts Payable support staff, providing improved supplier and operating unit support, as well as decreased operating unit administrative responsibilities.

Improving Accounts Receivable

Another large company placed Accounts Receivable as one of several Finance functions within its Shared Services Center. The PeopleSoft Accounts Receivable application performs basic cash application and collections processing for billing and credit card receivables. A lockbox receives cash and automates the flow of deposit data into the Accounts Receivable application. This information is then used to apply cash automatically to outstanding receivable items.

Accounts Receivable collections processing includes recording customer conversations and automatically scheduling follow-up activities to manage customer accounts proactively. In this company, collectors are now organized by customer to enable a more intimate relationship between the client and its customer base, as opposed to the previous operating unit, which was organized by a unit collections approach. With the introduction of the PeopleSoft Accounts Receivable module, the Shared Services Center can now use automated statement and dunning letter processing to help with basic collections functions. In addition, a customized follow-up letter functionality created within the PeopleSoft Accounts Receivable application allows collectors to produce letters easily documenting the results of customer conversations.

The business value this new Accounts Receivable process delivered includes:

- Centralized collections activities that improve the strength of the relationship between the client and its customer base
- Automated cash application and cash receipt processes, which have reduced processing time and improved overall cash flow.

ERP SOLUTIONS PROVIDE A TECHNOLOGY PLATFORM TO SUPPORT THE SHARED SERVICES MODEL

Shared Services Cost Structure

The Shared Services model can generate true economic value by fundamentally changing the cost structure of Finance, including facilities costs, personnel costs, and technology costs. For example, colocation with other facilities or perhaps switching to lower cost locations reduces facilities costs. Headcount reduction through end-to-end process standardization, automation, technology enablers, and low-cost locations reduces personnel costs.

Standard technology available in the top-tier ERP solutions provides important scalability. Through this scalability, ERP solution license fees can be reduced by eliminating multiple vendor products. However, when implementing a Shared Services model, organizations may actually see technology costs increase.

Why does this happen? Although the typical organization has a significant opportunity to rationalize multiple technology solutions (which should lead to cost reductions), creating the highly efficient, extremely effective, service-oriented operation of Shared Services often demands investment in leading-edge IT capabilities (see Figure 9.3). This IT investment is often needed to implement, upgrade, or perhaps reimplement a common ERP solution technology foundation, achieve process automation, facilitate numerous inbound and outbound interfaces through a robust technology enterprise application integration layer, and enhance the application foundation with third-party products and enablers such as imaging or fax solutions. All this additional technology requires ongoing system support, maintenance, and upgrade costs.

Shared Services and the Single-Instance ERP

The Shared Services and Business Process Outsourcing Association (SBPOA) indicates in its Shared Services survey that "Shared Services can be hampered by a lack of technological and contractual consistency" and

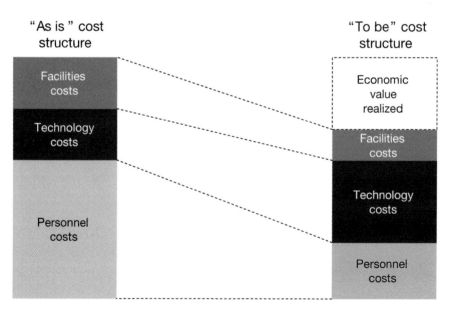

Figure 9.3 *Comparison of "as is" and "to be" cost structures*

that without standardized technology and processes, organizations are more likely to have a "centralized function than a true Shared Services center."[7]

The SBPOA research also concludes that "ERP continues to be a fundamental technology for Shared Services — however, only 44 percent of organizations operate a single-instance ERP solution that covers the same geographical area as the shared services center."[8]

Even though fewer than half the surveyed organizations have a single-instance ERP, many companies still view ERP solutions and their supporting technology as a fundamental requirement for Shared Services. For example, the Dow Chemical Co. implemented its Shared Services strategy with SAP as the technology foundation. Dow replaced 400 financial service centers around the world with four global centers with SAP, eliminated 70 percent of Finance positions, and reduced costs by 50 percent — results that far exceeded their initial goals.[9]

Ingersoll-Rand implemented Shared Services with Oracle financials and, according to Donald Janson, the director of the Shared Services Center, "The company needs ERP to create common processes and data standards." In fact, Ingersoll-Rand's policy was that each group being considered for the Shared Services Center had first to get on the common Oracle financials system.[10]

JDS Uniphase reduced IT costs by $35 million by consolidating servers and moving to Oracle software to support Shared Services. John Abel, the company's director of global IT, indicated that "a primary goal of our [Oracle] system was to simplify the various operations processes cost-effectively with technology into a more efficient, reliable configuration." JDS Uniphase considers the Oracle ERP backbone a key to their successful improvement of business operations.[11]

The right ERP technology platform is essential to optimized Finance Shared Services. In one global research project on Shared Services and government, the senior executives interviewed perceived technology as a key enabler for moving to Shared Services. The report summarized that "in many cases, the right technology had enabled simplification, standardization, and automation of previously complex, diverse, tedious, and duplicated manual tasks." The report also noted that of particular importance is a single ERP solution and that organizations that contemplate

Shared Services without a solid ERP strategy or are working in multiple ERPs are "starting with their hands tied."[12]

ERP Customizations and Shared Services

In unique situations, we see the leading practices and standard functionality provided by the "out-of-the-box" ERP solution are not enough, as discussed in Chapter 1. ERP technology can also be used to create custom applications not supported by the ERP solution or create extensions to existing functionality for an optimal Shared Services process.

For example, one leading company leveraged their ERP technology platform to develop and provide service to the Finance Shared Services customers for the cash management process. This company used development tools, provided within the ERP technology, to create a custom module to enable the Finance Shared Services Center to manage the overall cash flow through the center and to be able to associate the appropriate portions of the overall cash balance within the bank accounts to the "owning operating units." This functionality enables the Finance Shared Services Center to identify, on a daily basis, the portion of the overall bank account cash balance attributable to each operating unit and to apportion investment income and expense to the appropriate operating unit based on the daily cash balance each day throughout the banking month. A daily cash position report outlines the specific cash balance for each operating unit within the bank account structure.

This custom cash management module integrates with the Accounts Payable module for daily disbursement data by operating unit, as well as with the Accounts Receivable module for daily cash receipts data by operating unit. Wire transfers and other banking entries are input and distributed automatically to the General Ledger.

Another company used ERP functionality to create a custom credit model. Using this custom credit model enables its Finance Shared Services to evaluate requests for credit automatically based on a comparison between the amount of the request and the customer's assigned credit limit, as well as information on any outstanding receivable balance and any previously authorized credit events. Credit limits are assigned using Dun & Bradstreet credit data (which are also integrated and interfaced directly into the ERP application) and are reviewed regularly after a significant receivable payment history is available.

Using this customized credit model gives the company enterprise-wide visibility into an individual customer's payment history and eliminates the need to evaluate a customer for credit worthiness at each operating unit.

For this company, leveraging the ERP technology platform for a customized credit model delivered:

- A standardized credit evaluation process, which resulted in a 5 percent reduction of bad debt expense as well as a consolidated customer database
- The ability to share credit data across the enterprise and an elimination of the need for customers to complete duplicate credit applications.

THE FINAL WORD ON SHARED SERVICES AND ERP

Aligning Deployment of ERP and Shared Services

We find that most organizations contemplating Shared Services with an ERP typically face the challenge of how and when to align the development of their Shared Services organization with the delivery of the ERP solution. Typical questions include:

- Should we implement the ERP technology solution before, during, or after the creation of Shared Services?
- Should we reengineer the end-to-end processes and then consolidate into Shared Services or centralize on existing systems and then reengineer?
- Should we start with one function's end-to-end process and then add additional processes into the Shared Services Center as business demands?

Although there is no one right answer for every situation, it is generally recommended by Shared Services experts that consolidation of multiple processes, reengineering, and related systems work be conducted simultaneously. Specific criteria that can be used to evaluate which approach is best for effectively delivering Shared Services within an organization include:

- Capacity of an organization to internalize change
- Degree of scope alignment between the ERP solution and the targeted Shared Services processes
- Time to benefits realization
- Cost of the approach
- Availability and constraints of resources.

The selected approach ultimately will depend on the organization's strategic intent, appetite for risk, and ability to manage large-scale, complex programs. Whatever the approach selected, our experience shows that creating Shared Services across multiple end-to-end processes, reengineering end-to-end processes, and implementing supporting ERP and other enabling technologies in parallel help to expedite the Shared Services program and manage costs effectively.[13]

Continuous Improvement

Shared Services depends on continuous improvement, and ERP technologies are continually being updated by the ERP software vendors to bring the next wave of innovation. Managing the growth of both the supporting technology and the Shared Services operating model together optimizes the contributions of both. Shared Services organizations should strive to achieve this synergy and ultimately build leading Shared Services organizations.

Shared Services will continue to be of importance and interest to organizations that seek to deliver better service at lower costs. Another cost-saving mechanism with proven success is the use of Finance Business Process Outsourcing (BPO). If an organization is considering Finance Shared Services, then it should also examine the potential of BPO. Some organizations that began their Shared Services journey years ago, transitioning from a decentralized operating model to a highly efficient Shared Services model, have elected to evolve further by transitioning their Shared Services operations to a third-party business process outsourcer. Others who have started a Shared Services assessment find that they can reap even more cost savings by skipping Shared Services as a step and moving immediately to BPO. Some of the benefits of BPO include:

- Step change in cost reduction through appropriate leverage of off-shore and/or near-shore personnel
- Minimal cash flow and Profit & Loss (P&L) impact to the organization
- Contracted business outcomes and service-level agreements
- Leading practices and repeatable/proven solutions, methods, technology, and tools that can be leveraged across the providers' portfolio
- Enabling a focus on information analysis and not transaction processing
- Allowing an organization to focus on business growth (organic and/or mergers & acquisitions) rather than back-office complexity.

THE HACKETT GROUP ON SHARED SERVICES

One of the biggest issues to confront Finance executives over the past few years is deciding which processes should stay with the business unit and which may be effectively performed by either Shared Services or outsourcing. Over the past few years, there has been a significant increase in the centralization of Finance activities.

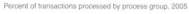

Percent of transactions processed by process group, 2005

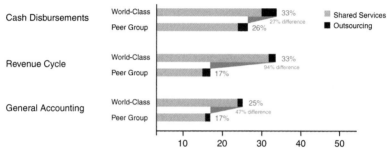

Source: The Hackett Group

Percent of centralization of accounts payable verification sub-process today and in three years, 2005

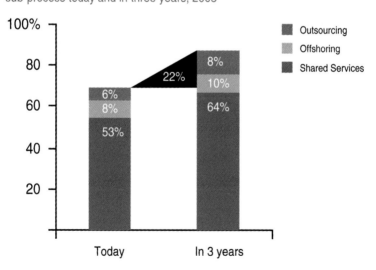

Source: The Hackett Group

continued

continued

However, there are many types of centralization techniques beyond traditional corporate and Shared Services. The Hackett Group recently surveyed its clients to identify forward-looking trends in centralization. The results were intriguing. The survey showed only a modest increase in movement toward Shared Services in areas such as Tax services, probably because of a saturation of work already done in this area and the attractiveness of lower priced offshore alternates. Accounts Payable and Billing are areas expected to shift more dramatically to Shared Services over the next three years. Although there has been a very steady increase in both offshoring and outsourcing, these approaches are still very small in comparison with traditional centralization techniques. The gap between average organizations and world-class Finance organizations is not trivial. In fact, these world-class performers are able to spend significantly less on running their Finance operations: $5.3 million per billion in revenues.

II. ENTERPRISE PERFORMANCE MANAGEMENT

OVERVIEW

EPM encompasses the analysis and management of the aspects of performance that consistently drive the current and the future value of the business. These key drivers are not limited to the financial indicators derived from the balance sheet and income statement, rather, they also include nonfinancial drivers, and the analysis often offers a new perspective by grouping different factors into tangible or intangible drivers.

Some of the key questions that EPM addresses are:

- What are the real drivers of current and future value?
- What tools are needed to make the best use of these drivers to support timely decisions?
- How can a long-term strategy be translated into a short-term business plan more quickly?
- Where in the organization is value created – and where is value destroyed?
- What are the right metrics to align incentives with value creation?

Although the ultimate, strategic goal of EPM is to ensure a sustainable increase in shareholder value for the long term, the more tactical goals of operational planning and performance measurement are focused on shorter time periods. These two processes are closely related. On the one hand, the operational processes translate the business strategy into actionable steps that ensure the profitability and liquidity of the organization over the next 12 to 18 months. On the other hand, the operational performance measurements provide feedback for corrective actions and adjustments to the long-term strategy.

This relationship summarizes the roles and interdependencies of an EPM solution and its underlying ERP solution.

The top-tier ERP vendors all have EPM components in their latest releases, even though they use slightly different terminology. For example, PeopleSoft calls its suite of products "Enterprise Performance Management." Oracle is offering similar functionality under the name "Corporate Performance Management." SAP, meanwhile, has grouped the various components under the label "Strategic Enterprise Management." Even though there are some differences in the functionality of these packages, they provide key basic functionality and have plans for future enhancements that will make them compare even more favorably with the dedicated solution providers in the EPM space, such as Business Objects, Cognos, and Hyperion.

BusinessObjects XI Release 2 from Business Objects provides performance management, reporting, query and analysis, and data integration in one solution.

Cognos is combining tools for Business Intelligence, Balanced Scorecarding, and Planning and Consolidations into its Corporate Performance Management suite.

Hyperion offers its System™ 9 Applications +™ modular suite of integrated financial applications for performance management. Together with Hyperion System 9 BI +™, the complete management cycle, from strategic goal setting through execution and analysis, is supported.

Neither Business Objects, Cognos, nor Hyperion offers an underlying ERP solution for transaction processing. Therefore it is fairly common today to have a best-of-breed combination of their products with an ERP solution. The top-tier ERP vendors are aiming at this market segment. Their goal is to provide organizations with an integrated offering and make the best-of-breed solutions obsolete.

Figure 9.4 shows how the strategy of any publicly traded organization ultimately focuses on the Total Return to Shareholders, with the necessary operational steps in between.

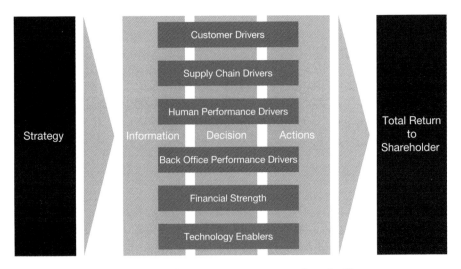

Figure 9.4 *Moving from business strategy to shareholder return*

ENTERPRISE PERFORMANCE MANAGEMENT TOOLS: CURRENT STATE

A recent *Harvard Business Review* study indicated that organizations with dedicated EPM tools can achieve up to 3 percent higher return on assets and more than 5 percent higher return on equity compared with other companies.[14] However, less than 25 percent of the organizations with EPM solutions actually achieve these results.

The question is why? Accenture research has shown that most organizations struggling to reap the benefits of their EPM solution deal with a common set of five issues; the first four can be addressed during the ERP and EPM solution design:

1. **Using the wrong metrics:** Only 23 percent of the organizations with a Balanced Scorecard have any proven link between the Balanced Scorecard and shareholder value. Knowing the metrics, and what is needed to calculate them correctly and consistently, has a major impact on the design of the ERP solution and the data-gathering environment that will provide most of the data.[15]
2. **Cost of data quality:** More than half of the cost of running an ERP solution and data warehouse solution is spent on data cleansing and reconciliation. Proper design of the ERP solution and the meta-data management can help reduce these costs.
3. **Lack of integration:** Oracle, PeopleSoft, and SAP solutions provide superior integration possibilities right out of the box. However, only with EPM in mind can the transaction-processing components, performance-measurement tools, and planning solutions be designed as an integrated solution to provide a single source of the truth. If the EPM solution is an afterthought, the integration will be much harder to accomplish.
4. **Lack of scope and breadth:** Even a seamless integration between the EPM solutions and the underlying ERP solution does not automatically guarantee that management is looking at the big picture. Since most ERP and EPM solutions are narrowly focused on traditional financial data, nonfinancial factors are not sufficiently measured and therefore ignored or undermanaged.
5. **Wrong incentives to drive performance:** Many organizations have the wrong incentives to drive performance. The lack of better measures is at least partially to blame, but the situation also indicates a certain persistence to stick with management tools that have been used for decades. A more radical change management and education effort is needed to make senior executives accept and embrace newer ways to drive performance.

Although these results are concerning, they are not surprising. An earlier study[16] found that:

1. The strategy of the organization often is not translated into tactical measures. Only 40 percent of middle management and 5 percent of the remaining employees understand the strategy of their organization.
2. Only 50 percent of senior management and only 20 percent of middle management have a compensation and bonus system linked to the strategy of the organization.
3. Fully 85 percent of the management team spend not even one hour per month on discussions of the strategy; 60 percent of the organization's resources are not directly related to the strategy.
4. Most performance measures are reactive and focused on past events. There is also too much emphasis on financial numbers and not enough on nonfinancial data.

What is more surprising is that after decades of large-scale ERP, data warehouse, and EPM implementations – with the complete process and enterprise-wide data integration heralded as one of the major benefits – the actual integration between ERP and EPM solutions is still not sufficient.

Over the last few years, corporations went through great efforts to implement ERP solutions. These were very often combined with financial and corporate data warehouse solutions and other strategic management technologies consolidations, business planning, forecasting, and Balanced Scorecards. Given the complexity and the cost of these programs, most organizations started out with a focus on improving transaction processing capabilities; in other words, they implemented ERP modules for core Finance, Human Resources, and Supply Chain components.

Well aware that any significant EPM component was missing, these organizations considered their narrow focus a stepping stone toward integrated and comprehensive technologies and processes – a temporary solution. However, few things last as long as "temporary" solutions, and the EPM piece was either never added to the puzzle or it was done as a stand-alone solution.

Our experience shows that the phased and staggered approach of implementing ERP solutions independent of planning and budgeting solutions or corporate data warehouses leads to a fragmented solutions landscape, in which every point solution is quite capable of doing what it is intended to do but in which the overall technology environment lacks cohesiveness. Data redundancy and inconsistent numbers and results across the various reports and metrics provide little value for decision making. Organizations are overwhelmed with the volume of information that ironically limits their ability to make decisions.

THE EPM FRAMEWORK

The Accenture EPM Framework in Figure 9.5 depicts the key activities of performance management, starting with the formulation of the high-level strategy through its translation into operational targets, which are subsequently executed, controlled, and monitored on a regular basis. The results and analysis from the controlling and monitoring stage feed back into the business strategy in a continuous EPM cycle.

The EPM framework centers around a set of organizational and technical enablers that are designed to drive technology behavior, as well as to provide a common IT and ERP architecture. Since the framework is scaleable, it can be adjusted to meet the requirements of the whole organization, as well as a single business unit.

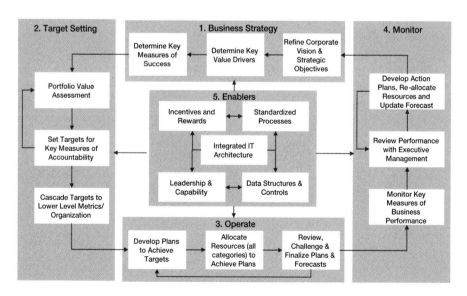

Figure 9.5 *Enterprise Performance Management framework*

Leading organizations use this EPM framework consistently to achieve better allocation of scarce resources. Their EPM solutions include ongoing processes that consistently define and model the key value drivers of current and future shareholder value.

The following case study describes how ING Group used a combination of ERP and best-of-breed solutions to achieve higher performance.

CASE STUDY

ING Group

ING Group is a global financial institution of Dutch origin, offering banking, insurance, and asset management to more than 60 million private, corporate, and institutional clients in 60 countries. Since the merger that led to the company's formation, ING experienced a decade of rapid expansion through autonomous growth and a series of large international acquisitions. This, in turn, led to the proliferation of numerous disparate financial management systems that weighed down its operations.

ING decided to develop a new financial architecture and supporting processes. It developed a solution based on a combination of best-of-breed systems:

- *PeopleSoft General Ledger*
- *Hyperion Essbase XTD Business Intelligence Platform*
- *Hyperion Brio Portal.*

In effect, the ING team launched a complete business transformation program, which involved system and process design, development, testing, implementation and rollout, and training to maximize user acceptance. The effort provided ING with a common financial language for enabling the effective integration of its banking processes, in addition to providing a data-driven versus report-driven architecture for more meaningful financial performance analysis.

EPM FRAMEWORK DELIVERY

In this section, we will discuss how organizations can effectively deliver each component of the EPM Framework, as previously illustrated in Figure 9.5, with the implementation or enhancement of an EPM solution.

1. Business Strategy

As one of the very first steps in the EPM cycle, the organization must identify the key value drivers that must be managed not only to be successful but also to provide superior and sustainable shareholder value. An astonishingly low percentage of organizations can actually establish a link between their Balanced Scorecard and shareholder value. The strong dependencies on Finance data for the Balanced Scorecard severely limit the reporting dimensions, since most key figures will be derived from the Balance Sheet and the P&L statements. Future value, however, cannot be explained solely from past performance.

Simply having an EPM solution, even one that is nicely integrated with an ERP solution and built around advances in Business Planning and Forecasting processes, does not guarantee that the organization has identified and is tracking the right value drivers. The best tools will still deliver suboptimal results when the value drivers are too narrowly focused on financial data alone and do not consider nonfinancial data, such as customer relations, distribution networks, human capital, and so on. However, the EPM tools that are provided by the two large ERP providers (Oracle and SAP) allow for the inclusion of these value drivers into the data model. Examples of these EPM tools are SAP's Strategic Enterprise Management SEM™ suite, PeopleSoft's Enterprise Performance Management™, and the Oracle Corporate Performance Management line of products. They all have similar functionality for data modeling, business planning and forecasting, Balanced Scorecards, and data warehouse-based reporting.

The table in Figure 9.6 shows the many different key value drivers we believe should be considered for inclusion in the business strategy. Selecting the right mix of measurements for a particular organization is a key activity in the design of the EPM solution.

2. Target Setting

We recognize that the business strategy is not necessarily immediately actionable. During the EPM program the business strategy needs to be further detailed and cascaded to lower level metrics within lower levels in the organization. Clear accountability can then be established. These more detailed targets, or performance measures, should also drive desired management behaviors and compensation.

	Back Office Performance	Financial Strength	Customer	Supply Chain	Human Performance	Technology Enablers
Tangible	Cost Efficiency Service Effectiveness Headcount Process Standardization	Cash Investments Receivables Payables Property, Plants and Equipment Capital Productivity Debt/Equity Mix	Customer Growth and Retention Market Penetration Sales Force Effectiveness Customer Profitability Contract Management	Demand Management Transportation Management Operational Excellence Inventory Values	Employee Retention Diversity Management Contracts Documented Accessible Skills Inventories	Operational Efficiency / Cost Reduction Centralization / Standardization of Systems and Data Level of Automation
Intangible	Informal Processes Organizational Reputation Operational Risk Compliance Level of Internal Control	Credit Ratings Borrowing Capacity Bad Debt Balance Sheet Strength Quality of Investor Relations	Customer Satisfaction and Loyalty Brand Awareness Customer Preferences	Plant Flexibility Plant Modernity Access Rights Inventory Quality	Management Quality Employee Loyalty Leadership Capabilities Problem Solving Abilities	Level of Internal Control Data Integrity Customer Service

Figure 9.6 *Tangible and intangible value drivers*

We have determined that a valuable guideline to determine the right level of detail for the performance measures is to assess whether they are:

- Meaningful and aid in the decision-making process
- Manageable and can be controlled by the responsible person or entity
- Measurable and can be captured and reported by the EPM or ERP solution
- Material and quantifiable enough while not distracting from the overall strategy.

These "four M's of performance management" have a significant impact on the design, implementation, and ongoing maintenance of the EPM solution and even the supporting ERP solution. They drive the data model that has to be developed, the structure and hierarchy of cost centers, and other management reporting entities, as well as the data volume. They can even drive the decision of whether to use a more standardized EPM/ERP solution or to deploy a best-of-breed combination of specialized products from different solution providers (for example, combining Oracle's ERP solution with Cognos's CPM, or SAP's ERP with Hyperion's System 9 Applications™).

3. Operate

Operate is the subprocess of the EPM cycle that usually has the strongest link to an ERP solution. Today, all the major ERP packages have highly robust capabilities to develop the detailed plan, capture the actual results, and compare the plans versus actuals – the major activities within Operate. The tight integration enables a seamless flow of information and data sharing between the components. Common master data and hierarchies are used across the solution. Besides the Balance Sheet- and P&L-driven data from the General Ledger, the operational systems provide comprehensive tools for management accounting, for example, for product costing and break-even analysis and allocation engines for overhead cost.

An organization's operational systems also provide tools for more advanced management accounting and reporting methods, such as SAP's tools for Activity-Based Costing (CO-ABC) and profitability analysis (CO-PA). Here, the boundaries between ERP and EPM solutions become more fluid, especially when the tools provided by ABC are combined with the reporting and analysis capabilities in a multidimensional profitability analysis.

In traditional ERP solutions, management accounting information is largely based on profit and loss data and the subsequent allocation of expenses. However, that method does not provide any information on which product is driving the success of the organization. On the other hand, ABC links actions to their cost and thereby identifies the factors that cause expenditure. As a result, ABC is an integral step to managing performance by analyzing and changing cost behavior.

In a well-designed ERP solution, all the necessary information is captured in the General Ledger, management accounting, and Supply Chain components and is accessible for reporting and analysis.

Figure 9.7 shows the importance of an integrated design for EPM and ERP solutions. If the ERP solution does not capture the data at the necessary level of detail (for example, activity cost) or with the necessary attributes, the EPM solution will be severely hampered in its potential functionality.

4. Monitor

Management should monitor key performance measures on a regular basis, some more frequently (e.g., product profitability) than others (e.g.,

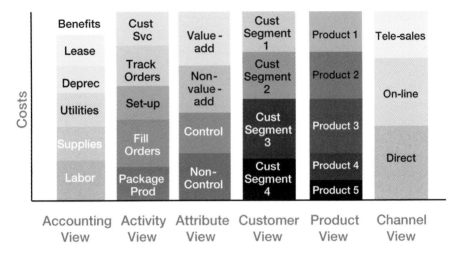

Figure 9.7 *Multidimensional cost analysis*

headcount). In addition to the tools that are used to "Operate," the monitoring activities also make use of variance analysis, scenario simulation, and analysis. Here again the boundaries between EPM and ERP blur. For example, plan versus actual analysis uses the transactional data from the ERP (Oracle Financials, PeopleSoft Financials, or SAP R/3) and combines them with the planning and forecasting data that are captured in the EPM solution, as discussed in Chapter 3.

Profitability analysis concentrates on reporting and analyzing product, customer, distribution channel, or geographic dimensions. The combination of ABC and profitability analysis allows:

- **Multidimensional Profitability Analysis:** the ability to conduct profitability analysis by relevant segment in the organization (such as customer, product, business unit, or sales channel)
- **Cost Object Margin Analysis:** the ability to report the contribution margin of customers, products, segments, or channels and to evaluate the convergence of cost objects and the combinations of cost objects that maximize profitability

- **Process View of Costs:** the ability to analyze the cost associated with performing key business processes and activities
- **Cost Attribute Analysis:** the ability to quantify aspects of the business process to build focus and prioritization of the cost management initiatives (including value-add/non-value-add or controllable/non-controllable)
- **Traceback Reporting:** the ability to trace costs from any point in the model back to the lowest level of detail (typically the General Ledger)
- **Scenario/"What-if" Analysis:** the ability to change and recalculate the model, applying expected or potential future changes
- **Intercompany Chargebacks:** the ability to charge business units for Shared Services, corporate overhead, and intercompany transfers.

Based on this analysis, management usually triggers short-term action plans to correct unplanned variances. Management also considers any changes to the medium-term strategy and determines whether and how to reallocate resources to more profitable activities and investments.

5. Enablers

Our experience shows us that leading organizations will show a long-term commitment to their EPM framework. On the organizational side, we recommend that the whole EPM solution should be anchored with a set of incentives and rewards and should have the unconditional support of senior leadership.

The key enabler on the technology side is the integrated system that ensures a seamless flow of data, from a feeding system all the way to the data marts and the reporting applications that present the data to the end-users.

The sample architecture in Figure 9.8 applies either to an EPM/ERP solution from a single provider or to a best-of-breed solution. It shows the modular, yet integrated architecture of a successful solution. Key to this architecture is the controlled flow of data and information from the core Finance and management accounting systems through a data warehouse to data marts for further analysis. The controlled flow ensures a single source of the truth and automatic reconciliation between data that are used either for multidimensional customer or for product profitability analysis or for planning and forecasting.

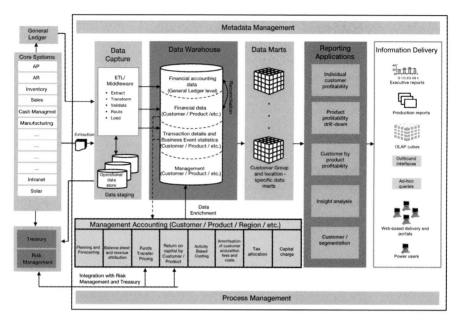

Figure 9.8   *Illustrative integrated ERP/EPM architecture*

CASE STUDY
Integrated Oil and Gas Company

An integrated oil and gas company in the Central European Region active in domestic and international Exploration & Production, refining, wholesale, and retail as well as the gas, power, and chemicals businesses launched a major business process reengineering initiative. The organization wanted to:

- *Streamline management reporting-related processes for ease of information analysis*
- *Improve corporate planning capabilities*
- *Enhance reporting and forecasting effectiveness*
- *Increase operating efficiency by cost reduction*
- *Improve decision-making capabilities through access to higher quality information in logical formats*
- *Develop a long-term Business Intelligence strategy.*

252

By implementing SAP R/3 and streamlining the organization, the company was able to gain considerable budgeting and planning process efficiencies (50% reduction in planning time), reduce system costs, decrease reporting time from 24 days to 6 days on monthly reports and eliminate redundant interfaces, operations, and costly and uncontrolled off-line databases.

A key component of the initiative was a Business Intelligence implementation, which led immediately to a common source of business information that supports multiple levels and analysis of performance indicators, among other benefits. Over the long term, the organization hopes to maximize its profitability through a better understanding of what the new system provides its customers, financials, and supply chain and how to improve its performance matrix.

REQUIREMENTS AND ATTRIBUTES OF SUCCESSFUL EPM SOLUTIONS

Accenture research finds that leading EPM software packages, whether they are ERP/EPM based or a best-of-breed solution, share the following key characteristics[17]:

1. A focus on the Total Return to Shareholders
2. A comprehensive, quantitative method to identify key value drivers
3. An external, market-based approach to setting targets
4. Evaluation of decision tradeoffs on key investments
5. Enhanced performance monitoring and decision support
6. Enhanced business reporting and disclosure
7. Incentives and rewards aligned with performance targets.

These key attributes of EPM solutions are independent of the supporting software applications. However, they must be considered when one is designing a new EPM solution, preferably in conjunction with the underlying ERP solutions and corporate data warehouse. The EPM solution has to be an integrated part of the ERP solution design, implementation, ongoing maintenance, and enhancement. Otherwise, an organization will find it hard to achieve the results and benefits of a world-class ERP and EPM solution.

The basic requirements for an integrated design of an ERP and EPM solution include[18]:

1. Information integration, or integration of meta-data and data definitions, master data, and transactional data across the whole organization. This includes financial as well as nonfinancial data, and both tangible and intangible data.
2. Function integration, or the ability to drill down from a high-level performance metric to the underlying plan and actual data.
3. Module integration, or using the same functions and definitions across all components of the integrated solution. For example, the organizational hierarchy or the key value drivers are only defined and maintained once.
4. Process integration, or the translation of strategic goals into actionable steps that trigger a complex chain of events, coordinated planning, budgeting, and data collection in a decentralized organization.
5. Global access to the solution via the Internet or intranets.
6. Multidimensional structures, or all relevant data collected, managed, and displayed to meet the reporting aspects that are relevant to the organization.
7. Easy to learn, consistent look-and-feel. The users should feel comfortable using the various EPM and ERP components, once they have mastered the basic navigation steps that apply to all components.
8. Interpretation models and visualization models that provide graphical assistance to show the cause and effect relations between key drivers and the value of the organization.

Connecting the dots – in other words, combining the more strategic and process-related attributes of a leading EPM solution with the more technical and basic requirements of an integrated EPM and ERP solution design – should position an organization to get the most out of its investment dollars. The resulting EPM framework will cover all the necessary steps of the performance management process, as well as the integrated ERP architecture that sits at its core.

THE HACKETT GROUP ON ENTERPRISE PERFORMANCE MANAGEMENT

In an increasingly competitive environment that lives by the "knowledge is power" credo, world-class CFOs have recognized the importance of gathering the right information and disseminating it to leaders throughout the organization. World-class organizations do a far better job than peer organizations at focusing on analysis of data, rather than investing most of their efforts in the less strategic, value-added activity of simply collecting and compiling the data. (Only 35 percent of their time is spent on collecting and compiling, versus 65 percent for the peer group.)

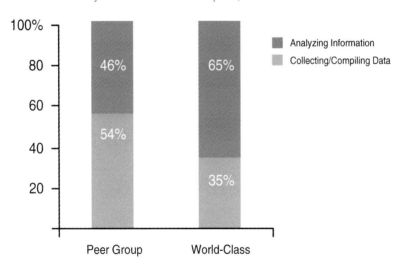

Allocation of analysts' time for standard reports, 2005

Source: The Hackett Group

continued

continued

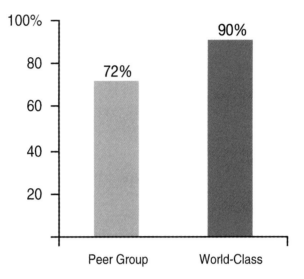

Percent of internal customers who describe
cost analysis provided as "on target," 2005

Source: The Hackett Group

Despite the availability of sophisticated reporting tools, we believe that many Finance managers, although comfortable with numbers — the lingua franca of their specialty — struggle with the concepts involved in being a proactive partner and in providing the reasoned analysis that can assist with decision making across the enterprise.

In today's increasingly regulated and complex global environment, speed and accuracy of information are a critical currency. These are dimensions in which world-class performers clearly outstrip their peer group. The cost analysis provided by 90 percent of world-class organizations is judged to be on target by their internal customers, compared with only 72 percent of their median peers. Moreover, top performers generate ad hoc reports faster than their peers, providing timely information to executives within their operating unit and in other operating units to support decision making.

continued

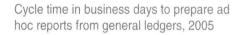

Cycle time in business days to prepare ad
hoc reports from general ledgers, 2005

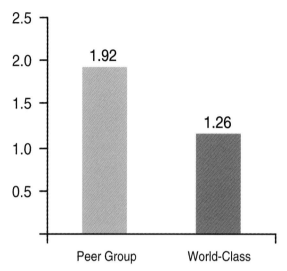

Cycle time in business days to prepare ad
hoc business performance reports, 2005

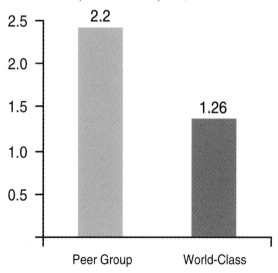

Source: The Hackett Group

III. TOTAL COST OF OWNERSHIP

OVERVIEW

The implementation of an ERP solution is likely to be the single most expensive IT acquisition an organization will make. As a result, organizations often contemplate this decision for years – anguishing over the business case, which compares estimated costs versus anticipated benefits over an assumed time horizon – before actually embarking on the ERP journey.

During this analysis period, we find it is critical that Finance partner with IT to make this major investment decision jointly. Evaluating IT purchases such as an ERP solution can involve complexities and scenarios that are quite unique, and the decision-making process often includes many diverse stakeholder groups, including IT, Operations, Supply Chain, and Human Resources. To become a valued partner in these large IT purchases, the Finance personnel must understand the unique cost dynamics associated with IT investments.

Certainly, discounted net cash flow analysis, net present value (NPV), and internal rate of return (IRR) calculations still apply. However, our experience shows that a firm understanding of the more visible ongoing cost drivers associated with IT investments, as well as the sometimes hidden costs, is essential for estimating the stream of cash outflows that must be considered when one is evaluating such a large IT investment.

Unfortunately, many financial analyses of ERP investments only focus on the up-front investment and often underestimate the ongoing costs associated with these ERP solutions. The initial investment can be staggering considering software/hardware acquisition costs, implementation costs (such as external consultants and workforce training), and roll-out costs (such as productivity loss during stabilization). Ongoing cost items such as IT overhead, annual licensing agreements, a permanent support organization, and expected future upgrades also have a significant impact on the business case and therefore require adequate attention during the investment analysis.

TOTAL COST OF OWNERSHIP DEFINED

The phrase "Total Cost of Ownership" (TCO) became part of the Finance vernacular years ago, when it was seen as a way to measure the entire cost of an investment better over its expected lifecycle. TCO takes into account not only the up-front investment but also the expected ongoing cash outflows that accompany an investment for several years after the initial investment (see Figure 9.9). These costs are compared with the quantifiable benefits or positive cash flows generated as a direct result of the investment, ultimately generating an objective financial measure such as Net Present Value or Internal Rate of Return.

TCO is often applied to operational capital investments, such as new production equipment or new retail outlets; here quantifiable costs and benefits are readily available in the form of increased rate of operation, reduced utility consumption, or additional revenue. When applied toward ERP solution investment decisions, however, the inputs to a TCO calculation can be somewhat subjective, and business case authors struggle to achieve established corporate NPV and IRR targets when conservative estimates are used.

The primary reason for the struggles is that ERP solutions are often regarded as back-office investments with few easily quantifiable near term benefits. Some of the more tangible benefits may include labor savings owing to process improvements and reduced IT costs associated with legacy system retirements, as described in Chapter 1. Benefits that are harder to quantify may include the value of better information to the business and cost avoidance associated by implementing an ERP solution.

Software Licensing	Annual licensing agreements can contribute significantly to TCO, and are calculated in various ways (e.g., per registered end-user, per module, per CPU). Vendors have attempted to simplify their licensing structures recently, in order to encourage expansion of the ERP footprint at existing clients while providing an equitable cost structure.
Hardware	Consists of two components, the initial infrastructure investment and ongoing maintenance costs. The initial investment includes the necessary servers, telephony, storage, and tools. Ongoing costs include maintenance agreements, upgrades, and routine repairs.
Internal Support Staff	This is one of the largest ongoing components of the TCO calculation, including all support staff required to maintain the ERP solution. Examples include functional support staff, help desk, and database administrators.
Professional Services	This is one of the largest up front investment components of TCO, and includes integrators and vendor experts who assist the organization with the design and implementation of the ERP. Upon cutover to the ERP solution, this cost should diminish and not be a significant part of the ongoing TCO cost stream. However, it is important to note that ERP solutions require regular upgrades and this category should be estimated in the out years according to the established release schedule for the ERP solution.
Overhead	This category represents the typical fixed and variable costs associated with any investment and organizational function including taxes, depreciation, utilities, and management. Organizations typically maintain driver-based metrics for overhead allocations, and these should be included in the TCO calculation.

Figure 9.9 *Typical cost components of IT investments*

ERP SOLUTION COST DRIVERS

Whether you are considering the implementation of a new ERP solution, the addition of an ERP module, or the upgrade of an existing solution, we find that two keys areas of focus can dramatically impact on the overall cost structure of an ERP program: technology and standardization components.

Technology Components

Technology costs and benefits are associated with the hardware, software, and infrastructure required to support the ERP solution. Two of the key technology decisions that impact on TCO include Instance Design and Release Strategy.

Instance Design Strategy

For many organizations, the ERP landscape has evolved over a period of time, resulting in numerous applications and instances. Often, ERP solutions from multiple vendors on multiple instances are spread across operating units and regions of the world. These disparate application structures and instances often carry high support costs.

The single-instance concept has been a long-standing ambition for all ERP vendors and organizations. This concept provides for a single global instance of the ERP solution, in which every end-user around the world accesses the same application, and management has real-time visibility into all information routinely collected within the ERP solution.

Gartner has noted the implications of multiple ERP instances: "The consequences of a decision to decentralize are higher initial implementation and ongoing ownership costs. The implementation of a single vendor's ERP solution in many locations without centralized standardization and control will result in multiple (often widely varied) configurations, or instances, of the ERP application. Each deviated configuration will require unique training and support capabilities."[19]

The benefits of the single-instance concept are enormous, from both a process standardization and a business intelligence perspective.

- A single-instance ERP makes standardization in its purest form possible, as validation rules, forms, and reports are common and available to all end-users, without the instance synchronization efforts required in a multi-instance format.

- Transactional efficiency improves through reduced errors at the entry point because of real-time, global validation rules. Cross-instance transactions are avoided, since transactional activity is performed entirely within the global instance, thereby reducing transactional volumes and the associated reconciliation.

- End-users have real-time visibility into applicable global master data, such as items, suppliers, and customers, to perform their daily tasks.

- The reduction in the number of different software solutions may reduce overall IT support costs and can result in ERP licensing cost savings. For example, organizations may operate software from multiple ERP vendors such as Oracle and SAP. The consolidations of end-to-end processes onto a common application provided by a single provider will allow for economies of scale for software support and licensing agreements.

As Finance attempts to move to a single-instance environment, it should consider the efficiencies and cost savings that can be realized from these efforts. With fewer sources of data, the quality of information will be higher, which in turn can be used to enable greater cooperation and productivity throughout the organization. Our experience shows that single instance offers simplicity by eliminating duplicate entries and redundant IT functions.

Release Strategy

Leading organizations establish a release strategy, which consists of a structured deployment plan for an ERP solution. This includes not only the initial deployment of the ERP solution but ongoing maintenance including patches and upgrades. The initial release strategy for an ERP solution will most likely be driven by business requirements. However, the ongoing upgrade strategy can have a dramatic impact on the overall TCO for the organization. An organization should consider different options when it is developing an upgrade strategy:

- Following a vendor through every "dot" release may reduce support costs and should improve internal Service Level Agreements, leading to a lower TCO. However, upgrading at each release requires testing and migration work, which can be costly and will negatively impact on the overall TCO. In addition, maintaining an ERP solution to the newest version of the software may expose an organization to unexpected software glitches.

- Another upgrade approach suggests operating with an older, fully supported version of ERP software as long as possible and only advancing when major releases with new required functionality are made available. This approach avoids the step-costs of upgrading at each dot release, but the organization may cope with somewhat outdated functionality and go without the benefits of upgrading to new capabilities.

We realize there is no single answer that describes the best upgrade path for an organization. This path should be driven by the requirements of the organization, with an eye on the affects on TCO.

The following case study describes how Constellation Energy methodically built its business case, factoring in a comprehensive look at TCO, to justify its investment in a single-instance ERP.

CASE STUDY

Constellation Energy

Constellation Energy, a FORTUNE 200 company based in Baltimore, is the nation's largest competitive supplier of electricity to large commercial and industrial customers and one of the nation's largest wholesale power sellers. It is a major generator of electricity with a diversified fleet of power plants strategically located throughout the United States. The company delivers electricity and natural gas through Baltimore Gas and Electric Company, its regulated utility in Central Maryland. To achieve a higher level of performance and operating efficiency, the company's Corporate Finance and IT divisions teamed up to address the pressing need to consolidate and align its financial and supply chain business processes. The solution included global business processes and the consolidation of all the company's business units onto one integrated Oracle enterprise solution, establishing a single, centralized source for financial data.

An extensive business case analysis was conducted to justify this large ERP investment. Cost savings incorporated into this analysis included the avoidance of operating and forecasted upgrade costs associated with the numerous existing ERP platforms, efficiency gains associated with the standardization of business processes and controls, and the reduced IT maintenance costs associated with the adoption of a single-instance strategy. TCO cost components included costs associated with the implementation, as well as ongoing operating costs of the consolidated ERP

solution. To complete the business case picture, the "enabler" benefits of a standard-
ized, single-instance global ERP platform were also factored into the business case.
These enabler benefits included anticipated savings associated with shared services,
strategic procurement, and growth scalability, all strongly dependent on a global,
standardized ERP solution. This comprehensive analysis, consisting of hard benefits
as well as enabler benefits, yielded a highly compelling business case, which was
used to justify this significant investment.

Standardization Components

Standardization spans all aspects of an ERP program, including process
design, configuration, and hardware design. Standardization is actually a
design guiding principle that can dramatically impact on the TCO of an ERP
program. Often, we see organizations set out with this guiding principle at
the beginning of the design phase, only to veer off in some key areas potentially leading to increases in TCO and negatively impacting on the business
case. A key design area that can present considerable challenges for the
implementation team during the design phase is end-to-end process design.

An important trend among ERP solution implementations is "ruthless
standardization." Common and simple end-to-end processes drive standard configurations and fewer software customizations. This simplification
in turn reduces overall TCO by minimizing the ongoing cost of maintenance during the upgrade and maintenance process.

This trend is a dramatic departure from past philosophies, whereby
ERP solutions were designed with configurations that stretched the capabilities of the latest release, and the software was customized to fit the
unique requirements of the organization. In the past, customers would
often pressure vendors for enhancements in future releases to achieve an
optimal fit for their requirements. This drive for a custom-tailored ERP
solution has subsided recently, as organizations began to discover the
true recurring cost of these stretched configurations and customizations
in the form of incremental costs in the areas of support, upgrades, process
efficiency and training.

The implications of these design decisions must be considered when
you are evaluating the ERP investment. In fact, ERP vendors are now
being pressured to provide offerings that are more economical to run,
striking an appropriate balance between configuration flexibility and TCO.

Of course, ruthless standardization does not happen by itself. No matter what the organization, the industry, or the end-to-end process, the phrase "but we are different from everyone else" creeps into ERP design sessions. We often hear this point of view offered during discussions of such common end-to-end processes as invoice processing, entering journal transactions, and recording receivables. This desire to be different often has its roots in a desire to have the new ERP solution look and feel like the legacy system the users know.

Following this approach drives up-front costs, complexities, and implementation challenges, as discussed in Chapter 1. Therefore, strong executive support from the highest levels down is often required to ensure that this ruthless standardization actually happens.

INVISIBLE COST OF OWNERSHIP

Most TCO analysis performed while one is evaluating an ERP solution investment will incorporate the typical operating cost categories associated with an IT purchase. Traditional TCO-based financial analysis, however, may miss other costs, which we refer to here collectively as the Invisible Cost of Ownership (ICO). This section seeks to uncover these "rogue" ongoing ownership costs, which are classified into three categories:

1. **Design creep.** These costs stem from design decisions made during the implementation that have business merit but are not fully "costed" to take into account their long-term impact. In a typical ERP implementation, the design team will attempt to satisfy functional requirements by configuring the solution accordingly and proposing configuration changes and customizations for all identified gaps. The decision to accept the proposed configuration change or customization rarely takes into consideration the long-term cost/benefit implications of this decision.

   We recommend that the TCO developed during the business case be continually updated to account for these changes, with a reasonable amount of due diligence applied around the TCO impact. Although some configuration changes may not necessarily have a dramatic impact on TCO, other customizations might. When evaluating an ERP investment, it is wise to include some incremental TCO in the cost model to account for design creep impacts.

2. **Evolutionary Costs.** Once ERP solutions are implemented and stabilized, they tend to expand and flex to the changing shape of the organization. Most vibrant, growth-oriented organizations expect their ERP investment to grow with them, and vendors have responded with scalability and flexibility features within their products to enable their ERP solutions to keep up with their customers.

Another aspect of this category pertains to the organic expansion of the ERP solution once users become comfortable with the delivered design. Most users crave more features and functionality to improve productivity or obtain better information to perform their job. This force can be most easily seen in the area of reporting, in which the initial set of reports provided at go-live are likely to be mostly generic and only meet the expressed business requirements. Most ERP solutions provide end-user reporting tools that enable "power users" to build their own reports. These two drivers lead to evolutionary operating costs, as additional reports consume processing resources, generate additional support calls, and tempt end-users into potentially inefficient development behaviors.

Another aspect of ICO in this category pertains to patches and upgrades that are released into an ERP solution over the course of its lifecycle. Although intended to enhance the base functionality of the applications, resolve system bugs, and potentially reduce TCO, the additional functionality sometimes yields unintended cost side effects as end-users latch on to these enhancements and unintentionally expand the cost structure of the ERP solution as they derive business benefits. These evolutionary costs are often not included in the up-front TCO analysis for ERP solution implementations, because they are quite difficult to predict and are influenced by numerous external factors including upgrade timings, business growth, and even end-user creativity levels.

3. **Exit Costs.** Most TCO analyses for investments include accounting for "salvage" value and "disposal costs." These costs are included in the expected cash flows when one is calculating the TCO of the investment.

ERP solutions are not often seen as an asset with a defined service life, which will be replaced at some point in the future and which requires consideration of exit costs. Most ERP solutions have long lives, spanning scheduled upgrades according to a planned release schedule and as-needed patches to resolve vendor-acknowledged issues when they surface.

Exit costs are defined as the costs required to move the organization off the ERP solution, presumably to another ERP solution. Costs associated with the design and implementation of the new ERP solution should not be included here as an ICO item, but components such as data conversion and hardware decommissioning could be considered in the overall TCO. Although this element may seem remote and difficult to estimate, it deserves some consideration during the investment analysis. The possibility is even more plausible now, with the consolidation of the major ERP vendors. Current users of the acquired vendors' products could not have foreseen this major development, but those who are about to start or who are in the midst of an implementation of one of these packages need to consider these costs in their TCO analysis.

The concept of ICO is quite difficult to quantify credibly during the financial analysis, given the vast number of dynamic variables at play. However, we feel that some due diligence around this topic is justified, considering the magnitude of the potential associated costs and the impact ICO could have on the investment decision. Also, we recommend that the Finance organization stay engaged throughout the project, updating the TCO calculation and the business case to make sure the ICO has not exceeded the expected levels assumed during the TCO analysis.

THE HACKETT GROUP ON TOTAL COST OF OWNERSHIP

World-class Finance organizations spend 0.15 percent of revenue on technology, slightly less than the peer group's 0.17 percent. In absolute terms, this is not a significant difference; however, when we consider the issue of technology/labor swap and look at metrics such as technology cost per employee, an interesting pattern emerges. World-class companies spend 20 percent of their Finance cost on technology — fully 33 percent more than the peer group. This higher proportional spend drives a significantly higher ROI on technology. Whereas the peer group spends slightly over four times as much for labor as for technology, world-class organizations spend only three times more. This translates to combined labor and technology costs that are fully 31 percent lower than the peer group.

continued

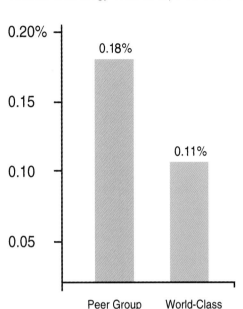

Finance technology costs as a percent of revenue, 2005

Source: The Hackett Group

World-class Finance organizations also spend 39 percent less than their peers on technology. However, this is not because they use less technology, rather, they make better use of the technology they have by simplifying and optimizing their infrastructure. For example, world-class Finance organizations rely on just one enterprise-wide Finance platform, whereas typical companies rely on two. World-class Finance organizations also process a larger percentage of their payments electronically and rely on on-line systems for Travel and Expense submissions more than twice as often as typical companies. Effectively leveraging technology to achieve an acceptable return on investment is an ongoing challenge for many Finance executives. The difference between average companies and world-class organizations is that world-class performers have realized a significant return on their financial investments — including their ERP solutions — by incorporating leading practice processes, organization design, and the technology that enables their use of these systems.

CFO INSIGHTS

Shared Services

- Shared Services should not be confused with centralization. Shared Services involves consolidating and redesigning business processes into service centers to deliver the optimum balance in cost-effective, high-quality services based on an agreed-on service management framework.

- ERP and Shared Services are perfect together. Shared Services drives an end-to-end process and organization redesign that requires the standardization, automation, and leading practices built into today's ERP solutions. ERP solutions are a key enabler for Shared Services. Organizations that contemplate Shared Services without a solid ERP strategy or work with multiple ERP solutions are starting from a disadvantage.

- Shared Services has a critical emphasis on "service." Redesigning processes and implementing an ERP solution to support a highly efficient service requires investment in technology. Shared Services depend on the continuous improvement and updates provided by ERP vendors.

Enterprise Performance Management

- The ultimate strategic goal of Enterprise Performance Management (EPM) is to ensure a sustainable increase in shareholder value. Operational planning and performance management translate the strategic plan into actionable steps and provide feedback for corrective actions and adjustments for the long term.

- Top-tier ERP providers are penetrating the value-based performance management market with increasingly sophisticated technology that goes way beyond standard transaction processing capabilities. An integrated ERP/EPM solution is a viable alternative to a best-of-breed solution.

- Designing an EPM solution integrated with an ERP solution enables the organization to answer key questions about value creation and plan the strategies and associated tools to reach its long-term goals. The EPM Framework is scaleable and can be adjusted to meet the requirements of the entire organization, as well as a single business unit.

Total Cost of Ownership

- An ERP implementation is not a one-time project with a fixed cost. Ongoing maintenance, support, and upgrades should be considered when evaluating your ERP strategy. Total Cost of Ownership (TCO) takes into account not only the up-front investment, but also the expected ongoing cash flows that accompany an investment for several years.

- Technology, including instance design strategy and release strategy, as well as standardization, are two key areas that can dramatically impact on TCO.

- Standardization often drives down overall ERP program costs. Nonstandard ERP configuration and software customizations need to be supported by a defined business need.

FROM INSIGHT TO ACTION

SHARED SERVICES

LINK THE ERP SOLUTION TIGHTLY WITH SHARED SERVICES
Organizations need to reengineer existing processes to support the high efficiency required by the Shared Services model. A holistic change program results in significant productivity gains and reduced operating costs.

MANAGE THE GROWTH OF THE ERP SOLUTION AND THE SHARED SERVICE
Leading organizations continuously leverage the evolving ERP technology solutions to optimize their Shared Services operating model.

CONSIDER BUSINESS PROCESS OUTSOURCING
When assessing the feasibility of Shared Services or opportunities for continuous improvement for an existing Shared Service, Business Process Outsourcing (BPO) is the next logical step. BPO enables an organization to focus on value-added activities and organic or M&A growth, as well as additional cost reductions.

continued

---

continued

ENTERPRISE PERFORMANCE MANAGEMENT

FOCUS ON FINANCIAL AND NONFINANCIAL METRICS

The strategic goal of EPM is to ensure that the organization has a sustainable increase in shareholder value. Leading organizations tightly link their ERP and EPM solutions to translate the business strategy into tactical, actionable planning and performance measurement.

DEMONSTRATE LONG-TERM COMMITMENT TO THE EPM FRAMEWORK

Approach your EPM and ERP solution as an ongoing program based on organizational incentives and rewards and enabled by integrated technology. The integrated technology solution ensures the seamless flow of data while providing a "single source of the truth."

TOTAL COST OF OWNERSHIP

INCLUDE ALL TCO COMPONENTS AS PART OF THE BUSINESS CASE AND VALUE REALIZATION

Leading organizations incorporate the upfront investment (implementation and rollout costs), as well as ongoing costs (IT overhead, licensing and maintenance, support and upgrades).

FOCUS ON TCO DURING DESIGN, IMPLEMENTATION, AND SUPPORT OF THE ERP SOLUTION

Successful ERP programs update the business case throughout the program lifecycle and focus on key TCO cost drivers such as instance design strategy, release strategy, and standardization.

UPDATE TCO WITH INVISIBLE COST OF OWNERSHIP COMPONENTS

Invisible cost of ownership (ICO) components, including design creep, evolutionary costs, and exit costs, should not be overlooked and can have significant impacts on the investment decision.

REFERENCES

1. Accenture, *Boise Cascade Corporation: Profound Impacts through Shared Services*, http://www.accenture.com.

2. Accenture, *Shared Services: The Evolution of Higher Performance*, April 2004, http://www.accenture.com.

3. Rowan A. Miranda and Shayne C. Kavanagh, "Achieving Government Transformation through ERP Systems," *Government Finance Review* 21 (2005): 36–43, http://www.gfoa.org.

4. A. Pfeffer and B. Hayes, "Filling Today's ERP Performance Gaps with Technology Enablers," *Hackett Perspective*, April 2005.

5. PeopleSoft, "PeopleSoft Financial Management and Supplier Relationship Management First to Receive Hackett Group Best Practices Certification," *Business Wire*, April 30, 2003, http://www.peoplesoft.com.

6. Rowan A. Miranda and Shayne C. Kavanagh, "Achieving Government Transformation through ERP Systems," *Government Finance Review* 21 (2005): 36–43, http://www.gfoa.org.

7. The Shared Services and Business Process Outsourcing Association (SBPOA), *Key Findings of our Shared Services Survey 2002*, September 2003, http://www.sharedservicesbpo.com.

8. Ibid.

9. Tim Reason, "Share Where?," *CFO* 16, (2000): 101, http://www.cfo.com.

10. Ibid., 101.

11. John Abel, "Shared Services, Single Instance Real Time ERP Database: Key to Operational Excellence," *Insight*, Winter 2005, http://www.jdsu.com.

12. Jim McDade, *What about the Technology and ERP? Maximizing the Value of Public-Sector Shared Services*, Accenture, 2005, http://www.accenture.com.

13. Accenture, *Shared Services: Enabling Finance Mastery and High Performance*, 2005, http://www.accenture.com.

14. C. D. Ittner and D. F. Larcker, "Coming Up Short on Non-Financial Performance Measurement," *Harvard Business Review* 81, (2003): 88–95, http://www.hbr.com.

15. Brian McCarthy, et al., *Enterprise Performance Management, A Unique and Differentiated Approach*, Accenture, 2005, http://www.accenture.com.

16. D. Norton, *Building a Management System to Implement Your Strategy,* Point of View, Renaissance Solutions, 1996.

17. Brian McCarthy, *Enterprise Performance Management, A Unique and Differentiated Approach*, Accenture, 2005, http://www.accenture.com.

18. Marco Meier, Wener Sinzig, Peter Mertens, *Enterprise Management with SAP SEM™/Business Analytics*, Springer, 2005.

19. Brian Zrimsek and Derek Stephen Prior, *Comparing the TCO of Centralized vs. Decentralized ERP*, Gartner Note Number LE-18-6282, January 24, 2003, http://www.gartner.com.

Biographies

CHAPTER 1: OVERVIEW OF FINANCE SOLUTIONS LEVERAGING LEADING PRACTICES

C. Cristian Wulf

Cristian Wulf is an executive partner in the Accenture Finance & Performance Management service line. He is the global lead of the service line's Finance ERP practice and sponsors the Next Generation Enterprise Solutions offering. Mr. Wulf's client experience includes full lifecycle Finance and Human Resources ERP programs (including Oracle, PeopleSoft, and SAP), business architecture, Finance transformation programs, and Finance and Accounting operations. He has assisted organizations across many industries, including wireless communications, high technology, media and entertainment, professional services, automotive, retail, and financial services. Mr. Wulf holds an Accounting degree from the Universidad de Buenos Aires in Argentina and an MBA from the University of Washington.

CHAPTER 2: LEVERAGING THE FINANCIAL CLOSE TO GAIN A COMPETITIVE ADVANTAGE

Oksana M. Kukurudza

Oksana Kukurudza is a senior manager in the Accenture Finance & Performance Management service line. Ms. Kukurudza has extensive experience assisting organizations with design improvements to their accounting, management reporting, performance management, planning, budgeting, and forecasting capabilities. She has worked across many industries including telecommunications, media and entertainment, financial services, insurance, chemicals, and paper products. Ms. Kukurudza is a Certified Public Accountant in New York and has an MBA from the Emory University Goizueta Business School.

CHAPTER 3: FINANCIAL AND MANAGEMENT REPORTING

Reese Hawkins

Reese Hawkins is a senior manager in the Accenture Finance & Performance Management service line, specializing in Finance business process improvement, Enterprise Performance Management, and SAP Finance/Controlling implementations. His career started in public accounting with specializations in oil and gas upstream accounting and related industries. He has held positions as CFO and Controller. His consulting experience covers industries including natural resources, utilities, communications, and high technology. Mr. Hawkins has extensive experience in all aspects of financial reporting and management processes, including financial control systems. He has an MBA from Houston Baptist University and a BA from Jackson State University in Accounting. He is also a licensed Certified Public Accountant in Texas.

CHAPTER 4: PROCURE TO PAY FOR THE NEXT GENERATION

Stephen H. Wassmann

Stephen Wassmann is a senior manager in the Accenture Finance & Performance Management service line, specializing in Finance and Accounting operations, process reengineering, post-merger integration, Shared Services, and transfer pricing. Mr. Wassmann has worked on engagements in the pharmaceuticals, communications and high technology, oil and natural gas, and consumer goods industries within the United States and internationally. He has assisted clients to design and build new Finance and Accounting processes in ERP solutions and has also helped clients to combine existing environments following mergers or acquisitions. Mr. Wassmann has a BS in Civil Engineering and an MBA from the University of Illinois at Urbana-Champaign.

CHAPTER 5: ASSET LIFECYCLE MANAGEMENT

Todd J. Sheerman

Todd Sheerman is a partner in the Accenture Finance & Performance Management service line. Mr. Sheerman has deep expertise in managing large-scale Finance, Supply Chain, and Order to Cash transformation programs for clients spanning multiple industries. He has specialized in leveraging technology, particularly ERP software, to implement new operating models and leading practice business processes. Mr. Sheerman holds a BS in Finance and an MBA from the University of Missouri.

CHAPTER 6: ORDER TO CASH MANAGEMENT

Alex Rahm

Alex Rahm is a senior manager in the Accenture Finance & Performance Management service line. He has extensive Finance experience and specializes in working capital improvement, shareholder value analysis, Finance and Accounting, and application outsourcing. He has experience across multiple industries including financial services, high technology, and manufacturing and has worked with clients on a global basis. Mr. Rahm has assisted clients with merger integration activities and Finance transformation programs. Before joining Accenture, he worked at a national accounting firm and also has significant experience in forensic accounting and private equity. Mr. Rahm holds a Masters of Accountancy from Brigham Young University and is a Certified Public Accountant in Illinois.

CHAPTER 7: TAX MANAGEMENT

Andrew Cheung

Andrew Cheung is a senior manager in the Accenture Finance & Performance Management service line. Mr. Cheung specializes in large-scale Finance change programs and has deep expertise in Finance process design and Shared Services. He has significant experience designing and implementing

ERP solutions across industry sectors and leads the Accenture Next Generation Enterprise Solutions for Tax Management offering. Mr. Cheung is a Chartered Management Accountant, earned an MBA at the Ulster Business School, and holds a Bachelor of Engineering degree from Queen's University, Belfast.

CHAPTER 8: IMPLICATIONS OF REGULATORY COMPLIANCE

Eric R. Noren

Eric Noren is a manager in the Accenture Finance & Performance Management service line. Mr. Noren has considerable industry experience in financial reporting, accounting operations, budgeting and forecasting, strategic planning, and decision support. Mr. Noren primarily focuses on Enterprise Performance Management solutions including complex consolidations and shareholder value analysis. Mr. Noren is a Certified Public Accountant in New York and holds a Masters degree and a BS in Accountancy from the University of Denver.

Les S. Stone

Les Stone is a partner in the Accenture Finance & Performance Management service line, specializing in Finance business process improvement, Finance operations, Finance strategy, and Enterprise Performance Management. He leads the Financial Close Improvement Market offering in North America. Mr. Stone is also the Accenture global lead in helping clients understand how to transform Sarbanes-Oxley Act compliance into competitive gain. His career started in public accounting with specializations in manufacturing, distribution, and retailing. He has held senior Finance positions in a Fortune 150 company. In addition, he has held senior Operations positions, responsible for Strategic Planning, Transportation and Logistics, and IT. Mr. Stone has a BS in Accounting from The Pennsylvania State University and is a licensed Certified Public Accountant in the Commonwealth of Pennsylvania.

CHAPTER 9: IMPLEMENTATION AND OPERATIONAL IMPERATIVES FOR ERP

ENABLING SHARED SERVICES

David T. Cousineau

David Cousineau is a partner in the Accenture Finance & Performance Management service line, specializing in Finance and Accounting operations, Shared Services, Finance ERP solutions implementations, Procure to Pay processes, purchasing cards, and financial and management reporting. He has worked with numerous clients to assess and implement Shared Services operations, including the design and build of Shared Services centers with new or existing ERP technology and the improvement of operations in a fully functioning Shared Services center. He has considerable experience in implementing PeopleSoft applications for his clients across multiple industries. Mr. Cousineau holds an MBA from Brigham Young University.

ENTERPRISE PERFORMANCE MANAGEMENT

Martin Traub

Martin Traub is a senior manager in the Accenture Finance & Performance Management service line, specializing in SAP Financials, Finance and Accounting business processes, and financial reporting. He has worked on engagements in the United States and Europe. Mr. Traub has been working with SAP applications for many years, concentrating on the Financial, Management Accounting, and Treasury modules and the underlying Finance business processes they support. His experience covers several industries including financial services, utilities, manufacturing, pharmaceutical, communications, and high technology. He holds a Master's Degree in Economics from the Eberhard Karls University of Tuebingen, Germany.

TOTAL COST OF OWNERSHIP

Thomas R. Gall

Thomas Gall is a senior manager in the Accenture Finance & Performance Management service line, specializing in Oracle Financials, Finance and Accounting business processes, and financial reporting. He has worked on engagements in a variety of industries including travel and transportation, utilities, manufacturing, and banking in the United States and Canada. Mr. Gall has been working with Oracle applications for many years, concentrating on the financial and manufacturing modules, as well as the underlying Finance business processes they support. He has an MBA from The University of Minnesota and is a Certified Public Accountant in Minnesota.

PREFACE

Daniel London

Dan London is the managing partner of the Accenture Finance & Performance Management service line. His responsibilities include developing new service offerings and alliance relationships, and managing Accenture's consulting services of interest to senior finance executives. Mr. London is also managing partner for the Accenture Enterprise Performance Management market offering. He oversees engagement teams that enable successful enterprises to make extensive use of business insight to identify the best value creation opportunities within and outside the organization. Since joining Accenture, Mr. London has focused on global finance transformational efforts across industries and functional areas. Mr. London has expertise in finance visioning and strategy, enterprise performance management, shared services and outsourcing, financial management, billing and payment, and procurement.

THE HACKETT GROUP

Richard T. Roth
Chief Research Officer, The Hackett Group

Richard Roth is responsible for The Hackett Group's overall research methodology and is a member of its executive team. With extensive experience in benchmarking and best practices, he is responsible for the quality of the firm's analysis and published research and for architecting its benchmarking methodology. Mr. Roth has more than 20 years of experience working with executives to achieve world-class performance in all areas of the sales, general, and administrative functions and has employed his expertise to guide employees at a wide range of organizations.

Index